Y0-CCB-014

Isobelle Gidley and Richard Shears have written widely on Australasia and the Pacific. Isobelle Gidley was brought up in Vanuatu, then a French–British condominium, and still spends much of her time there. Richard Shears has been the Australia based correspondent of the London Daily Mail for ten years, during which time he and Isobelle have written on a number of dramatic events in recent Australian history, including the best-selling *Azaria*

Who will rid me of this turbulent priest?

(William Shakespeare, Henry II)

The RAINBOW WARRIOR *Affair*

Isobelle Gidley

&

Richard Shears

IRWIN PUBLISHING
Toronto Canada

Copyright © 1986 Richard Shears and Isobelle Gidley

Canadian Cataloguing in Publication Data

Shears, Richard
  The Rainbow Warrior affair
  ISBN 0−7725−1608−1
  1. Oceania − Strategic aspects. 2. France − Politics and government −
  1981. 3. France − Foreign relations − 1981. 4. Rainbow Warrior (Ship)
  I. Gidley, Isobelle. II. Title.

DU29.S48 1986   990   C86−093055−6

No part of this publication may be reproduced or transmitted in any form or by
any means, electronic or mechanical, including photocopy, recording or any
information storage and retrieval system now known or to be invented, without
permission in writing from the publisher, except by a reviewer who wishes to
quote brief passages in connection with a review written for inclusion in a
magazine, newspaper or broadcast.

1 2 3 4 5 6 7   92 91 90 89 88 87 86

Published by Irwin Publishing Inc.

Printed in Great Britain by Cox & Wyman Ltd, Reading

Contents

Maps

Acknowledgements

The authors are extremely grateful to a vast number of people for their help in the compiling of this book. Because of the sensitive nature of their information and their past or present employment, many cannot be named.

However, the following provided important background information or aided with translations: Anita De Botton, Eva Lopez, Leni and Johnny Ruegg, Claude Demorest, Mary Berkemeier, Dorothy Durley, Marcel Dupin, Gerard Chabot, Dick Kluczniak, Marty Owen, the Professional Divers Association of Australasia, Marcelina Ercoreca, John Anderson, and residents of New Zealand's Northland.

We would also like to thank the French Embassy in Canberra whose staff were courteous and always available.

And special thanks are given to the members of Greenpeace UK, Australia and New Zealand.

Cast of Characters

Petty Officer Gerald Andries. Aliases Eric Audrenc, Eric Andreine. Wanted for murder by New Zealand Police. Member of the Ouvea crew. Ten years military service. DGSE agent for six years. Based at Navy Frogmen Training Centre (CNIC) at Aspretto, near Ajaccio in Corsica, before its closure in October.

Christine Cabon. Alias Frederique Bonlieu. Wanted for questioning by New Zealand Police. Joined French army in 1977, later seconded to the Direction Générale de la Sécurité Exterieure (DGSE) in the intelligence-gathering and evaluation wing. Assigned to infiltrate Greenpeace.

Petty Officer Jean-Michel Bartelo. Alias Jean-Michel Berthelo. Wanted for murder. Member of the Ouvea crew. Ten years military service. DGSE agent for four years. Formerly based at Navy Frogmen Training Centre.

Lieutenant-Colonel Louis-Pierre Dillais. Aliases Philippe Dubast, Jean Louis Dormand. Wanted for questioning by New Zealand Police. Commander of CNIC base. Overseer of DGSE Rainbow Warrior Operation.

General Roger Emin. Second in command of DGSE. Heard various suggestions by agents within the service about ways to prevent the Rainbow Warrior from sailing to Mururoa Atoll. Told government investigator that agents had followed instructions to provide information about Greenpeace and infiltrate movement if necessary.

Admiral Henri Fages. Former Commander of DIRCEN, centre of nuclear experimentation. Expressed concern about Greenpeace plans to Defence Minister.

Laurent Fabius. French Prime Minister since 1984. Youngest man to hold position this century. Under pressure from Press and politicians he finally confessed that the French Secret Service sank the Rainbow Warrior.

Detective Superintendent Allan Galbraith. Dedicated Auckland police officer, formerly from Scotland, in charge of Rainbow Warrior investigation. Experienced in explosives, drugs and major crime investigation.

Charles Hernu. French Minister of Defence since Mitterrand came to power in 1981. Became Socialist Party's defence spokesman in 1971. Dedicated to the military and France's nuclear test programme. Resigned in the wake of the Rainbow Warrior scandal.

General Jeannou Lacaze. Commander-in-Chief of the French armed forces at the time of the laying of the plot against Greenpeace. Denied to government investigator that he had given any orders or received any information about the preparations.

Admiral Pierre Lacoste. Appointed Commander of DGSE in 1982. Was asked by Defence Minister Hernu to look into the Greenpeace problem. Sacked in September amid political storm over Rainbow Warrior sinking.

David Lange. Prime Minister of New Zealand. Has adopted a strong anti-nuclear position.

Colonel Jean-Claude Lesquer. Head of DGSE's Action Service (SA). Told government investigator that the team of agents had kept strictly to surveillance instructions.

Major Alain Mafart. Alias Alain Turenge. DGSE agent. Deputy Commander of CNIC base and commando instructor. Used false passport to travel to New Zealand as Swiss businessman on honeymoon. True role: support sabotage team. Pleaded guilty to charge of manslaughter which had been reduced from murder. Sentenced to 10 years imprisonment on November 22.

Dr Xavier Maniguet. Specialist in treating victims of diving accidents. Travelled to New Zealand with DGSE agents on yacht Ouvea. Claimed to have been tourist all along and been 'used' by agents.

President Francois Mitterrand. In 1981 became first Socialist president of France since the founding of the Fifth Republic in 1958. Personal friend of Charles Hernu for 30 years. Amidst political storm after Rainbow Warrior sinking demanded to know details of DGSE action.

Captain Dominique Prieur. Alias Sophie Turenge. DGSE controller in the intelligence-gathering and evaluation wing. Christine Cabon's controller. Specialist in European pacifist movements. Arrived in Auckland on June 22 posing as schoolteacher on touring honeymoon with bogus husband, Major Mafart. Pleaded guilty with Mafart in Auckland on November 4 to reduced charge of manslaughter. Sentenced to 10 years imprisonment on November 22.

General Jean Saulnier. Head of President's military staff at Elysee Palace during planning of Rainbow Warrior operation. Since promoted to Chief of General Staff of French Armed Forces. Told government investigator that he approved a plan to spy on Greenpeace only, and gave his approval for funds to be released. Denied giving any orders or that he received information about preparations for an attack on the boat.

Bernard Tricot. Highly respected Gaullist politician appointed by Prime Minister Fabius to investigate French involvement in Rainbow Warrior sinking. Concluded there was no French official responsibility but admitted later the truth may have been held back from him.

Chief Petty Officer Roland Verge. Alias Raymond Velche. Wanted for murder by New Zealand police. Fifteen years military service. DGSE agent 11 years. Based at CNIC base, Corsica. Worked under cover for Secret Service on numerous operations, including posing as professional skipper in Cuban waters.

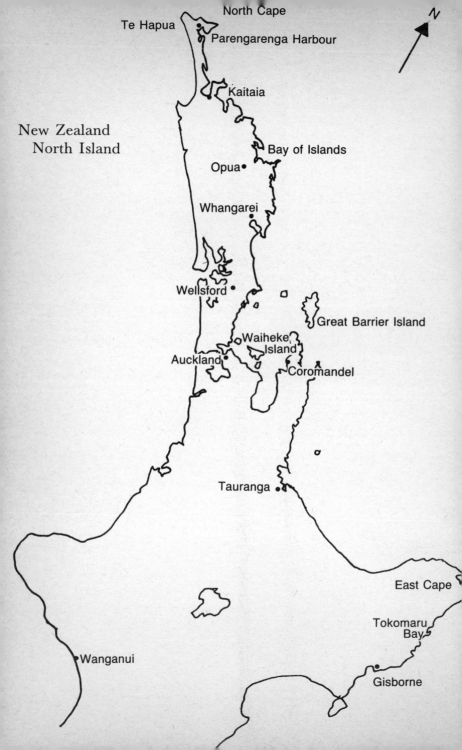

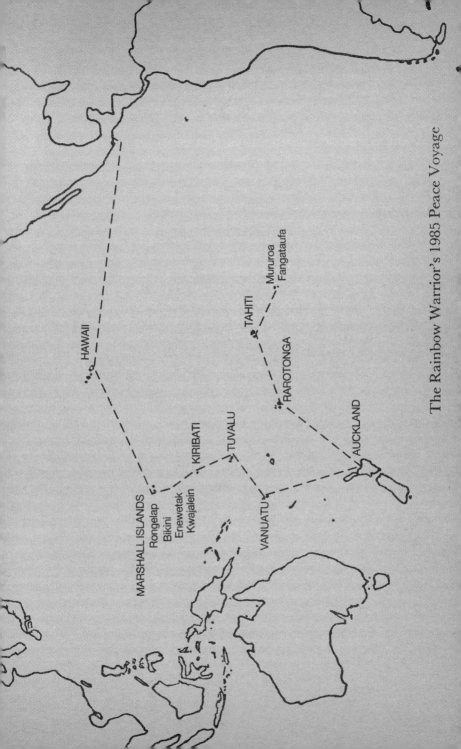

The Rainbow Warrior's 1985 Peace Voyage

HAWAII

MARSHALL ISLANDS
Rongelap
Bikini
Enewetak
Kwajalein

KIRIBATI

TUVALU

VANUATU

AUCKLAND

RAROTONGA

TAHITI

Mururoa
Fangataufa

1

Auckland, 10 July 1985

The hardiest would have cursed the chill that night. The frogmen crouched low into the wind as the Yamaha outboard motor pushed the Zodiac dinghy across the icy waters of Waitemata Harbour. It had been early summer when they had left Paris. Here, on the other side of the world it was the depth of winter.

Ahead they could see the lights of the Auckland office blocks and, high on the hill, the illuminated sign of the Hyatt Hotel. The wharves were brightly lit, but they did not see that as a problem. The sea was as black as pitch.

They were close enough now to switch off the motor and paddle in. It was a silent operation, bringing out all the skills they had been taught at the base in Corsica. When they reached their dark, pre-arranged position, they secured the dinghy with a grappling iron. Then, lifting their re-breather rigs over their heads, they strapped them onto their chests and with practised efficiency proceeded with an equipment check — the mouthpiece which was attached to the fat flexible rubber breathing hoses, the rubber breathing bag, the two litre high pressure oxygen bottle, the demand regulator.

The closed-circuit scuba gear, which re-used the diver's expelled breath, converting it back to oxygen, released no bubbles. For an operation such as this, the system was essential, but the slightest mistake could be fatal.

Opening the valves on their oxygen bottles, they inflated their breathing bags. These remained full with no sign of leaks. Using his mouthpiece, each man drew in the dry oxygen, deflating the breathing bag, then exhaled, inflating the bag again. The bad air passed through a special absorbant powder which 'scrubbed' it. Now, only a check of the regulator remained. Once the re-usable air was all gone, it would be necessary to call on a reserve supply from the bottle. Sucking hard on the deflated bag, and so automatically opening the regulator, they felt the sweet, fresh oxygen fill their lungs. Satisfied, they closed the mouthpiece switch to seal the O_2 inside and twisted the valve closed. They were ready to go.

They spat into their face masks and dunked them in the sea to prevent fogging. After attaching them, they pulled on rubber gloves, then reached down and lifted up the mines lying in the bottom of the boat. The heavier weighed some 15 kilograms but it would be weightless in the water: the buoyancy problems had been well taken care of. The extra tools they'd need would be no problem either. Fixing the mouthpieces and opening the valves, they gave each other a brief signal, then slipped backwards off the dinghy into the sea.

The water was icy. Even a gasp could throw the whole res-piratory system out. For an instant, both frogmen concentrated on controlling their breathing. Then, everything normal, they silently moved off through the water. They were not unaware that naval and security experts were likely to unravel the logistics of the operation at a later stage. At least, they would come pretty close to it.

Swimming in the dark with heavy weights is no problem. Some mines are manufactured with built-in synthetics to make them weightless under water. Others can be carried in special buoyancy bags which can be inflated. Night manoeuvres often involve the use of a specially-made 'attack board', a square foot of light plastic material with a depth gauge, compass and a watch, all with flu-orescent dials, arranged in an approximate triangle.

The divers were closing in on their target. Now, they had to be particularly careful, for although the re-breathing equipment prevented bubbles, it could give them away — drawing an excess of new oxygen into the breathing bag would make them too buoyant and send them surging to the surface. The pair had, in any event, kept close to the top, not wanting to risk dropping below 50 feet; this would have upset the chemical balance and turned their pure oxygen into deadly poison.

Ahead of them now, the rumble of the ship's generators was clearly audible. But there was plenty of time. They could swim 1,000 metres in less than an hour and their re-breathers gave them up to two hours use.

They reached the ship and set to work on the starboard side of the hull, which was up against the pilons supporting the concrete wharf. A mine blast would find the line of least resistance. If the wharf had been solid underneath they would have needed less powerful mines — the wall would have bounced the blast back against the hull.

At last, the work finished, the frogmen headed back to their concealed dinghy. There were still a couple of rendezvous to be made, but they were in good time. The difficult part was over.

It was Steve Sawyer's birthday and a small celebration had been planned. There was plenty of wine, beer and rum, herbal tea for the purists, baked potatoes, various salads and a chocolate cake, ablaze with 29 candles.

Since the Rainbow Warrior had reached Auckland three days earlier, there'd been little time to discuss details of the planned protest voyage to Mururoa Atoll. A constant stream of visitors — anti nuclear campaigners, Labour politicians, journalists — had called, all wanting to hear about the voyage through the Pacific. But tonight, after a few drinks with Steve, an international director of Greenpeace and the campaign co-ordinator, some of the crew and the skippers from the other yachts would get down to business.

They began arriving early. Dutch-born Rien Achterberg, 36, a veteran Mururoa campaigner now living in New Zealand took it upon himself to welcome people on board the Greenpeace flagship, handing out glasses of wine and slices of birthday cake as they congregated in the vessel's L-shaped mess room. Someone had put on a tape and the music and increasing chatter floated out over Marsden Wharf.

'Bloody cold out there,' commented Russ Munroe, New Zealand skipper of the tiny yacht Django as he came aboard. The Auckland harbour front in July is not the most hospitable of places.

'Happy birthday, Steve!' shouted Tony Still from another yacht, Alliance, tucking into a piece of cake.

By 7.15 p.m. there were close to 30 people of all nationalities on board and Achterberg wandered among them, ensuring everyone was catered for.

Then he saw a face at the porthole. A young man was crouched on the wharf peering inquisitively into the mess room. It was obvious the stranger was interested in what was going on inside and Achterberg, ever affable, decided to extend the group's hospitality to the onlooker. Ambling over to the porthole, he signalled him to climb on board, stepping up on deck himself to greet him.

Well groomed, youngish, probably in his early 20s and slim, with dark blond hair, the stranger was dressed in the style of a well off European student. He introduced himself to the Greenpeace man, his voice pleasantly French, and added that he was very interested in the organisation's work. 'Come on in and have some cake,' said Achterberg, leading him back towards the mess. As they made their way along the corridor, Achterberg was sidetracked for a moment by one of the other crew members, losing sight of his charge. Eventually, he discovered the newcomer had, in fact, found the mess room for himself. Achterberg gave him a piece of birthday cake and since he hadn't caught his name clearly the first time, asked for it again. And what, he inquired sociably, was the stranger's interest in Greenpeace?

'My name,' he said, 'is Francois Verlon. I'm on my way to Tahiti. I've heard about your plans to protest at Mururoa and I might be able to arrange further help through some of my friends over there.' As he sipped a glass of red wine, the Frenchman explained that he was a member of a 'semi-religious' group and that he had been working for them in Singapore. He had only a few hours left in Auckland before his flight out and because of his interest in the work of Greenpeace he had decided to come down to the wharf to have a look at the Rainbow Warrior.

For some reason that Achterberg could not put a finger on, he felt uneasy. Only weeks earlier, a French woman, in New Zealand for several weeks, had offered her services to Greenpeace and had worked in the office during her stay. Now there was this man, who had suddenly turned up on this cold night . . . odd that the French, the target of Greenpeace's' protests should be crawling out of the woodwork offering their services. Deciding he was being over-suspicious, Achterberg set his doubts aside and guided Verlon to meet Australian Chris Robinson.

Robinson was a veteran of protest voyages and was about to embark on his third trip to Mururoa as skipper of the yacht Greenpeace 111. The Australian didn't have to be informed of Verlon's nationality: he could pick a Frenchman from a mile away. He had been one of three Greenpeace crew members arrested by the French in French Polynesian waters and deported from the Tahitian capital of Papeete.

'And how do you think you can help us?' Robinson asked Verlon.

'Well, I think you are trying to get some canoes to sail to Mururoa from some of the atolls and I may be able to help organise that through some of my friends,' the Frenchman replied.

Achterberg was aware Greenpeace could do with all the help it could get at Mururoa this year. He invited the Frenchman and Robinson to come to his cabin to discuss further details. But once there, Verlon was very vague, saying that his friends in Tahiti 'might' be sympathetic to the Greenpeace cause. He would just do the best he could.

Robinson didn't like the man and threw suspicious glances at Achterberg. Finally the Frenchman was told that a meeting of skippers was due to begin and he would have to leave. Before going out of the cabin, Verlon wrote his name on a piece of paper, along with a Post Office Box number in Papeete. As he led the man towards the deck, Achterberg was once again waylaid by one of the visiting crew members and he had to dash quickly

5

after Verlon when he realised he was heading for the bridge. Expensive radio and radar equipment was installed there, and it was the ship's policy that all strangers were to be kept away from the area.

Achterberg realised as he stepped onto the deck that he hadn't been aware of Verlon's movements all the time he had been on board. Looking back, there had been one or two occasions when he hadn't seen him in the mess, but that could have been been because he was hidden behind other crew members.

'Good luck,' the Frenchman called as he made his way along the wharf, illuminated by half a dozen lights on the warehouses.

It was now after 8 p.m. and the campaign committee had already begun to assemble in the old fish hold which had been coverted into a theatre-cum-conference room. There were some experienced campaigners among the 14 who gathered there.

Rien Achterberg, now based in the Greenpeace office, had worked on the protest yacht La Flore in 1974. Lloyd Anderson, the Rainbow Warrior's American radio operator, had sailed with Greenpeace many times and had been on the Vega when it sailed to Mururoa in 1981. First mate Martini Gotje, a Dutchman, had sailed through the Pacific on the yacht Fri.

The role of the old campaigners was to discuss with the skippers and crews of the smaller yachts — Django, Alliance, Kliss II and Varangian — the problems they might encounter. Kliss II was only a 24 foot trimaran and there was some discussion whether it could be taken to Mururoa on board the Rainbow Warrior. Certainly when it was in the area it and the other vessels would be relying on the Rainbow Warrior for food and water supplies. Radio communications were also discussed as well as the positioning of vessels. The more boats that could descend on French Polynesian waters, the more confusing it would be for the French navy, whose commandos were ready to arrest any Greenpeace vessels and their crews. While the meeting was in progress, various Greenpeace supporters remained in the mess room, drinking wine and discussing plans for the next few days. There wouldn't be too much time for socialising in the weeks to come and they were making the most of what they could snatch.

By 10.30 p.m. the 'get-to-know-you' conference in the theatre had broken up. But for Steve Sawyer and a few others the evening was far from over. Just before 11 p.m., they set off for yet another meeting at Piha Beach, about half an hour's drive away, to prepare for a conference to be held in Britain in September.

After his colleagues had left, Achterberg made his way to the mess room, poured himself a glass of red wine, and sat on a bench seat in the corner. People were still coming and going and there were some nine or 10 standing and sitting around when Achterberg started chatting with Russ Munroe; Hans Guyt, a Dutchman from the Greenpeace Amsterdam office who had joined the Rainbow Warrior in the Pacific a few weeks earlier; and Richard Rae, New Zealand skipper of the Kliss II.

Somebody said they might hit the sack. Skipper Pete Willcox, who had been on the Rainbow Warrior since 1981 and had been involved in many campaigns, had already gone to his cabin in the foreward part of the ship for a relatively early night. In a nearby cabin, radio operator Anderson had fallen asleep with his glasses on while reading in his bunk. Elderly Mrs Margaret Mills, who had jumped at the chance to come from her home on Waiheke Island to give the regular cook, 20 year-old Natalie Mestre a break, had also gone to bed in a lower-deck cabin she had been provided with. Achterberg tossed back his wine. An early night wouldn't go amiss. He'd been given Martini Gotje's cabin and Achterberg's black bearded compatriot hadn't complained one little bit. He'd been bunking up on the voyage across the Pacific with Hanne Westlund Sorenson, the Danish second engineer, and he needed little excuse now to foresake his cabin.

The explosion lifted them off the bench. Then the lights went out. For a split second, they flickered back on. White faces. Then darkness. Somebody yelled: 'Jesus Christ!'

Suddenly, the ship started to shift, listing over to starboard. Achterberg, his body shaking, thought: 'Engine room. It's gone up!' He'd been on a cargo ship once when the engine had blown. It was just like this. Except the keeling. They were going over.

He felt an iron grip on his shoulder. Russ Munroe, 6 feet 4inches, said: 'Walk Rien! Let's go!'

Achterberg felt someone in front of him. He grabbed an arm and said 'Come on!', putting out his own arm to take hold of somebody else. From all over the ship came shouts, curses, orders to get off, get off, up to the deck!

Spreading through the chaos was the smell of burning metal. And a hissing. As if a poker had been dipped in ice cold water.

Achterberg thought he should go quickly to his cabin — he was sure he could find his way there in the dark — and rescue his files. But the scorched smell filled his nostrils and he heard water bubbling, as if the sea was on fire. Don't be a fucking idiot! Don't be a fucking dead hero, man. He pushed, others pushed him, as they all dragged each other out, past the galley and onto the deck.

Englishman Davey Edward glanced at his watch. In the gloom he saw that it was just after 10 minutes to midnight. The problem was evidently in the engine room. As chief engineer, he needed to find out what the hell had happened down there. There was time. The Warrior was keeling over, but there was time. He raced to the engine room door. Eight seconds. He flung it open and went down three steps. The water was up to his knees. The engine room was 15,000 cubic feet and in less than 30 seconds it was half full. He slammed the door. There was a bloody great hole in there somewhere, thought Davey Edward, and he'd better run like hell out of there. But there was still time . . . time to check the cabins nearby. He barged into the compartment occupied by elderly Mrs Mills, the relief cook. That saved her life. She was fumbling around for her glasses, without which she couldn't see. But there was nothing to see anyway. Edwards could just make her out. As he took her arm a second blast sent the sea gushing in. Davey called on everything he had and dragged her up to safety.

Fernando Pereira, who had hurried up to the main deck after the first blast, had been wringing his hands and shouting: 'We're sinking! We're sinking!'

His camera equipment . . . it was all down below in his cabin, next to the engine room. 'I'm going down,' he shouted and left the confused group who had gathered on the listing deck.

Skipper Willcox had sat bolt upright in his bunk when the explosion occurred. His first thought was that they had hit something in the water. Then, through his porthole, he saw the dock lights. Still disorientated, Willcox jumped from his bed and hurried to the engine room. Diesel fuel would never blow up like that, he thought, but he'd better check. The water was three feet below deck level. Shit, it just didn't make sense. Half dressed, he ran to the deck. 'Abandon ship!' he yelled. 'Everyone get their ass onto the wharf!'

But Pereira had already gone back down. So had Martini Gotje. The Dutchman was frantic. His girl, Hanne, where the hell was she? He raced to her cabin, but found it empty.

'Hanne! Hanne!' His voice rang through the darkness, high above the rush of water, the bubbling sea. There were shouts coming from everywhere, but he couldn't hear Hanne's voice. 'Oh Jesus,' he cried 'where is Hanne?' It was as he was hurrying back up the stairs that the second blast rocked the Rainbow Warrior.

Moored on the port side of the flagship was the 34 foot steel keeler Django, a Waiheke island yacht, with second crew member Treesa Tutt on board. She had decided to go to sleep while her fellow crewman, Russell Munroe stayed chatting on the Greenpeace flagship. Jolted awake by the first explosion, she had clambered out through the hatch, terrified. As she watched the big vessel keel over the second explosion occurred. The sea lit up, as lightning illuminates a black sky.

Mururoa . . . a blast under the water . . . a flash of light . . . death . . . it all rushed through her mind. As the Rainbow Warrior shuddered from the effect of the second blast Rien Achterberg thought: 'Bombs. We've been bombed. Why the hell didn't they give us a warning? The bastards don't give a damn whether we die or not.'

The thought of bombs raced through other minds, too. So did the feeling that if there had been two, there might be a third.

They scrambled onto the wharf, Mrs Mills, bewildered yet amazingly calm in her soaking pyjamas, being helped by a couple of the men.

'Who's here? Who's missing?' The same frantic question was on everyone's lips.

'Hanne's missing!' yelled Martini Gotje. 'Jesus God, she's missing!'

'Fernando,' someone else shouted. 'He went down there!'

They yelled out names. 'Hanne! Fernando!'

But there were others who could still be on board. Nobody really knew just who had been on board when the explosions occurred. It was chaos. Orders were flying everywhere. Get the police. Get the ambulance. For Christ's sake, we gotta get somebody down there to get them all out!

Rien Achterberg and Richard Rae dashed along the wharf. At the end, behind the red railings and over the other side of Quay Street, was the Wharf Police office. But they were stopped by a fisherman who said he had a radio telephone on board his boat, moored a short distance away and it would be quicker to use that. Then Warren Sinclair, captain of the passenger ship Gulf Explorer, also moored nearby, ran up to tell everyone he had already sent a radio mayday call.

However, the police were already on their way. You didn't need to make phone calls to tell half of Auckland that something big had gone off in the harbour. The sound of the blast echoed up through the main shopping area of Queen Street, some 500 yards away and woke guests in the Hyatt Kingsgate Hotel, high on the hill.

As police and ambulance sirens provided an ominous echo to the two explosions, the wet, confused Greenpeace members were taken to the police station to describe their terrifying ordeal. Martini Gotje, convinced that Hanne had gone down with the Rainbow Warrior, was overcome with relief and burst into tears when she turned up at the quay. She'd been for a long walk and had not told anyone of her plans.

While police questioned crew members, other officials got busy on the telephone and telex. Steve Sawyer, still at the meeting at Piha, received a call at one a.m.

'Is this a joke?' he asked.

'No Steve. It's no joke. The Warrior's been bombed.'

The telex machine started to chatter at the Lewes headquaters of Greenpeace, in Britain. It was late afternoon. In North America the day was just beginning. Time made no difference to the impact of the message that flashed around the world:

ATTN: GREENPEACE, ALL OFFICES

10 JULY, 1985

FROM GREENPEACE INTERNATIONAL

URGENT URGENT URGENT

APPROXIMATELY TWO HOURS AGO, RAINBOW WAR-RIOR SUNK BY TWO EXPLOSIONS IN AUCKLAND HARBOUR, NEW ZEALAND. SABOTAGE SUSPECTED. VERY LITTLE NEWS FORTHCOMING AT PRESENT. ONE CREW MEMBER MISSING . PLEASE DO NOT, RE-PEAT NOT, CALL AUCKLAND OFFICE, AS TELE-PHONES ARE JAMMED. WILL HAVE MORE INFO IN HOUR OR SO.

As stunned Greenpeace officials read and re-read the message, navy divers in the harbour dragged the body of Fernando Pereira from his flooded cabin.

At dawn, with a drizzle sweeping in across Waitemata Harbour, the Auckland members made their way back to the wharf to look at the corpse of their flagship. Half submerged, it listed towards the wharf at an angle of 45 degrees. The wing of a flying white dove painted on the port bow was below the water line, as if the bird was struggling for freedom from an unseen hand. Some-body asked Rien Achterberg what he thought it was all about.

'I have no doubt,' he said, as stunned and tearful Greenpeace officials stared at the sunken emblem of their campaign to keep the Pacific free of bombs, 'that somebody wanted to stop us going to Mururoa. And they didn't give a damn how many people had to die in the process.'

At Auckland International Airport, Peter Bahouth, Greenpeace USA board chairman was greeted by a customs official with these words:

'Good morning, Mr Bahouth. I take it you haven't heard. Your trawler's on the bottom of the harbour.'

Bahouth went straight to the wharf. The crew were standing, some still partially dressed, gazing at the Rainbow Warrior. Weighing 418 tonnes, 48m long, it had sunk in just four minutes. They weren't saying anything. Just staring. Just thinking.

The frogmen were well away now. Changed. Dry. They would be pleased in Paris.

2

Paris, March 1985

The file ran to only a few pages, but by the time he had read the first sheet, the Minister knew that his fears had been correct. He sat back in his chair and tried to contain the tide of anger that threatened to engulf him. Although not given to fits of irritability, one word made his blood boil: Greenpeace.

It had come up several times around the Defence Ministry in Rue St.Dominique and, he had little doubt, around the quartier des ministeres of the seventh arrondissement. Greenpeace had become the *bête noir* of the French nuclear defence programme. And, to some extent, his own career in defence. The organisation had shadowed him almost from the start . . .

Only a year after he became the Socialist Party's defence spokesman in 1971 the first of the protest yachts, Vega, made its way to the waters around Mururoa, capturing world headlines when rammed by a French minesweeper. Then, in 1973, while he was in the process of setting up a defence committee within the party, the same yacht — also known as Greenpeace III — was back in the Pacific, creating more headlines when its Canadian skipper, David McTaggart, was hit in the eye with a truncheon swung by a member of the French boarding party.

That incident had done nothing to stop the protests. And almost every year, France's image had eroded even further. But through it all, he, Charles Hernu, had staunchly defended his country's stand on the nuclear issue.

A keen advocate of the modernisation of the army, he was, in a way, the pin up of officers and men. He maintained a popular image by visiting his troops — he was responsible for nearly 500,000 military personnel — as often as possible, at home and abroad.

Although he kept a low public profile, never flamboyant enough to steal the headlines very often, he regarded himself as a buffer between the military and the pacifists. It was he who had cemented better relations between the Socialist Government and the generals, who had been appalled by Francois Mitterrand's ascendancy in May, 1981. He'd paved the way to some extent five years earlier when, virtually single handedly, he had persuaded the Socialist Party to support a nuclear weapons policy.

Charles Hernu had always insisted that party politics had no part to play in France's defence and he had persuaded the top brass that a left wing President could live happily with the officer corps. He vowed that as Defence Minister he would get them just about anything they wanted. And he had not let them down. He set up the crack Rapid Action Force and Europe's first helicopter air cavalry division. More recently, he had promised to win increased defence spending in the 1986 budget. A promise that drew him even closer to the hearts of the military chiefs.

But he did have the majority of the people behind him, too, when he reaffirmed to visiting dignitaries France's intention to retain a military presence in the South Pacific and continue nuclear tests at Mururoa Atoll. In that, he was supported by his close friend, Francois Mitterrand, whom he had faithfully served for 20 years since the time when today's Socialist Party was being blueprinted. Charles Hernu, had, in fact, talked Mitterrand into eating his words after promising before winning the Presidency that he would abolish nuclear testing.

The Minister absently fingered his greying beard as he studied the next page of the highly sensitive report from Admiral Henri Fages, Director of the nuclear test centre in the Pacific. The ecologists were going to hit France hard this year. Admiral Fages wrote of convoys of small craft and canoes filled with Polynesians opposed to the tests being urged on by Greenpeace in an invasion of the test atolls of Mururoa and Fangataufa. Even if the main flotilla of large protest boats could be stopped at the edge of French territorial waters, it would be difficult to round up crews from a myriad dinghies.

Charles Hernu was well aware that French military and sea-going commandos could certainly handle such trouble. But at what cost? More bad publicity? For there would undoubtedly be confrontations, just like before, and the world would jump up again and demand that France stop its tests and get out of the Pacific.

But as he'd said so many times before, and was to repeat a few months later, to abandon the tests would be the equivalent of accepting the obsolescence of France's nuclear programme. No government, whether it be to the left or the right, could afford to do that — especially as American and Russian nuclear stockpiles were becoming increasingly sophisticated. And how could France drop away now when she was ranked as the world's third greatest nuclear power?

Charles Hernu had been told by his defence chiefs that within two months the country's sixth nuclear-armed submarine, the Inflexible, fitted with 15,000 kilotons of multiple warheads, would be ready for launching off Ile Longue. The Americans, who had been made privy to this information, welcomed the news. Already granting nuclear testing facilities to Great Britain in Nevada, the US saw French and British weaponry build up as an added deterrent. Between them, France and Britain had boosted their combined warheads to close to 1200.

The new French submarine was armed with 16 M-4 missiles tipped with six kilotonne independently targetable thermo-nuclear warheads. With a range of some 4,500 kilometres, the M-4s could penetrate deep into the USSR. The Inflexible was France's pride and joy, a triumph for her engineers and scientists and an acknowledgement that President Mitterrand intended to keep the *force de frappe* urged by General de Gaulle.

The 16 M-20 single-warhead missiles carried on the older, Redoubtable-class nuclear submarines would be replaced soon with M-4s and when all six submarines were equipped with this

MIRV system France's total nuclear warheads — close to 600 — would be well ahead of Britain's.

In addition, the Hades tactical missile system was under development. It was capable of carrying a neutron bomb to any area of Eastern Europe to destroy people but keep homes and buildings intact. Charles Hernu had built up a good relationship with US defence officials and his determination to maintain his nation's military strength had earned him a valuable prize — in return for keeping up his good work and providing greater solidarity for the Western military alliance, Washington had reversed a policy introduced in 1969 and provided a sophisticated computer system to the French nuclear industry. The secret agreement had in fact been struck within 12 months of President Mitterrand coming to power. In August, 1982, the first of eight Cray 1 supercomputers — each worth $36 million — was despatched to Paris under tight security. These highly sophisticated units, handed over to the French Atomic Energy Commission which is responsible for domestic and industrial power supplies as well as nuclear energy, have proved their accuracy in research in aerospace, weapons and nuclear reactors. The military have also found them invaluable in code breaking.

What had particularly pleased the Reagan administration was Mitterrand's and Hernu's support of the tough US policy towards the Soviet Union and the fact they had set up a rapid deployment force of close to 50,000 men who would join NATO forces in any action against Communist units. There had also been support from France for the NATO decision to use US-controlled Pershing II and cruise missiles in Europe.

Charles Hernu had to agree with Admiral Fage's concern about Greenpeace. They were not a government and had shown no respect for international laws or boundaries. They carried no authority to make demands of any nation, yet what they had in mind for France constituted war on the high seas: an organisation, with no official ties, challenging the rights of France whose scientists had led the world in many aspects of physics. As early as 1896, the Paris scientist Henri Becquerel had published seven papers on radioactivity while at about the same time the physical chemist Pierre Curie and his wife Marie discovered radium. Thirty years later Irene and Frederic Joliot-Curie were awarded the Nobel Prize for Chemistry for their discovery of new radioactive elements prepared artificially. And 40 years ago, when most of the world was still awed by the bomb, Charles de Gaulle created the French Atomic Energy Commission. In 1985, 59 per cent of all power in France was being generated by nuclear energy.

With such a technological background, France could claim to rival the United States in sending commercial satellites into orbit and as a developer and exporter of nuclear knowledge and components. As for Mitterrand and Hernu, they could bask happily in the knowledge that they had patched up old wounds between Washington and Paris, created by de Gaulle. The old General, who had unceremoniously tossed NATO headquarters out of Paris in 1967, had seriously damaged relations between France and the United States.

The new-found international friendship was strengthened by President Mitterrand's determination to set up a big military base in French New Caledonia in the South West Pacific. The Americans saw it as some consolation after New Zealand's Labour Prime Minister David Lange declared that no nuclear armed ships would be allowed to enter his country's ports. The United States was also worried about its presence in the Philippines where the Marcos regime was threatened by a communist take over. In a way, Mitterrand was promising to plug the hole. The base in New Caledonia would accommodate at least one nuclear submarine and at the nearby Tontouta airport more than 25 Jaguar strike aircraft would be maintained.

The new base envisaged by Hernu and Mitterrand would have a 3000 metre runway and at a nearby bay a 300 metre wharf would be constructed for naval vessels. With the exception of the American bases at Subic Bay in the Philippines and Pearl Harbour, the French base would be the largest on any island nation in the Pacific. At the moment, this claim is held by the Hao airfield in French Polynesia, which was extended in 1984 at the request of the Americans who wanted a support landing strip for its space shuttle.

French defence chiefs were not so concerned about protesters or espionage agents from the Eastern Bloc learning about developments at Hao. Nor were they particularly concerned about reports that the Greenpeace ship carried sophisticated equipment to monitor the neutron bomb tests due to be conducted in October. The prototype was now ready after five years of work and the tests were no different from other nuclear explosions. There was nothing that anyone could learn except register that a test had taken place.

The real concern was the damage environmentalists could do to the French presence in the Pacific. The United States wanted France there and had pledged their support to help them remain. But it would be an uncomfortable existence if world opinion continued to demand that the French get out and if, each year, the protest flotillas increased to such a degree that there was a possibility of accidents or loss of life.

Charles Hernu had often spoken about such things to military officials. The time would come, it had generally been conceded, when France would have to do something about the thorn that pricked her flesh.

The Defence Minister was proud of his country's past achievements and had every confidence in its current nuclear explorations and plans for the future. He had broken from traditional left wing policies and supported the use of nuclear power. And those close to him at the Ministry knew he would guard the work of France's scientists jealously.

Charles Hernu was the longest serving Defence Minister of the Fifth Republic and a practising Catholic freemason. He was a man not easily understood. Many considered him a paradox: a man with an air of mystery, yet with an openness that immediately set strangers at ease, who, through his ready use of the familiar, left them with the feeling that they had known him for years.

Nor was he without style. From the gold-rimmed half-spectacles that had become his trade mark over the years right down to his fashionable shoes, he presented a picture of affluence and his well cut suits and striped shirts were well known in some of the best restaurants in Paris. His generosity and dry sense of humour won him many friends with whom he shared the same loyalty he endowed upon his political colleagues. Yet there were those among his circle who found him aloof, displaying a proud arrogance his defenders put down to his success in arranging the marriage between the generals and the Socialists. Nevertheless, behind his back, and sometimes even within earshot, some left wingers who had not agreed with his noble act of saving France's nuclear deterrent from the Socialist axe, referred to him as 'Hernucleaire'.

In four months he would be 62. True, his hair was receding a little, but he was still a fine figure of a man who had lived a full life which had seen him married three times.

As a child, Eugene Charles Hernu moved with his family from Breton to Lyons, where he joined the Youth Camp, a training group for young members of the Resistance. His attachment to the Resistance gave him a taste for the army and at the end of the war he volunteered for military service in Germany. He rose to the rank of sergeant and after the armistice, civilian life found him working as a trade reporter on a Lyons newspaper, *Le Patriote*, followed by his appointment as Director of *Le Jacobin*, the newspaper of the Club des Jacobins.

In the early 1950s, Charles Hernu joined ranks with Pierre Mendes-France, hailed as one of the spiritual fathers of the French Socialist Party. Francois Mitterrand, who had run through the woods of Morvan with Hernu in the dark days of the Resistance, was also a protégé of Mendes-France and their political paths were destined to follow the same line. Hernu was elected as deputy for Mendes-France's Radical Party in 1956, but in the legislative elections in 1958, he and Mitterrand were beaten when de Gaulle came to power. But he remained faithful to the Socialists and in 1965 he worked for Mitterrand's election campaign. Within six years, he was helping Mitterrand set up the French Socialist Party, becoming its defence spokesman. His aim was to persuade the left to drop its nuclear disarmament campaign, a seemingly impossible task, but by the mid-1970s he had succeeded.

For long Charles Hernu had maintained an interest in municipal affairs and in 1977 he became Mayor of Villeurbanne, in the Rhone. The townspeople adored him and were enchanted by his obvious delight with his car telephone. The mayor found it irresistable and was always on the phone as he drove through the town. He was sad when he eventually left his domain for Paris following his re-election to the National Assembly. But he found his true love in the capital: he was re-united with defence affairs when Mitterrand came to power and Prime Minister Pierre Mauroy named him as Defence Minister.

Charles Hernu finished reading Admiral Fages' report. It speculated that the flagship of the proposed flotilla, the Rainbow Warrior, would charge through French naval lines and head straight for Mururoa. There was a determination to make a real mess of the French test programme this year. Again, it was only speculation, but word was around that one of Greenpeace's financial backers was British Petroleum, which, in an attempt to preserve Britain's market in Europe for North Sea oil, would be happy to see French development of nuclear power delayed.

Whatever the reasons behind the new Greenpeace campaign, Charles Hernu realised the assault on Mururoa would once again hurt France. His blue eyes went back over one particular passage in the report. It called for 'intensified intelligence gathering on the positions and movements of Vega and Rainbow Warrior in order to predict and anticipate the actions of Greenpeace'.

The Defence Minister contemplated the word 'anticipate' for some moments, underlined it, as he had underlined many important passages in official documents, then reached for the telephone.

3

The Rainbow Warrior

A North American Indian legend tells how a Cree grandmother known as Eyes of Fire looked into the future and saw poisoned fish in the rivers, deer dropping dead in the forests, birds plummeting from the skies. The sea was black and the sun did not shine. The Indian race would come close to losing its spirit, but, unlike other creatures of the earth, they would not succumb entirely to the White Man's technology which had brought such desecration. They would gather together all the races of the world under a rainbow, and the group would be taught how to revere Mother Earth. Then these Warriors of the Rainbow would set out to educate others on how their world could be saved.

Two hundreds years later in March 1985 the symbol of the ancient seer's vision moved gracefully through the South Pacific. The water was not black and the sun shone brightly. The crew of the sailing vessel Rainbow Warrior were on a mission to help those who had already been knocked aside as man rushed along an unswerving path towards a nuclear doomsday. The purpose of their voyage was in fact twofold: they were going to evacuate a group of islanders from Rongelap Atoll, in the Marshall Islands, who had suffered from the effects of nuclear tests three decades earlier. And then they would sail to New Zealand to lend support to Prime Minister David Lange's 'nuclear free' policy and co-ordinate a flotilla of protest vessels to sail to the French nuclear testing grounds at Mururoa Atoll. As Greenpeace declared at the beginning of what was to be the longest campaign in the organisation's history:

'The Rainbow Warrior's name descends from legend and carries with it magic; those who meet it as adversaries struggle to escape from its spell. Its history pays tribute to past campaigns and crews, while for new friends, it gives reason to hope.'

In preparation for the Warrior's epic voyage, Greenpeace had placed an appeal in the October issue of its American magazine, the *Examiner*:

Help Wanted:
The pay is poor, the hours are long, the rewards are great. The Rainbow Warrior has limited openings available in the following areas:
Engineers: People experieneced with GMC diesel engines of the 71 and 92 series. Should also have experience in maintaining ship-board fuel systems, water systems, air and hydraulic systems.
Mates: Individuals experienced in celestial and electronic navigation systems. Should be qualified radar observers. Licensing is not required.

The positions had been virtually filled before the advertisement appeared. On its files, Greenpeace has the names of some 100 available crew members from past campaigns. But this time, because of the length of the proposed campaign to the Pacific, it was important to find a crew who had no commitments for at least six months. All of those who were picked were veterans of past campaigns. They all knew how tough it was going to be. They'd all stated their commitment to Greenpeace by their previous actions. They knew the risks and were willing to accept them.

In preparation for its epic voyage, the 418-tonne former British cod trawler had undergone a seven-month refit in dry dock at Jacksonville, Florida. For the first time since Greenpeace bought it for 30,000 pounds from the British Ministry of Agriculture in 1978, the flagship of the environmental group had been equipped with sails to use natural energy as much as possible. They billowed out from two steel masts, 30m and 20m high. The bridge and its doors were rebuilt with aluminium and the only original part left was the wheel. The engine was overhauled, decking refitted and a new radar screen installed. The work was badly needed — the 27-year-old trawler which once fished the North Sea under the name Sir William Hardy had seen some tough battles.

In her first year under the Greenpeace banner, the Rainbow Warrior took on the Icelandic whaling fleet in the North Atlantic. She was arrested by the Icelandic authorities in September 1979, and $US25,000 worth of equipment was confiscated.

Within a few months, the 48 metre vessel was under arrest again — this time off the French port of Cherbourg while trying to disrupt the unloading of nuclear waste destined for a reprocessing plant. Then it was Spain's turn, with the Warrior becoming involved in one of Greenpeace's most spectacular exercises as she attempted to disrupt that nation's whaling fleet.

It was while under Spanish custody that the Rainbow Warrior emerged as a force to be reckoned with. After being held at the northern port of Ferrol for five months pending payment of a $US80,000 release fee, the crew staged a dash to freedom, resulting in the admiral guarding her being dismissed. Hardly had the waters calmed from that episode when the peace boat turned up in Canadian territory in February 1982 with Greenpeace members trying to thwart the annual seal cull at Nova Scotia. This time it was the Halifax coastguards who detained her.

Britain was the next target that year. During the summer, the Warrior tried to interfere with the dumping of nuclear waste in the Atlantic and only a High Court injunction obtained by the Atomic Energy Commission kept her at bay. June 1983 found her clashing with Japanese salmon fishermen in the North Pacific and then she sailed on to Soviet waters four weeks later to disrupt a Russian whaling fleet. There was more: seven crew members — six Americans and a Canadian — were held for several days after an illegal landing on Soviet territory in the Bering Sea to photograph whaling operations. Headlines around the world read: 'Greenpeace Invades Russia'.

Now in March 1985, with the green and yellow Greenpeace flag rippling on the tallest mast, she was on her longest campaign, her Pacific Peace Tour, the crew unaware that in Paris interest was already being shown in her movements.

On board were 12 international crew members — Peter Willcox (US), captain; Lloyd Anderson (US), radio operator; Fernando Pereira (Holland), photographer and deckhand; Andy Biedermann (Switzerland), doctor; Davey Edward (UK), engineer; Bene Hoffmann (German), mate, Grace O'Sullivan (Ireland), deckhand; Natalie Mestre (Switzerland), cook; Martini Gotje (Holland), mate; Bunny McDiarmid (New Zealand), deckhand; Hanne Sorenson (Denmark), engineer; and Henk Haazen (Holland), engineer. They'd been seen off from Florida by a team of experienced campaigners and the importance of this particular mission had not escaped any of them.

The planning, headed by Greenpeace director Steve Sawyer, had been going on for months. Wherever the Rainbow Warrior had sailed in the past, she had attracted the maximum publicity. Whenever ecologists took their vessels to the French testing grounds at Mururoa, they had also captured headlines. Put the Warrior at Mururoa and . . . well, the ecologists had agreed, the publicity was immeasurable.

In May, the Rainbow Warrior, laden with supplies it had picked up in Hawaii for the islanders of Rongelap — fishing and sewing equipment, medical supplies, books — sailed into the Marshall Islands, where, between 1946 and 1958 the United States had exploded 66 nuclear weapons. For the past few weeks the crew had been listening to horror stories related by three Rongelap leaders they had taken on board. The islanders had recalled the day of two sunrises. One sun had risen, as usual, in the east. The other loomed over the west. That was the sun of doom, the Americans' bomb, said the leaders, who related stories of death from leukaemia, still births, miscarriages, uncontrollable vomiting and diarrhoea, cancers and 'jellyfish babies', who breathe and move but have no human shape and die within hours of birth. Now they would see for themselves. And then they would take those people away from their irradiated paradise.

Fernando Pereira, the 33-year-old Portuguese-born photographer who, after working as a freelancer for alternative publications and activist groups throughout Europe was now an employee of Greenpeace, grabbed his camera gear excitedly. As much as he deplored the plight of the islanders who he, like the rest of the crew, believed had been abandoned by the Americans, he knew he would find sensational picture material here. But for the handsome environmentalist with the dark, droopy moustache, the re-location project was more than a photographer's dream . . . his work would be an important historical record. His pictures would show the world how, in testing weapons for 'defence', a government had in fact interfered with the genealogy of a race.

He had had his taste of governments. In the early 1970s he fled the repressive Salazar regime before its overthrow and settled in Holland, taking out Dutch nationality. He found work as a photographer with the Amsterdam daily newspaper *De Waarheid* (The Truth) but his interest in conservation issues resulted in him leaving to devote his time and talents to what he said was 'saving what was left of our world.'

His first Greenpeace campaign was in 1982, when he joined the Sirius, a Dutch-based sister ship of the Rainbow Warrior. From the decks of the Sirius, he took hundreds of pictures of the British ship Gem dumping nuclear waste off the coast of Spain. Pereira was never without his camera. He lived with it. Four months later he was to die with it . . .

Hardly had he stepped ashore when the islanders directed him to the graveyard where, they said, lay the victims of atomic testing 30 years earlier. Pereira took shots of the white headstones with their engraved crosses and listened to the words of 68-year-old Muvenarik Kebenli who recalled the fallout that rained down and turned her hands black after the US exploded a 15-megaton Bravo nuclear bomb, 1,000 times more powerful than the weapon which wiped out Hiroshima in 1954.

Pereira, himself a father of two children, Marelle 8 and Paul 5 took pictures of Rongelap youngsters, the healthy ones and those who had been born with birth defects. He was stricken with pity as he moved among them, listening to statistics quoted by the elders who told of twisted arms, shortened legs, blindness.

For the next two weeks, Pereira photographed the Rongelap people moving house, many with tears in their eyes, others with expressions of bewilderment, for this land had been their home long before the white man came with his bomb . . . this land was their sacred possession. His colour shots captured the beauty of the island girls in their bright dresses and garlands of frangipani, hibiscus, bouganvillea and cowrie shells. He focused on young mothers with babies in their arms and he snapped their men as they waded out to small boats to load their meagre possessions to be carried out to the Warrior, moored a few hundred metres off shore. He shot the large white church with its steeple as tall as the trees and promised to send the people his pictures as a memento — there was nothing like that on the island of Mejato, 90 miles away, to which they were all moving. The photographer stood discreetly in the church recording the last Sunday service at which the women sang specially composed songs about their homeland . . . songs they would sing on Mejato as they viewed Pereira's pictures.

The Rainbow Warrior transported people, pigs, chickens, building materials, schoolbooks and even prefabricated homes to Mejato Island, and when the islanders, spanning three generations, arrived they were greeted by 20 residents of the nearby Ebadon Atoll who sang songs of welcome, the Greenpeace photographer moving among them.

At last an independent organisation had done something for a people ignored by governments, particularly Washington. The islanders said they had received hand-outs, but that wasn't what they wanted; it was independence they had sought. They had dreamed of self-sufficiency and now the seeds had been sown. Greenpeace had removed them from proximity to beaches and soil that in 1979 were still showing dangerously high levels of radiation. It was in that year that the US government advised islanders to abandon the northern islands of their atoll . . . a warning that came 22 years after Rongelap had been declared safe. As one of the elders said: 'They told us to leave the northern islands, but the fish we eat and the birds — who can stop them from going to the northern islands, from swimming and flying throughout the atoll?'

Despite the warning to move from the north, United States scientists, technical experts and Government officials felt that the evacuation of the Rongelapese people to another island was unnecessary and inadvisable. The main island, they insisted, was safe and radiation measurements of islanders were far below recommended maximum exposure limits.

But Greenpeace preferred to listen to the islanders' health complaints and if ever the organisation needed encouragement for their relocation plans for the Rongelap people, it came through the words of a 38-year-old woman, Lijon Eknilang, when the Rainbow Warrior was already heading through the Pacific. Lijon, in a testimony submitted to the US House Sub Committee on Public Lands on March 14 1985, said she was only seven when the Bravo test was carried out.

'In 1981, I had surgery for thyroid problems. Every day of my life, I must continue to take thyroid medicine given to me by the Department of Energy doctors. Like many of the women exposed during the bomb tests, I have had miscarriages, seven. The people of Rongelap ask that the United States look into our problems with a humane conscience. I feel and fear that not only our health, but also our food and lands have been seriously harmed.

'We were told that the radiation would not hurt us, but it has hurt us. We ask you for a totally independent radiation study; a study we can trust. Only then will we know when it will be safe for us to return to our homelands, or, if we will ever be able to go home again.'

There was the testimony, too, of Kiosang Kior, who was 15 when Bravo was exploded. She had her first baby in 1958. Clutching a piece of paper, she said: 'It was born without bones — like this paper, it was flimsy. It lived half a day. After that I had several miscarriages and stillbirths. Then I had a girl who has problems with her legs and feet, and thyroid trouble.'

There was further encouragement for Greenpeace's plan to sail on to Mururoa to protest against the French nuclear tests. One of the Rongelap leaders who had sailed on the Rainbow Warrior, Julian Riklon, watched his people loading their possessions onto the peace ship and commented: 'The fact that we must leave our islands so long after suffering radioactive fallout from a hydrogen bomb is probably the great argument one can make in support of the abolition of all nuclear weapons from the face of the earth.'

When at last the Rainbow Warrior sailed away, the islanders gathered on the beach at Mejato and waved goodbye to the green-hulled vessel with the stripes of the rainbow painted on its bow. Many had tears on their cheeks, but Fernando Pereira was too far away to photograph them now. But it was a scene he and the crew would keep in their memories.

In his office in the eight-storey Paris headquarters of the French Secret Service on Boulevard Mortier, Admiral Pierre Lacoste perused the document passed on to him four days earlier by the Defence Minister. The 61-year-old head of the DGSE (the General Directorate for External Security) had spoken briefly with Charles Hernu, but had received no firm oral instruction. It was left to him to look over the report that had originated from test director Admiral Fages and take the appropriate action. Hernu had underlined the word 'anticipate' . . . 'forecast and anticipate Greenpeace actions.'

Was the Defence Minister trying to tell him something by underlining that word? To forecast the movements of the so-called peace group was clear enough, but what was the exact interpretation of the word 'anticipate'? That was to become a vital question in the months following, but for the time being Admiral Lacoste had little doubt that the Minister was giving him a free hand to look closely at the Greenpeace plans for the Pacific that summer.

The Secret Service chief had already been approached by Admiral Fages a few months earlier and had been asked what his agency planned to do about Greenpeace. Fages had received

reports from Tahiti that the organisation planned a huge operation and he hoped that did not mean that the important neutron
bomb tests scheduled for the summer would be shrouded in bad
publicity. Lacoste was left in no doubt that Admiral Fages was
unhappy with the lack of initiative the DGSE had taken. Now
Lacoste had received this official note from Fages endorsed by
the Defence Minister.

In fact, the DGSE had not been all that slack. The secret service
had been keeping a watch on Greenpeace for at least 12 months
and had its own files on the organisation which had been such
an embarrassment to the French government. Several agents
had already been briefed to infiltrate the group and the ground
had been prepared to give them a good cover.

'Honorable correspondents'— unofficial agents posted abroad
— had already reported the plans, first mooted in 1983, to send
the Rainbow Warrior to the Pacific. And at least one Frenchman had been operating in the New Zealand port of Whangarei
nearly a year before the Peace Ship reached Auckland. Not
only that, he had actually befriended a Greenpeace sympathiser,
a professional carpenter, who had helped carry out the
conversions on the Rainbow Warrior some four years earlier.
The layout of the ship, then, was well known to the French Secret
Service.

For more than a year within the dark and secret corridors of
the DGSE headquarters, men whose names never made the newspapers had suggested one grand solution to thwart the Greenpeace plan to send a protest flotilla to Mururoa — sink the
Rainbow Warrior!

Such ideas came easily to the men who hid behind the screen
of the DGSE's Action Service. They remembered clearly a similar
plan proposed two years earlier by France's best-known anti-
terrorist policeman, Captain Paul Barril, then head of the heav-
ily-armed Gendarmerie Intervention Group. After locating the
hideout of an extremist left-wing terrorist organisation on a hou-
seboat on the Seine, Barril put forward a plan involving a team
of underwater saboteurs fixing mines to the hull. The idea was
eventually turned down by the chief of the Elysee Palace's Security.

Now a similar idea was floating around. And the pressure was on from the top. Admiral Lacoste was aware that he had to pull something out of the hat. Well might he have done a great deal of groundwork by building up a dossier on Greenpeace, but it clearly was not enough. It was time to produce.

Since his appointment in November 1982 as head of the DGSE, things had not worked out too well for Admiral Lacoste. President Francois Mitterrand had been appalled by what he described as the 'trite incompetence' of DGSE position papers on the Falklands crisis and the Soviet Union. The President had been further angered in 1984 when the Secret Service presented a report stating that Libyan troops had pulled out of Chad. Contradicting this were US satellite pictures showing they were still comfortably ensconced.

A quietly-spoken man with virtually no espionage experience before his appointment, Admiral Lacoste had proved himself in the running of maritime affairs. But the DGSE was a completely different kettle of fish. A naval man since 1943, he had shown himself to be a worthy commander of escort vessels before his promotion to Vice-Admiral in December 1979. In September 1980, he became Commander of the Mediterranean squadron and 18 months later was promoted to the rank of squadron vice admiral. His new appointment as head of the Direction Générale de la Sécurité Extérieure was a tough task, but he was kept on in 1984, even though he had reached the age limit of his rank.

Under his wing he had gathered a corps of secret service operatives who were not altogether loyal to those who had had no intelligence experience. Indeed, Pierre Marion, a civilian who had preceded him, had been so unacceptable to the Action Service that shortly after his appointment in 1981, a group of hooded men had burst into his flat, gagged and blindfolded him and bundled him into a van. He heard the whirr of a helicopter, the splash of the sea — and woke up in a dinghy in the Mediterranean.

Yes, Lacoste had taken on something of a monster when he moved into DGSE headquarters, jokingly referred to in France as La Piscine — the swimming pool — because it is located near a popular municipal pool. But the Admiral was a staunch patriot, a necessary quality in anyone who took control of a government agency that could hardly hold its head high with pride for its good works.

The French equivalent to Britain's MI6, America's CIA, Russia's KGB and Australia's ASIO, the DGSE restricted its dubious international activities to French-speaking Africa, Eastern Europe, the Arab world and the South Pacific. Established in the war years by veterans of Gaullist resistance groups, the agency was then known as the Service de Documentation et de Contre-Espionage — SDECE. 'We don't want choirboys,' one of the founders declared. An unwritten rule gave members the right to kill for 'reasons of state' . . . the security of the nation. It operated efficiently, its agents carrying out risky missions throughout occupied France. But when the war ended, the service, like the Foreign Legion, attracted some dubious characters and in 1946 it had to be purged of no less than 10,000 members when it was shown to be a refuge for wartime cheats and crooks.

The underlying purpose of the service was to control Communist influence at home and abroad. In 1948 agents kidnapped a top Nazi commando, Otto Skorzeny, from a US prison in Darmstadt in order to obtain information about the Soviet Union. The agency showed equal audacity the same year when one of its pilots flew secretly into Czechoslovakia to bring out Hubert Ripka, an opponent of the Communists who had just seized power in Prague.

It became more daring. Under its wing it had a branch known as the Action Division — still active today — its members highly-trained to carry out seemingly impossible missions, and these are credited with a string of assassinations, back-street assaults and disappearances. Right wing elements from regular army paratroopers joined the division and the Seine and other internationally known rivers began to entertain more corpses than the usual run of suicide victims. Many of the Service Action's activities were said to have gone beyond the realm of orders.

In one larger-than-life operation French spies planned a brazen mission on the Orient Express. The trans-continental train was the most common means of transporting important documents before international air travel became dependable and the Soviets used it frequently. Every day, two Russian couriers left their embassy in Paris and boarded the express to take secret papers to Istanbul, via Strasbourg and Vienna. From Turkey, they travelled to Budapest from where they could safely despatch the material to Moscow by air mail.

The SDECE decided there was one batch of documents they wanted to get their hands on. Two agents were put on the train. The Soviet couriers, as usual, remained in their compartment tucking into hard boiled eggs, sandwiches and tea. When the train entered a long tunnel, the French drilled a hole in the compartment wall and pumped in a syringeful of a powerful sedative powder. With the Russians lying unconscious, the agents entered their compartment, photographed the documents and made good their escape at the next station.

One of the SDECE's longest operations was during France's ultimately futile eight-year struggle against the National Liberation Front in the Algerian war. Agents are said to have tried several times to assassinate the Front's leader, Ahmed Ben Bella, including one horrific bungle with a car bomb in Cairo which killed 30 people. Finally, the SDECE got their man by forcing his plane to land in Algiers on a flight between Morocco and Tunisia. The ensuing political storm resulted in resignations from Guy Mollet's government, but one minister who stayed on was Francois Mitterrand.

The bombing of three cargo ships carrying arms for Algerian independence forces in Tangier harbour in 1958 and 1959 was credited to the SDECE. So, in the same period, was the death of two German arms dealers who were blown up in their booby-trapped cars. A mysterious organisation calling itself 'The Red Hand' claimed responsibility for the attacks. The 'Main Rouge' turned out to be a front for officers of the Service Action.

The end of the Algerian war in 1962 saw the SDECE shifting the core of its operations to Africa, under the supervision of de Gaulle's legendary aide, Jacques Foccart, whose name was associated with a number of cloak and dagger operations which included supplying arms to Biafran rebels in Nigeria and attempts to overthrow the Guinean leader, Ahmed Sekou-Touré. But the agency was active on other fronts and received a pat on the back from the Americans in 1962 when one of its operatives, based in Washington, discovered that Soviet missiles were being deployed in Cuba.

In fact, there have been other occasions when the SDECE has collaborated with the Americans. When a Soviet Tupolev jet broke down at Le Bourget airport in Paris, French agents, following a CIA request, photographed the faulty engine and took scrapings of its metal while Russian mechanics were installing its replacement.

But scandals followed. And scandals followed scandals. There were allegations of the secret service being involved in heroin smuggling, planning *coups d'état* and recruiting hit-men and mercenaries. Their consciences were always clear, for their orders, they confided to those they could trust, came from right wing heads of state.

In 1965, four agents, along with others, were implicated in the abduction and murder in Paris of exiled Moroccan opposition leader Mehdi Ben Barka. Only one SDECE agent was ultimately convicted of organising the kidnapping, but the mud stuck and the service's boss was forced to hand in his resignation. President de Gaulle, deciding that the agency should be kept under a tighter rein, transferred responsibility from the Prime Minister's office to the Defence Ministry. To add to its cleansing, President Georges Pompidou purged it in 1970 after accusing it of being behind a plot to smear him and his wife with allegations of sex orgies. Pompidou's shakeup resulted in the weakening of civilian resistance connections and the SDECE came more under the control of servicemen who had been trained for James Bond style action, rather than inquisitve counter-espionage.

During a decade of revival in the 1970s, the SDECE came out looking a little rosier, at least as far as its government was concerned. SDECE agents correctly forecast the date of the Yom Kippur War in 1973 and also established that the Russians were about to invade Afghanistan in 1979. In the same year, French agents were responsible for helping the Saudis recapture the Grand Mosque in Mecca after it had been taken over by Moslem rebels.

But in 1980, cries of 'Dirty Tricks' rang out following an explosion which destroyed a Corsican nationalist radio transmitter on the island of Elba. President Valery Giscard D'Estaing, accused of giving the go-ahead, has not commented.

Then, in 1981, the Socialists came to power and the trouble associated with the SDECE turned in on itself. Members of the Action Division, convinced they could not work with a Socialist Government, mutinied and carried out a 'scorched earth' policy, burning documents that carried details about previous missions. The strongest opposition was at the marine commando base at Aspretto in Corsica where crack underwater saboteurs are trained. Right wing officers displayed their opposition to the ascendancy of Mitterrand by keeping a photograph of former President Giscard in their mess room. In addition, a number of NCOs believed to have left wing sympathies were booted out.

The SDECE found itself under the control of Pierre Marion, a close friend of fellow freemason Charles Hernu, and who had once worked as an 'honorable correspondent' while employed by Air France in Japan. The appointment caused further disruption in the service: officials believed Mitterrand's government would go soft on the Communists, the very people the SDECE was working against. What's more, Marion, with his prickly temperament, was not easy to communicate with and experienced operators questioned his attempts at reorganisation.

Lacking morale, the service became shoddy and turned in inaccurate reports, to the embarrassment of the new President. Unable to put up with it further, Mitterrand installed Admiral Lacoste in the hope that the service — now known as the DGSE — would pull up its socks, move away from violence and revert to intelligence work. But it did not go as well as the President had hoped. The service continued to show its ineptitude in intelligence gathering, but proved it still had muscle. In particular, the Service Action maintained its links with mercenaries and recently provided teams of fighting men for guerrilla operations in Chad. Right wing rebels in Angola have also been supported, as well as Afghan freedom fighters. Bodyguards from the 'mercenary pool' have also been provided by the service for African leaders who have right wing convictions.

Since Mitterrand won leadership of the nation, relations between his government and the DGSE, particularly the hard-bitten Action Men, have not been rosy. After four years of Socialist rule, there remained confusion over who really controlled the 2,000 employees of the service and its worldwide network of honorary correspondents.

One of the biggest grumbles among the ranks has been the lack of funding. Certainly the DGSE's annual budget of about $US50 million is a pittance against the allowances granted to its allied and opposing agencies in Britain, the US and Russia.

With this chequered history behind the service he now commanded, Admiral Pierre Lacoste fully realised its potential for success . . . .and failure. Whatever action he may anticipate for the future, of one thing he was certain. He needed to establish exactly what Greenpeace planned for its South Pacific campaign. That information could only come from inside the organisation. Like his superior, the Defence Minister, a few days earlier, Admiral Pierre Lacoste studied the underlined word 'anticipate' on the document for a moment before reaching for his telephone . . .

4

Christine Cabon

Like the brilliant operator that she was, the blonde woman with the short cropped hair who was winging her way to New Zealand was well aware of the need to move in at the top. As one of the DGSE's best intelligence-gathering agents, her experience had proved that penetrating the heart of any organisation or government was the only way to gather reliable information. She was well versed in the methods of Western intelligence agencies. And although the KGB and all that it stood for was far removed from her own principles, familiarity with their methods had also been invaluable. They had planted moles in every major Western government and, she and her superiors at the General Directorate for External Security were convinced, they had their informants within the ranks of Greenpeace. Whatever Greenpeace found out about France and its nuclear programme, the Soviet Union, it was believed, found out too. Well, with any luck, she'd be able to establish that within the next few weeks. That would be a bonus to the main purpose of her mission which was to discover the exact movements of the Rainbow Warrior and the plans of those who intended sailing her to Mururoa.

At 33, the stocky army lieutenant now seconded to the DGSE was not unattractive although some who met her later were to say she was aloof with men; she was much warmer to women she befriended. In her handbag, she carried a French passport in the name of Frederique Bonlieu; occupation, geomorphologist. Her true identity was Christine Cabon, a former member of the French equivalent of Britain's crack Special Air Services, who had been invalided out after hurting her spine in a parachute accident. Handed over to the foreign intelligence service, she was trained in the art of infiltration — and passed with flying colours.

One of her major assignments was the dangerous task of infiltrating the Palestinian Liberation Organisation in the Lebanon, where she worked as an interpreter and lived with members of various PLO cells. The information she gathered was sent back to DGSE headquarters and vital aspects of it was passed on to the Israelis. She left the PLO on good relations — there was always the possibility that her services would be required again.

Also in her handbag was a letter from a prominent French nuclear protester, Jean-Marie Vidal, Director of the School of the Sea of Port Camargue, west of Marseille. She had met him 'by chance' in August 1984 on the quay at Ajaccio in Corsica, and during the course of their conversation she had spoken of her admiration of the exploits of the renowned French naval officer and ocean explorer, Jacques-Yves Cousteau. She told Vidal that she had read a number of Cousteau's books, which might well have been compulsory reading for the DGSE 'Action Service' frogmen being trained at that moment further around the coast at the combat base at Aspretto — it was Cousteau who had invented the aqualung diving apparatus and a process for using television underwater. Cabon convinced Vidal that she was a sympathiser of those who fought for the protection of sea and land and expressed the hope that one day she would meet up with him again.

It was not to be long. Nine months later she found him at the Salon Nautique in Paris and explained that she had decided to go to the Pacific to carry out some archaeological exploration. While there, she had said, she hoped to get in touch with various ecological groups, particularly Greenpeace.

'I would be grateful if you would write me a letter of introduction,' said Christine Cabon.

Vidal did not hesitate. Having listened to her background he wrote his introductory letter by hand, saying of her: 'She is a scientist and historian and an excellent navigator who shares our convictions.' And he added in his letter, dated April 3: 'Accommodate her and make known to her your positions and actions.'

Indeed part of that was true. After studying at Pau, in South West France, she had started a post-graduate course in modern history. She had given up her studies in 1977 when she was accepted by the French army to maintain a family tradition — her late father had been in the services and her brother Bernard, 12 years her senior, had also persued a military career.

The woman spy had no trouble passing through immigration and customs in Auckland and made her way to a city youth hostel. It was now mid April. Although older than the average guests, she did not attract any undue attention. Besides, she had no intention of staying there for long . . .

The Greenpeace office on the fifth floor of Nagel House in Courthouse Lane keeps its doors open for strangers who come to offer voluntary help, make donations, purchase booklets . . . or just chat. With the Rainbow Warrior on its way to New Zealand, the office was particularly busy and it was some time before anyone paid any attention to the 163cm woman in a neatly pressed jumper and jeans who stepped through the doorway.

At last, when she explained she had called to offer her services for the forthcoming campaign to Mururoa, she was introduced to various officials, among them Elaine Shaw, secretary-general and official spokesperson; Carol Stewart, the group's national co-ordinator; and the tall, bearded Dutchman Rien Achterberg who was co-ordinating local boats for the protest voyage to Mururoa. The letter from Vidal dispelled any reservations the group may have had about a French person entering the office — Vidal had been to New Zealand in 1974 and had been involved with the protest yacht Fri. Certainly, Elaine Shaw remembered him and any friend of Vidal's was more than welcome in the Greenpeace office.

Although dressed down, the woman who introduced herself as Frederique Bonlieu stood apart. She carried an air of independence — typical French arrogance some said — and took it upon herself, even on that first day, to decide with whom she would hold conversations. 'I am actually here,' she said in good English, as she sat on a sofa in the main reception area, *'en route* to Tahiti for an international conference on coral reefs and atolls, organised by the French Government. I have also been asked to plan a holiday itinerary for a couple of friends who will be coming through later. I would like to use some of my time to help Greenpeace. I can translate, type letters for you; sell things if you like.'

She was asked who she worked for in France. 'Ah, I am employed by a freelance scientific consultancy,' she said. 'They have done work all over the world. I am lucky. I travel a lot for them.' She had even lived and worked in Senegal, a former French colony, as an archaeologist.

In an adjoining office a telex was clattering. Someone was on the telephone discussing the movements of the Rainbow Warrior. Christine Cabon was shown around. The office was cluttered with posters and stickers depicting Greenpeace campaigns — window stickers calling for a nuclear free Pacific, bicycle stickers with the Greenpeace name, bumper stickers demanding the protection of Antarctica (another blow at the French who have been destroying penguin habitats to build an airstrip).

It was hardly a spy's dream world, but Christine Cabon had learned to be patient. The vital material, the contents of the telex messages, the filed documents . . . all would be made available to her in good time.

Within those first few days Rien Achterberg tried to be friendly with her, but she often cut him dead. He thought she got on much better with women. Her only conversations with him at first were strictly business. She carried a military authority that clashed with his own easy-going nature,

'It is going to be a strong campaign at Mururoa,' she said to him one day. 'How many New Zealand boats are going?'

There was no reason not to tell her. It had been in all the papers. He started to explain his role as co-ordinator and she interrupted to say that yes, she knew what he did. She was interested to know what he had been able to arrange so far.

Achterberg grinned and said he was rounding up whatever boats he could get. Certainly on the island of Waiheke where he lived — a haven for ecologists, painters, potters and boatmen — there had been a great deal of support. He reckoned three or four vessels from Waiheke alone would be heading for Mururoa this year.

'And what do you hope to achieve?' asked the Frenchwoman.

It seemed an obvious question, but he answered it nevertheless. 'We believe the tests have gone on long enough. They should never have been started. France has taken no notice. It is time they were made to sit up and take notice.'

Frederique Bonlieu shrugged. Someone who had overheard their conversation asked what she as a Frenchwoman thought about the plans to protest against her government.

'Nuclear tests are a very delicate subject,' she said. 'But national security problems are always more important to us.'

Some in the office thought she held a conflict of interest, particularly with statements like that, but nonetheless they were eager to make her as comfortable as possible. She had turned up regularly every morning and seemed more than keen to do whatever jobs were required. She wasn't happy, she said, at the youth hostel and wondered if Greenpeace could suggest somewhere else that she could stay.

She had picked them well. The answer from Carol Stewart a former clerk in an insurance office and a Greenpeace worker for six years was not unexpected. 'You're welcome to stay at my place until you can find somewhere that suits you,' said Carol.

The first two days were particularly difficult at Carol's home. She thought that for a so-called environmentalist, Frederique had some surprising attitudes. Greenpeace supported the fight for independence by the indigenous Kanaks in New Caledonia. Frederique did not. With elections due to be held there later in the year, Frederique expressed the wish that the Kanaks would lose heavily although it was a foregone conclusion that with the way the electoral divisions were being restructured they would gain a big foothold.

Sometimes the conversations between the two women became quite strained. There was little doubt the Frenchwoman was a staunch patriot. She spoke of the wishes of her nation, which had the largest nuclear arsenal after the United States and the Soviet Union, to become completely independent of the super-powers. For despite the importance of her undercover job, Christine Cabon regarded her role as some sort of ambassador for her country. Her French pride would not allow her to totally dismiss her country's nuclear stance and she believed that she could discuss such things in open forum with Greenpeace members who had proved in her short period with them how much they enjoyed talking about all aspects of conservation and nuclear issues.

'Trying to find peace with weapons is a very big paradox,' she said, 'but without this defence, we risk becoming like Finland, which is so influenced by Russia. Since we've had nuclear weapons we haven't been threatened nationally.'

Frederique Bonlieu was herself a paradox, wearing the cloak of a conservationist but propogating views that were for the advancement of nuclear weapons. She was neat and clean and did not smoke. And, at times, patronising.

'I consider myself an honoured guest in your house,' she remarked. So honoured, in fact, that she did nothing to contribute to the upkeep of the house although it would have been obvious to her that Carol and her housemates were not well off. She assumed the attitude that her hosts would do all they could to help her — which they did.

Sometimes when Carol and her friends went out, Frederique remained alone in the house, making the excuse that she did not often socialise. These were golden opportunities to search through the Greenpeace documents that Carol often brought home with her . . . letters from other branches, telex messages, reports of meetings.

But she also listened. She was around when Carol and other officials discussed tactics at Mururoa. She learned that the international director, David McTaggart, had written from England explicitly ordering them to keep the Rainbow Warrior outside the 12 mile limit. This would mean there would be no arrests and Greenpeace would be able to drag out its publicity for many months, causing France prolonged discomfort.

The French mole heard some Greenpeace members demanding to go ahead with the initial plan of charging through French waters. She made mental notes of all the discussions, wrote up her reports at the end of each day, and despatched them to a post office box number in Paris.

When she moved out of Carol's home, she accepted an invitation to stay with a group of young Greenpeace members and sympathisers who were sharing a house. One worked for an Auckland newspaper — a particularly useful contact, for the young woman would have acquainted herself with many aspects of Greenpeace. Again, Frederique Bonlieu showed herself to be a woman of contrasts. Although claiming to be relatively poor, she dressed extremely well and revealed that she was going to hire a car to travel around a bit to do some sightseeing and plot her friends' travel itinerary.

Once again she became involved in discussions that revealed a conflict in her environmental direction. Unlike her work inside the PLO, Christine Cabon-Frederique Bonlieu found herself playing a role which was in direct contrast to her firm nationalism. For the first time in her brilliant career she did not play her part very well. Her disguise was thin. The one thing she had going for her was that Greenpeace did not believe that anyone would betray them. As Carol Stewart was to remark much later, when it was too late:

'I felt physically ill when I realised who she really was. I had been so gullible, so trusting. Looking back, I should have realised there was something terribly wrong about her story. But I didn't. Nobody did. Even in our wildest dreams we were not thinking of betrayal. We Greenpeace people trust each other.'

Frederique Bonlieu's patriotism continued to show through in her conversations. She made it clear on several occasions that because the French were dependent on electricity powered by the country's 15 nuclear stations and were themselves exposed to side effects of radiation, they did not consider the Mururoa tests dangerous.

Her story changed slightly now. Not only was she in New Zealand for sightseeing and 'professional geographical and archaeological reasons' — she also wanted to find out just what was going on in the Pacific because the region was far away from France and news was slow to get through. In addition, she said, she wanted to learn the truth about the New Caledonian issue.

'French people are very confused by the political debate,' she remarked one evening in a conversation with another woman journalist. 'They don't know as much about New Caledonia as they do about Chad, where France has also been involved. And you know, criticism of France's colonial attitudes are really so hypocritical because other countries such as Britain and the United States also have colonial traditions.'

She spoke from experience about the French presence in Lebanon, saying that was an example of the peace-keeping role her people were proud to be playing.

While defending her nation in such discussions, the bogus Frederique Bonlieu was not wasting time. Her orders were to gather as much material about Auckland Harbour as she could muster and also study the New Zealand coastline for a suitable landing point for a team of agents who were likely to be sent to the country later. Armed with a 35mm camera, she wandered around the harbour area taking photographs of the wharves and purchased a number of maps of Auckland and its waterfront.

Relying on the trust she had built up with the young women she stayed with, despite her often conflicting views, Frederique Bonlieu asked where in Auckland she could hire and fill oxygen diving tanks for her friends. She also wondered how much these would cost on daily and weekly rates. And where, she wanted to know, was the best place to go to hire small boats and dinghies? Obligingly, one of the Greenpeace girls found the information for her and pointed out that there might be a problem in just one or two divers trying to hire their own small boat. Hiring firms usually insisted on larger groups in case of accidents.

In the privacy of her room, Christine Cabon wrote down all the details, adding the names of hire firms that she had found herself in the Yellow Pages telephone book. She had also collected pamphlets giving details about yacht, car and campervan hire. These, too, were duly despatched to Paris, along with all the maps and her processed photographs. The contents of her package would have made dull reading for even the most avid of tourists, but for her DGSE controllers it was important time-saving information.

Always, she was vague with her temporary friends about the purpose of her visit. At one stage, preying possibly on what newcomers to the country mistakenly see as a naive innocence in New Zealanders, she revealed that the scientific consultancy which employed her was very interested in sending a mission to the country later in the year. Nobody pressed her for more information. It didn't really seem to matter.

She also got hold of a detailed map for her tour of the North Island. She hired a car to travel to the area north of Auckland known as Northland, a narrow peninsula no more than 100 km across at its widest and reaching 250 km from just south of Whangarei to its furthest point. The area has countless sheltered bays — including the spectacularly beautiful Bay of Islands — harbours and white sandy beaches on its eastern coast which looks onto the Pacific Ocean. As she travelled, Christine Cabon took more photographs and picked up whatever tourist brochures she could lay her hands on.

If anything, thought the Greenpeace people, Frederique Bonlieu was a keen worker for the cause. So much so that she made up for the time she lost while away on her 'sightseeing' trips. On several occasions she worked late in the office, up to 9 p.m., translating brochures from English into French for sending to supporters in Paris. She had access to all the files, particularly those of Elaine Shaw, which contained much of the correspondence received from abroad. Some of the information she gleaned was already known to the DGSE. It was no secret to her bosses that New Zealand had been pushing the Mururoa campaign for the last 10 years. Neither was it a revelation that the Pacific Peace

Campaign, with the Rainbow Warrior as the spearhead, had been proposed by New Zealand and accepted at a general council meeting in Lewes, England, in 1983. However, she was able to gather new information on the names of several organisations which supported Greenpeace and these were to be used later by at least one pro-French magazine as 'proof' that the world-wide organisation was backed by a number of Communists.

After several weeks, relations between the cool Ms Bonlieu and Rien Achterberg improved. With hindsight, he realised she had done the rounds of the ladies of the organisation, milked them of whatever information she could, and was ready to try new ground. Thus it was that when Achterberg invited her to come across to Waiheke Island, an hour and a quarter on the ferry, to stay with him and his lady, Linda, for the weekend, she readily accepted.

There were three boats from the island — Kliss II, Django and Alliance — that were planning to sail to Mururoa and he'd be happy to show her around, give her a chance to chat to some of the crews if he could round them up. Achterberg thought it was a bonus having a French person working in the office because the work of the organisation, through her translations, could now penetrate deep into the very heart of the nation they were all protesting against.

Frederique Bonlieu brought a bottle of wine across on the ferry that Friday evening. The three of them sat in Achterberg's modest home and drank the wine with a vegetarian meal and once again the French woman defended her country's right to continue its nuclear test programme. Achterberg thought she argued objectively and she raised no suspicions in his mind. He understood French pride.

She was given a room under the house which offered some privacy, but he made it clear to her that she had to treat the place as if it were her own — she could move as freely as she wished and help herself to whatever food she could find. In the morning Achterberg and Linda set off for the local market. The French-woman, who the night before had shown some interest in coming along now cried off, saying she did not really feel like going.

And so for the morning she was left alone in the house to search around for whatever documents she could find. When Achterberg returned he took her around the island on his motor cycle, pointing out to her where the boats were moored.

In retrospect, it was easy for him to understand that she had had military training. Muscular, she held herself well, breasts forward, stomach in and had a certain commanding air about her, disguised to some extent by what he was to recall as an 'aristocratic aloofness.' He remembered her as having hazel eyes, although others said they were blue, with a lot of character in her face. She wore just a trace of make-up and no jewellery. With her high cheek bones he thought that some might find something appealing about her--but not him; maybe no other man.

Perhaps Christine Cabon was not such a good choice for the DGSE to send to New Zealand. Apart from being obviously French, her patriotism and arrogance was drawing much attention. But she was getting away with her undercover mission because Greenpeace, and other New Zealanders she met, had no inkling of the event that was to thrust their nation into world headlines two months later.

She still had more work to do. With several packages of information already despatched and a number of phone calls made to France, Christine Cabon travelled in a hired car to the east of Auckland, to the finger-like peninsula known as the Coromandel, and further south to the East Cape, checking out the coastline.

Ninety kilometres north of Gisborne, on the east coast, nationally recognised potter Helen Mason found a sturdy French woman at her door one morning in the hamlet of Tokomaru Bay. It was an experience she was never to forget. The woman introduced herself as Frederique Bonlieu and said she was looking for some pots to give to her friends in Greenpeace.

Mrs Mason, 70, lives in the old harbourmaster's cottage. It has a commanding view of the disused harbour and isolated bay, sought out occasionally by yachtsmen wanting shelter.

The potter showed her visitor the kiln where she worked, then made her a cup of coffee. She wished she hadn't. As she was to say later: 'I have never met anyone quite so bitter. She quite shook me up. She harangued me for about an hour and a half about how hard it was to be French because everyone hated them.'

Frederique Bonlieu had arrived in a white rental car. She was wearing jeans and a sweatshirt and said she was an archaeologist working at present for Greenpeace in Auckland. Someone in the capital had given her Mrs Mason's address. The potter thought how unlike a member of a peace organisation her visitor seemed. 'She was very French,' she was to recall, 'and her bitterness quite upset me. I get all kinds of people calling in on me and some are ruder than others, but something about this woman put me on edge. Her bitterness seemed to run very deep and she talked a lot, as if trying to be accepted. She said her father had been an admiral in the French fleet and had to watch as his ship was scuttled during the war.'

The French spy purchased a few pots from Mrs Mason, then said she must be on her way. Despite her discomfort, the potter invited Frederique Bonlieu to stay the night — Gisborne was a long drive from anywhere. When the offer was turned down, Mrs Mason asked her visitor for her address for her contact book. Ms Bonlieu gave the address she was staying at in Auckland, and when asked for a French address, said she did not have one. Finally, she gave Mrs Mason the address of an Italian woman in France who would know where to contact her.

Shortly before midday her visitor set off in her car. She was going to Wanganui, she said, another coastal town in the west. Yes, she assured Mrs Mason, she knew how far it was; she had a good map.

In addition to the wealth of information she had collected, Christine Cabon came across one more little gem. Greenpeace were often in touch with Bengt Danielsson, a member of the Kon Tiki expedition now living in Tahiti, about Mururoa. A fervent conservationist, Danielsson had promised to do all he could to help the protest campaign from his end. In a letter to the New Zealand office, he had discussed possible tactics. That letter was lying around when the French spy was working late one evening. It told how several well-known Tahitian independence fighters and anti-nuclear church leaders were ready and willing to join the Rainbow Warrior in Auckland to take part in the protest voyage to Mururoa. Danielsson also made the point that since they were French citizens it would not have been legally possible to deny them access and toss them out of French Polynesia.

On May 24 Christine Cabon said goodbye to her 'friends' in Auckland and flew to Tahiti. To give credence to her cover as a geologist, she registered with the Coral Reef Congress. Again, she didn't do it very well. As Bengt Danielsson was to say later: 'It soon became clear to the participants that she knew next to nothing about the scientific problems under discussion.'

However, she made a point of calling on Danielsson to ask about the local attitudes to Mururoa and the plans to protest against the tests. He dug out copies of articles he had written for the Sydney produced magazine *'Pacific Islands Monthly'* about the testing site and local opinion and handed them to her. They hardly contained material that could be classified as top secret, but Christine Cabon sent them off to Paris nevertheless. As far as the DGSE was concerned, this was further proof that this year could be bad for France's image unless something was done to stop the protest flotilla.

Late in June, the spy flew to California where she contacted a Greek woman friend, Antigone Zournatzis. The two flew to Paris, where they separated. Cabon went to the DGSE headquarters and gave a verbal run down of all her inquiries. Then, to back up the cover story that she had given to Greenpeace members, she flew to Israel to join Ms Zournatzis on an archaeological dig at Pardes Hanna.

Her work was over. It had been clean, easy, and certainly not dangerous. Or so she thought.

5

Preparations

Hardly had the first of Christine Cabon's reports arrived at DGSE headquarters when the audacious plan to sink the Rainbow Warrior was set in motion. Admiral Lacoste, along with a number of DGSE and military officials, including General Roger Emin, the agency's second in command; Colonel Jean-Claude Lesquer, head of the Action Service; and the Defence Minister's Chief of Cabinet, Jean-Francois Dubos, had listened to various suggestions put forward by agents within the service.

The flagship's engines could be sabotaged. Storage facilities for distilled cold water for the engines could be damaged. Food supplies could be threatened by putting the cold store out of action. But the ideas were dismissed because they were impractical or impermanent. Whatever action was to be taken, the DGSE had to ensure that not only did the Rainbow Warrior not sail to Mururoa but that other protest crews had to be frightened off and the morale of Greenpeace members dented for a long time to come.

Sending the Rainbow Warrior to the bottom of the sea was going to be expensive. Overseen by a colonel, accountants at the DGSE drew up a *'dossier d'objectif'*, working out just how much it would cost to fly agents to the other side of the world to sabotage the peace flotilla flagship. Air tickets, the hire of boats and cars, accommodation, food . . . all these items were totted up by DGSE clerks who had been given access to the material sent from New Zealand by Christine Cabon.

The immediate questions were how, where and when the operation would be carried out. Obviously the old trawler could not be blown up at sea with the possible loss of everyone on board — apart from the physical difficulties of such an action, the secret service would be committing mass murder and even for an agency with such a dubious past as the DGSE that would be overstepping the mark.

One suggestion from the Action Service was to plant a mine on the harbour bed long before the Rainbow Warrior arrived at its mooring and set the explosive to go off either by a timer or radio control at low tide when the vessel was in dock. That would certainly break its back. But there were too many risks. The ship might be delayed, it might change its mooring, the radio control system might fail.

There was only one fail-safe method. Fix a mine on the hull when the vessel was securely moored. The question again arose about the crew. When was the Rainbow Warrior ever unoccupied? As Christine Cabon had already established from her conversations with Greenpeace members, hardly ever. But there was always a way of getting the crew off before the vessel went down. It would involve two explosions . . .

The accountants assessed that the operation would cost no less than three million francs — about $US383,000. But as the two DGSE paymasters, Prefect Philippe Parant and his assistant Alain Christnacht were to point out to their superiors, there was a cash flow problem. Although the DGSE receives an annual fixed budget — 196.7 million francs (about $25 million) in 1985 — from the overall defence budget, they do not get it all at once. Monthly payments are allocated by the Government Chief Secretary and no questions are asked at the time about its intended use, although at the end of every year a report from the French Accounting Court itemises the expenditure.

Early in 1985 the DGSE had already made great use of its allocated funds to develop its intelligence equipment, recruit new 'honorable correspondents' and intensify its anti-terrorism measures. To add to that, money had become tight as usual in the months before a general election, with funds being set aside for security purposes. But it was the custom to keep an emergency supply at the office and residence of Prime Minister Laurent Fabius at the Hotel Matignon.

Whenever this special fund was needed, it was the practice for it to be released with the approval of the Defence Minister and the chief military official on the President's staff at the Elysee Palace, General Jean Saulnier. When the money for the Greenpeace operation was suddenly demanded, and the release of the funds had been approved by the two defence heads, the Government General Secretary, Jacques Fournier, telephoned the office of the General Director of the State Budget asking for the endorsement of a special decree for what was known as 'accidental expenditure'.

This document, already 'legalised' by a rubber stamp bearing the signatures of Prime Minister Fabius (affixed by Government General Secretary Fournier) and one other official was then signed by Budget State Secretary Henri Emmanuelli. The money was later withdrawn from a government account numbered 200–00–18–852.

In the second half of May, as Christine Cabon was preparing to leave Auckland, three senior aides to President Mitterrand met with intelligence chief Admiral Lacoste at the Elysee Palace.

Present in the office of the Secretary General, Mr Jean-Louis Bianco, were Mr Hubert Vedrine, Diplomatic Advisor to the President; General Saulnier, who had approved the unblocking of the special funds; Admiral Lacoste; and Mr Bianco. The topic of discussion was France's presence in the Pacific — and the importance of propping it up. The government officials talked at length about the determination of some South Pacific nations to push France away.

There was a general feeling that there was no real danger of France's grip being weakened. It was then that Admiral Lacoste laid the hard facts before them. Despite France's rapid steps in nuclear development, her position as a colonial power in the Pacific was weaker now than it had ever been, due to a strong independence movement encouraged by outside conservationists and the Soviet Union.

In New Caledonia the independent movement was making great headway. Agitators were at work in Tahiti. And Greenpeace, which had always been a problem, intended that year to take advantage of France's weakening colonial hold. That indeed would suit the Soviets perfectly. To back up his conviction that the headlines were going to be bad within a few months, the DGSE chief repeated the information relayed by Christine Cabon. The French Navy, Admiral Lacoste emphasised, would have great trouble in keeping a vessel the size of the Rainbow Warrior away from Mururoa Atoll. It was big enough to batter its way through to the test site.

Admiral Lacoste's words burned into every heart. The three other men and their aides listened carefully to the hopes that action could be taken soon to meet the Greenpeace menace head on.

The Odyssee Travel Agency in Rue du Ranelagh, Paris XVl, is a small family run business operated by Mr Claude Leroy and his wife. It could be said of both of them that discretion was a virtue. Since the agency started in 1971 word had gone around that Mr Leroy was the man to see for the arrangement of private luxury cruises. The business is one of only a handful in France that handles bookings for the hire of boats from Noumea, in New Caledonia. A casual bystander would not therefore have been particularly surprised to hear an inquiry from a blond caller about renting a yacht to sail the waters of the Western Pacific.

What was unusual about this particular request, however, was the client's next demand. He was hoping to sail on for a vacation in New Zealand. It was the first time Mr Leroy had received such a request for the Southern Hemisphere's winter, but he took the applicant's details. He gave his name as Dr Xavier Maniguet from Dieppe and was willing to pay up to 90,000 francs, but he did not want to sail alone. If Mr Leroy could assist him in finding two or three co-sailors, that would be very nice . . .

Within a few days Mr Leroy had another inquiry about the hiring of yachts in New Caledonia. The caller gave his name as

Raymond Velche, a professional skipper, who was inquiring on behalf of himself and two friends. They were looking for a fourth person to make up a crew in Noumea. Why yes, Mr Leroy could certainly help them. Why, only the other day . . .

Although Mr Leroy has always remained a gentleman of discretion, refusing to divulge the identities of individuals, organisations, and government employees who have sought out his services, his *modus operandi* is not entirely unknown. The agent arranged meetings between solitary crew members, often assessing letters in lieu of personal introductions in order to avoid embarrassment should one applicant find another not to his liking. It was also his practice not to ask for identity papers or certificates of navigation. All that was required was a name on the hire contract, the maximum number of crew — and, of course, cash in advance.

It just so happened that by a remarkable coincidence Dr Maniguet and the crew he was to join up with shared a great deal in common. The so-called Raymond Velche and his two colleagues were DGSE agents, all highly-trained combat frogmen based at the Navy Frogmen Training Centre (CNIC) at Aspretto in Corsica. And Dr Maniguet was an adept parachutist, a skilled underwater swimmer, a devotee of combat sports, a reservist in the French navy, and a specialist in treating problems arising from diving accidents.

While the Rainbow Warrior headed through the Pacific on its mission of peace, Mr Leroy contacted charter companies in Noumea searching for a yacht that would suit his clients. From the Auckland central post office, just a few minutes walk from the Greenpeace office, Christine Cabon sent off her new information, indicating that there might be some difficulty in hiring small boats or rubber dinghies for parties of less than six. In a way, as was suggested later by intelligence agents in Britain and New Zealand, the dinghy problem suited the DGSE perfectly. It gave those who planned the fine details of the sabotage operation an idea that would, hopefully, divert any suspicion of French involvement.

By the middle of May, just before Christine Cabon handed out her farewell gifts of pots to her Greenpeace friends for the tremendous service they had given her, the intricacies of the plot had been worked out.

It was important that the yacht which Mr Leroy had found, the Ouvea, was suitable for the voyage from Noumea to New Zealand. It was also essential that it had areas where bulky equipment could be stored, hidden from sight from any casual caller who happened to come on board. The DGSE could not afford any last minute slip ups. And so on May 28, the fair, curly-haired man calling himself Raymond Velche caught a flight from Paris to Noumea specifically to look over the yacht.

His real name was Chief Petty Officer Roland Verge, with 15 years of military service behind him, 11 with the DGSE. Like many French secret service operatives, he had chosen a false name near to his own, yet different enough to suggest a mistake had been made should his cover be blown. There can be a problem in having more than one identity, as Verge was to demonstrate later. At Tontouta Airport he handed over his false passport showing that he was Raymond Velche, a professional skipper, born at Bayonne on July 10 1950. He gave his address as 52 rue de Chemin Verte, Paris X1, in reality a decaying block of 61 apartments, so poor that it does not even have a concierge.

He checked into room 302 at the Noumea Beach Hotel from where he made two overseas telephone calls. Also on the agenda was a visit to Noumea Yacht Charters from whom he was hiring the Ouvea. The manager, Mr Roger Chatelain, explained that Mr Jean Pelissier, a major shareholder in the company, always insisted on knowing the nautical experience of yachtsmen. The DGSE operative's first slip was to detail his age as 32 — not 35 as his false passport indicated. He also claimed to have had 10 years experience as a ship's captain, including two years of charter work in the Antilles.

Antilla, Cuba, would have been more accurate. For Verge, a highly-rated underwater sabotage diver, had worked under cover in Fidel Castro territory for a number of months, passing himself off as an adventuring yacht skipper.

He was taken down to the harbour front to inspect the vessel that was to launch him on a new espionage job. The $100,000 Ouvea, an 11.7 metre French-built First 38, had something of a history of sailing around Pacific waters. She had been taken to the North Island of New Zealand a few years earlier and sailed around Great Barrier Island. In 1983 she cruised to Honiara in the Solomons from where she was stolen. But Noumea Yacht Charters got her back, resolving to make sure they knew full details of everyone who hired their vessels in future.

On May 29, while Verge was dining out in Noumea, a second member of the team from the Aspretto base was arriving at London's Heathrow Airport under the name of Eric Andreine. Well-muscled, dark-haired, with puffy eyes and a broken nose, Andreine's true identity was Petty Officer Gerald Andries. He had served 10 years with the French Navy, six of them with the DGSE. Shortly after 9 a.m. he made his way through the early holiday crowds in Terminal 2 to the counter of Hotel Booking International. Mr Kirti Shah, an employee, thought the man's English was terrible but understood him well enough to know he wanted a room in London. Andries was given a docket, signifying a room had been found for him at the Vanderbilt Hotel in Cromwell Road, Kensington, West London.

Travelling lightly, he did not bother to go straight to the hotel but made his way to North London, to a nautical shop trading under the name of Barnet Marine. Located at the junction of Greenhill Parade and Grand North Road, New Barnet, it is acknowledged as an important retailer of boats and fishing equipment. Ironically, Greenpeace is one of its customers.

Manager Keith Chapman and his staff were very busy, and the Frenchman was left to wander around the store for a time, gazing at equipment. Finally, when he received attention, he explained in his broken English that he was a representative of a Belgian diving company. He was looking for a rubber boat, he explained, and an engine to go with it. After checking over various boats for about an hour, he selected a grey French-made Zodiac dinghy which was on display. Although Mr Chapman's staff brought an identical dinghy, packaged in two parts in plastic bags, from the store, the Frenchman insisted on it being inflated in front of him. Mr Chapman led the man next door to the workshop for a demonstration.

Next Andries selected a four horsepower Yamaha engine which surprised the store staff as the dinghy could have taken a 40 horsepower engine. There was another eyebrow raiser: he handed over 1,400 pounds in new 50 pound notes, showed no concern about the cost and did not bother about filling in an export form which would have meant he could have claimed back the Value Added Tax when he took the boat and engine out of the country.

Barnet Marine staff, understanding enough of the Frenchman's virtually incomprehensible English to realise he wanted a taxi, called a radio cab from a local company, Metro Cars. Andries demonstrated his strength by carrying the two dinghy bags, weighing a total of 67 kilograms and the motor, with a weight of 19 kilograms, out to the taxi.

At the Vanderbilt Hotel that afternoon, a porter helped the foreigner carry the heavy packages to his room. Later that day he went to the West End, to a hotel off Oxford Street, to meet a compatriot . . .

The following morning, before 11 o'clock, the man calling himself Eric Andreine paid his bill, 64 pounds and 90 pence, in cash and vanished, taking the dinghy and motor with him. But Andries had been careless, displaying a lack of expertise that caused some old hands at the DGSE to remark later that it would never have happened when they were in the field. For Andreine-Andries had made phone calls from his hotel room, booking them through the switchboard. Two of the numbers retained in the hotel records were of the Air France office. The third was a number at the DGSE.

Just how the Frenchman spirited his bulky packages out of Britain was to be queried by police much later. Checks at air cargo terminals at Heathrow Airport and Gatwick in the south east, showed no record of any package resembling the Zodiac and the dinghy being sent to either France or New Caledonia, leaving some detectives to believe the parcels had been taken back to France on a ferry crossing the English Channel.

While Andries was making his way back to Paris from London, Roland Verge, satisfied with his inspection of the Ouvea, was winging his way back to the French capital from the other side of the world. When he touched down at Orly on May 31 he had clocked up 60 hours of flying in less than four days.

Andreine-Andries, Velche-Verge and the third man who was to make up the crew of the Ouvea — Jean-Michel Bartelo, with 10 years military service, four with the DGSE — met for a final briefing with Action Service officers. Among those present was a heavy-set 49-year-old man who was to assume two false identities. His real name was Lieutenant-Colonel Louis-Pierre Dillais, Commander of the Aspretto base. At first, he would travel as an analyst under the name Phillippe Dubast, born at Reims on April 4 1936. His role in the affair would be overseer of the sabotage operation against Greenpeace.

Also briefed was a slender auburn-haired woman who would fly to New Zealand to assist the team. She would travel under the name of Sophie Frederique Clair Turenge. In fact she was Dominique Prieur, 36, a Captain in the French Army and a member of the intelligence branch of the DGSE. Her cover would be that of a newly-wed — and her 'husband' Alain Jacques Turenge, would in fact be 34-year-old Major Alain Mafart, a skilled underwater swimmer and instructor from the Navy Frogmen Training Centre in Corsica. These two bogus honeymooners were supplied with passports from a department within the DGSE that specialises in false identity papers. Secret Service agents are provided with passports from the department identifying them as either French or Swiss citizens. In the case of the 'Turenge' couple, they were given Swiss passports stating her occupation as a schoolteacher, his as a businessman.

The stage was now set. The right dinghy had been purchased and a suitable yacht lined up. Magnetic mines were available in New Caledonia where a French military base was maintained. The advance party was sent on its way.

UTA flight 566 touched down at Noumea on June 7, carrying Verge, Andries and Bartelo. Andries, who had earlier visited London using the name Eric Andreine, had now become Eric

Audrenc, 32, photographer of 2, rue de l'Atlas, Paris XIX. Bartelo presented himself as Jean-Michel Berthelo, 33, a commercial agent of 49, rue de la Victoire, Paris IX.

Verge, who had already got his age mixed up on his visit 10 days earlier, now made another mistake with his bogus identity. Instead of giving his address as 52 rue de Chemin Verte, he wrote it this time as number 58. The mistake was not picked up by the authorities, even though the three DGSE agents drew attention to themselves by arguing with customs about the size of the marine sacks that had been flown in with them. They hired a Volkswagen Combi van and travelled to the city, where they checked into the Noumea Beach Hotel, occupying rooms 302, 206 and 202. There was a fourth man on the UTA flight who booked into the same hotel, taking room 208. He was Phillippe Dubast, overseer of the operation.

For the next few days the four men busied themselves preparing for the voyage to New Zealand. However, Dubast kept a low profile and avoided being seen too often with the others. Onto the Ouvea they loaded a Satnav system for taking points by satellite, an automatic pilot, an 8 megahertz radio for international link-ups and an interphone connecting the cabin with the bridge. They also rented oxygen bottles and a compressor.

Mr Chatelain, manager of Noumea Yacht Charters, had just the slightest of worries as he watched the equipment being loaded onto the 38 foot one-masted keel boat.

Someone who understands communications remarked to him that the equipment being taken onto the Ouvea was not compatible. When this was pointed out to the crew, they brushed advice aside.

To add to his niggling unease, Mr Chatelain thought the men calling themselves Audrenc and Berthelo behaved like overgrown schoolboys. They threw mock punches at each other and larked around in a way that would have concerned any man who was about to hand over an expensive yacht. The man calling himself Velche, however, acted responsibly, trying to keep the others under some control. It eased Mr Chatelain's mind somewhat when Velche produced cheques to pay for the hire until

July 28. He wrote two, totalling 106,250 francs drawn, mysteriously, on the account of the Odyssee Travel Agency.

On June 11, Noumea received another visitor who was familiar with the Odyssee travel service — Dr Xavier Maniguet, 38, who had arrived to join his fellow crew members. During his adventurous career, Dr Maniguet had worked for five years as a 'diving medicine' expert in the United Arab Emirates centre of Abu Dhabi. For three years, before leaving Abu Dhabi in December 1984, he was seconded from the French State Oil Company (CFP) to an offshore oil company, Zadco. He had also worked in Asia as a specialist treating divers who suffered from the bends.

Later he was to explain his travels as 'a means of earning a living while embracing adventure.' He was to add: 'For me to be a doctor means to work wherever it is possible, provided that you can at least earn a minimum income. This may be an open door to adventure of many kinds. I have an inquisitive mind and my ideal in life would be to become an honest man in the sense as it was understood in the eighteenth century — by that I mean living until the end with a maximum of experience and the respect of everyone.'

Dr Maniguet dined out in style with his crew and looked over the yacht. He seemed to be well satisfied. Verge tried to call Paris from the Noumea Post Office but told staff he had not been able to get through. On June 13, after the Volkswagen had made numerous trips to the harbour and sacks and supplies had been loaded aboard the yacht, the Ouvea sailed out of Noumea for its voyage south to New Zealand.

Standing on the harbourside was a burly man with short brown hair. As the yacht picked up speed, Lieutenant Commander Louis-Pierre Dillais, alias Phillippe Dubast, turned and made his way back to the Noumea Beach Hotel. Booked to fly out the following day, he had some packing to do and yet another identity to assume.

The commander of the French secret underwater school had not wasted time during the past six days. While his three subordinates had busied themselves preparing the Ouvea, Dillais, a master planner who was aware of the need for more than one escape route on any undercover mission, made contact with certain Navy officials. Moored at Noumea since May 10 was the French nuclear submarine Rubis, which was to play a vital role in the Rainbow Warrior affair.

The Rubis had been ordered into the South Pacific to bolster France's strategic power in New Caledonia after 47 days of submerged cruising. Her presence in the Pacific was a demonstration of President Mitterrand's determination to maintain a strong French profile in the region. Her movements a month later were to have an added significance.

6

Paradise Threatened

It's a big playground. Occupying a third of the surface of the globe, it covers 165,250,000 square kilometres, reaching north for 15,500 kilometres from the ice-packed shores of Antarctica to the Bering Strait and stretching east to west for 21,300 kilometres from the Malay Peninsula to Columbia in South America. The Pacific is larger than the whole land surface of the world and with depths greater than the height of Mount Everest, it has more than double the volume of water in the Atlantic.

It is the playgound of whales, sea lions, dolphins and rainbow-coloured fish. Gulls plummet from great heights to snatch their shimmering prey. And tides gently wash the white sandy beaches of ancient coconut-fringed atolls. The ocean with its blend of colours from blue-black to turquoise green is an awesome place with no defined borders for the life forms that survive in it. Only the intruders seek to change the balance of nature.

On its surface and below glide the ships and submarines of the superpowers. Overhead fly their jets and bombers. From military bases sophisticated radar systems search for missiles; satellite communication systems punch out coded information; the bottom of the ocean vibrates as another underground bomb is exploded.

Close to 250 nuclear warheads have been tested in the Pacific region since Hiroshima and Nagasaki were destroyed and according to estimates based on Pentagon documents and other information, some 600 American and Soviet nuclear weapons are already deployed in the Pacific-Asia region. Another 1400 are said to be ready for deployment in the area. The United Nations estimates that some 150,000 people have died or are destined to die — many of them Pacific inhabitants — as a direct result of the testing of nuclear weapons by the British, the Americans, the Chinese and the French in the Pacific region. Nobody bothers to count the toll in terms of the creatures to whom the ocean belongs.

However, when Presidents and Prime Ministers of the 13-nation South Pacific Forum adopted a new treaty on August 7 declaring the region a 'nuclear free zone' it was immediately dismissed by some Pacific politicians and defence experts around the world as being far too late.

Between 1946 and 1962, the USA carried out more than 60 nuclear tests in Bikini and Enewetak in the Marshall Islands and on Christmas and Johnson Islands. The British conducted tests in central Australia, the Christmas Islands and the Malden Islands during the 1950s. In the Gobi desert at Lop Nor, in Sinkiang Province, China has been carrying out atmospheric tests — the latest estimate is 25 — and scientists estimate the fallout has been over the Pacific. But the biggest culprit of all has been France, carrying out 41 atmospheric tests between 1966 and 1974 in French Polynesia, with another 60 underground up to May, 1984.

Given these facts, it is not surprising that in mid November, 1985, a leaked independent report commissioned by the US State Department said rigid American policies and French colonial intransigence were the main source of instability in the South Pacific. Mr Peter Hayes, an investigator at the Massachusetts-based Nautilus Research Centre, commented: 'While the US says that the Soviets are the bull in the South Pacific china shop, in fact it is the US itself and its close ally France who are the bulls.'

Apart from providing a lot of space in which to explode nuclear weapons, the Pacific has become a vital trade route, with some 40 per cent of America's commerce passing through the region. Japan, Australia and New Zealand also rely heavily on using the

Pacific for trade. But the ocean is valuable, too, because of its huge fish supplies and enormous mineral deposits on its floor.

This important region has become the battleground for the new Cold War. Much of the in-fighting between Western politicians and ecologists, and the arrogance displayed by France and the United States towards Pacific islanders, has added to the threat of Soviet intrusion.

The Russians continue to extend their range of strategic interests in the South Pacific, reaching from bases in Vietnam, through newly-formed alliances in Vanuatu and Kiribati, to the Antarctic. The more the Labour governments of Australia and New Zealand argue with France and the United States over the nuclear issue, the happier the Soviets become.

Caught up in the wrangling are the Pacific nations, some of whom are not happy to be bounced around the political ring by the big Western nations, and the Russians have recognised this. In addition, Pacific island groups which started wearing the cloak of independence with Western Samoa's break-away from New Zealand in 1962 are now rarely influenced by their old leaders. With a new generation of university educated, anti-colonial politicians, they have turned their heads towards a socialist-style administration.

So far, attempts by the Soviet Union to form a recognisable political liaison with Pacific nations have been rebuffed and there has been no evidence of Russian attempts to intervene in the government of the island States. But complacency by the West could have given the Russians a foot in the door.

With bases dotted throughout the Pacific, the United States has assumed that it had the region nicely 'sewn up' and that there was no possibility of Russian intrusion. After all, the US Pacific Command, with headquarters in Hawaii and key bases in the Philippines, covers half the globe. Its zone, which also includes the Indian Ocean, reaches up from the Antarctic to the Arctic, from the southern tip of Africa to the west coast of America. To patrol this enormous area, the command employs some 365,000 Army, Navy, Air Force, Marine Corps and Defence Department personnel.

Without Philippine bases, a fully loaded US aircraft carrier would take some 25 days to reach the Indian Ocean from the West Coast. Aware of the precarious military future for the West in the Pacific, the Soviets have already made their move.

They have started nibbling away at several Pacific nations in the hope of obtaining 'fishing rights' in their waters. And one nation, Kiribati, has already taken the bait and signed an agreement with the USSR, annoyed that the Americans have taken them for granted. The Soviets stepped in with their irresistable offer as the bickering over French nuclear testing gathered momentum at the beginning of 1985 and American tuna fishing boats, ignoring the sensitivities of island nations, cast their nets indiscriminately.

Formerly known as the Gilbert Islands, the Micronesian nation of 33 islands and a population of 60,000, Kiribati's territory covers 5 million square kilometres of water in the central Pacific. It gained independence from Britain in 1979 and has been receiving $US1.3 million in aid from London as part of the decolinisation agreement.

As well as Kiribati, Russian diplomats approached the governments of Fiji, Tuvalu, the Solomon Islands and, it is believed, Papua New Guinea, asking for fishing rights. They knew exactly who to go to. These nations have been upset by the activities of the big US fishing boats in waters where local economies are dependent on fish. In fact, feelings were so high that the Government of the Solomon Islands was widely applauded when it arrested a poaching American boat, resulting in sanctions from Washington.

In March 1985, while Tuvalu, the Solomons and Vanuatu were being wooed by the Russians, Kiribati government officials held talks with Soviet envoys in Sydney and were offered a sum in excess of $US2 million a year — cash. Much to the dismay of the United States, Australia and New Zealand, Kiribati signed an agreement.

'It's simply a commercial deal,' President Tabai insisted. He had consulted with the governments of the United States, Australia and New Zealand and they did not misunderstand what his nation was doing. 'We belong to the West, but we are the only ones who know finally what is in our national interest.'

The contract allows up to 10 Soviet trawlers to work the tuna schools in the ocean within the 320 kilometre zones around the atolls forming Kiribati. The President has not denied that the activities of United States fishing boats have displeased him. The United States ignores the Law of the Sea convention and, in a display of what the Pacific nations see as American high-handedness, have harvested the waters within the various 320 kilometre zones. The Americans now find themselves in a dilemma — they cannot offer increased aid to newly independent nations in the hope of keeping the Russians out because the island states are not interested in hand outs; they want financial independence, with the US paying fishing licence fees.

This however, presents problems because the US does not recognise the Law of the Sea convention, a legacy of the pressure placed on Congress by the powerful US tuna-fishing lobby. The immediate answer would be for the United States government to spend billions of dollars in 'paying off' its tuna fishing industry, to keep boats out of the various zones and therefore improve relations with the Pacific islanders. But there is the added problem of French nuclear testing and President Mitterrand's flight to Mururoa in September, both of which signalled a mood of aggressive confrontation. The result: a growing dislike of Western imperialism.

The appearance of a new fleet of Soviet fishing trawlers in the central Pacific only serves to strengthen Russian intelligence-gathering machinery. Every trawler in the enormous Soviet fishing fleet sprouts an elaborate array of antennae and the skippers seem to think that the best places to fish are close to splash-down zones of space probes and naval exercises. Although Russia has an established and legitimate interest in Pacific fishing, there is now a growing fear among Western nations that a number of land bases will be set up within a few years.

President Tabai has said his agreement does not include provision for a shore base or for Russian staff on Kiribati territory — it would be the first permanent Soviet presence in the south-west Pacific — but he has not ruled out the possibility of a base being set up as a result of any future expansion of the agreement.

Malcolm Fraser, a former Liberal Prime Minister of Australia had no doubts what the Kiribati-Russian agreement meant. 'The Soviet Union is going to get a base in the Pacific with absolute certainty, probably in Kiribati,' he said during a meeting of former government leaders in Paris in April 1985. 'It will start as a fish processing facility, but that will have some refuelling facilities which will then require repair facilities and in turn an airfield — then it is a base.'

Even as he spoke, the largest Soviet naval task force to enter the central Pacific was conducting training manoeuvres about 2000 kilometres north of Hawaii. The 10-ship task force, headed by the anti- submarine carrier Novorossiysk,included the newest of the four Soviet Kiev-class carriers, four guided missile cruisers, two frigates and two oilers. The manoeuvres included frequent flight operations by vertical take-off and landing aircraft, YAK-38 Forgers.

The American Nautilus Research Centre reiterates that a nuclear war in the Pacific could result in a two-day exchange of more than 5000 Soviet and US nuclear weapons — about one tenth of their combined stockpiles, with targets stretching from the joint US-Australian communications base on the Australian mainland at North-West Cape to Japan. Weapons would include land-based intercontinental ballistic missiles, nuclear land mines believed buried in Korea, and an assortment of nuclear depth charges, short-range missiles, rockets and artillery shells.

The United States is by far the most dominant military power in the Pacific. It has more than 100 military installations in the Hawaiian islands and although it has less men and machines it is more advanced than the Soviet Union which freely continues to test its missiles in the North West Pacific. The landing spots being north of the Cook Islands and south of the Line Islands. Storage facilities for Russian weapons exist at Vladivostock and at other naval and air bases on the Russian mainland in the North West Pacific region and at Cam Ramh Bay, on the coast of central Vietnam overlooking the South China Sea.   It is from Cam

Ramh Bay that a big threat to the Pacific exists, US and Australian defence experts acknowledge. The Russians were given regular access to Vietnamese bases in 1979 after China attacked northern Vietnam as a reprisal for Hanoi's invasion of Kampuchea. Now, about 25 Soviet naval ships and submarines operate from there, and although that is not a particularly large force, the fact that there are support facilities for many more vessels and aircraft is of concern.

According to the US Pacific Command, Russia with its mobile force outnumbers the US in east Asia and the Pacific but America has the better fighting power. Figures supplied by the Americans reveal the strength of each power in the region: *Naval surface warships*: US 98; USSR 87. *Submarines*: US 42; USSR 128. *Tactical aircraft*: US 990; USSR 1820. *Bombers*: US 12; USSR 355. *Army troops*: US 47,000; USSR 450,000. *Marines and naval infantry*: US 259,000; USSR 134,000. *Air force personnel*: US 45,000; USSR 150,000.

But as long as Western nations continue to argue among themselves over nuclear issues, as long as ecologists turn the Pacific nations against France and the United States, the Soviets remain confident of further encroachment into the Pacific region. The Eastern bloc wants nothing more than to see the isolating of the US from its South Pacific allies and the cutting of its established links with Hawaii, Japan and the Philippines.

Certainly instability in the Philippines, with the Communist Party and insurgents gaining strength, threatens the future of US bases there — bases that are the heart of Pacific defence strategy and without which America's protective umbrella over Pacific nations, including Australia and New Zealand, is full of holes. The concern has increased with New Zealand Prime Minister David Lange prohibiting port facilities to American naval vessels carrying nuclear arms.

Worried by the growth of the New People's Army, with up to 15,000 members, another 10,000 sympathisers, and support from 100,000 members of the communist-dominated National Democratic Front, as well as 60,000 members of the Philippines Communist Party, America's Assistant Defence Secretary, Richard

Armitage sees the period between January 1986 and 1988 as being crucial to the political future of the Philippines and the balance of power in the Pacific. A Communist victory would pose a clear danger to South-east Asia. It would force the closure of the US facilities at Clark and Subic Bay and severely restrict the US capability to support operations in the Pacific.

With the two superpowers holding most of the cards, France's role in any Pacific confrontation would be more of a military and communication back up. But it is not solely for the defence of her island outposts or as a cheerleader in any Pacific war that France maintains a military presence there, with aero-naval bases in Noumea and Papeete employing 5,000 men in Polynesia and 3,000 in New Caledonia. It is also to guarantee her own independence and security.

In the mid-1950s, France was aware that it could not rely on the United States for protection should it, and it alone, be threatened by attack from the superior forces of the Eastern bloc.

As an answer to those who ask how many bombs France has to explode to ensure that they go off, Paris officials point out that while the Soviets continue to improve their weapons, so France must improve hers. It would be naive to believe that France would be prepared to pack up the nuclear testing facility at Mururoa Atoll until Paris had decided to do so.

Before the Greenpeace affair, French Defence Minister Hernu declared that the 'sun will never set on our armed forces'. For beyond the two superpowers, France is the only country in the world which feels obliged to keep a military profile in every ocean. Successive French presidents since Charles de Gaulle have claimed that maintaining a military presence is the one sure means of ensuring national independence. French defence officials point out that without her isolated atolls, it would be extremly difficult for France to modernise her nuclear armoury and keep abreast of nuclear technology.

While the United States, the Soviet Union and China have deserts in which to conduct their tests, France has no similar appropriate region. Britain doesn't have deserts either, but she has now reached an agreement with the US to develop an atomic arsenal in Nevada. The longer France remains in *d'outre mer* the louder the ecologists shout, which prompted one commentator to remark in Paris: 'To maintain the status quo, it is necessary to have dirtier and dirtier hands and to give and receive more and more blows.' And as far as the French Deputy Foreign Minister, Jean Michel Baylet, was concerned in August 1985, France would continue nuclear testing in the South Pacific as long as the superpowers failed to make significant strides towards disarmament.

Supporters of a French presence in the Pacific say that if one Western ally is to be asked to leave, the Americans should be asked to go too, taking their Trident intercontinental ballistic missile submarines with them.

In defence terms France has not been wasting time at Mururoa. The tests have given the nation the neutron bomb — the weapon that destroys people but keeps buildings intact. In the September 1985 edition of the French Army publication *Armees d'Aujourd'hui* (Armed Forces Today), it was revealed that the highly mobile Hades tactical missile system was being designed to deliver a neutron bomb which would replace the 20-year-old Pluton missile in the early 1990s. The Hades would have a range of some 4,000 kilometres, covering an area 10 times greater than the Pluton, and its purpose would be what the publication described as 'the last warning blow, signifying in a brutal fashion to the enemy our firm determination to have recourse to strategic arms of reprisal if he pursues his aggression.' Hades would be able to hit the enemy far away and earlier whatever strategic direction the invasion forces may take. For 'optimal penetration' two of the weapons would be carried on a fast semi-trailer, the size of a freight truck, loaded within minutes from a base stock and concealed until the last moment before firing. The missiles would be fired almost vertically and independently of the direction the vehicle was facing. Firing would be a simple operation carried out from the truck's cabin with no manual work involved.

Although some Pacific nations have at least shown some willingness to talk to Soviet envoys about the use of their waters for fishing, it is the development of weapons like the neutron bomb in their territory that has concerned a number of Pacific leaders. Which is why a majority of members of the South Pacific Forum, meeting in Rarotonga in the Cook Islands in August 1985, agreed to endorse a South Pacific Nuclear Free Zone Treaty.

Proposed by Australian Prime Minister Bob Hawke, who had been battered by complaints from the Solomon Islands and Vanuatu over Australia's exporting of uranium, it was signed on the 40th anniversary of the bombing of Hiroshima by eight of the 13 member states — Australia, New Zealand, Western Samoa, Nuie, Fiji, Kiribati, Tuvalu and the Cook Islands. The essence of the treaty is that no country now participating in it will develop, manufacture or acquire any nuclear explosive device and will not station or test nuclear explosive devices. It allows South Pacific countries to decide for themselves on issues like access to airfields and ports for nuclear armed aircraft or nuclear armed or powered vessels. Since it was first proposed in 1975 by the then Labour Prime Minister of New Zealand, Bill Rowling, the treaty was left in abeyance during intervening periods of non-Labour rule in Australia and New Zealand until Bob Hawke reintroduced the proposal in 1983.

Critics of the treaty say it was hardly worth signing. For a start the South Pacific Forum members do not include French Polynesia, to which the greatest concern is being directed. And the nuclear free zone will be anything but that. Nuclear armed ships will continue to cruise the ocean and American warships will go on visiting Pacific states which welcome them and continue carrying out exercises with Australia. France will continue with its tests, impervious to international opinion.

America's immediate reaction to the signing of the treaty was to regard it as a joke. Mr Bernie Kalb of the US State Department was asked at a Washington Press conference: 'In Raratonga in the Cook Islands, the South Pacific Forum has approved the nuclear-free zone for the South Pacific. What is the US position on it?'

Replied Mr Kalb: 'I asked that very question just before I came down here (laughter) and . . . I was told that the official, final text has not yet been received here. That being the case, I'm in a position of total bankruptcy.'

Question: 'May we get the bottle from the sea or . . . ?'

Mr Kalb: 'I don't know whether the bottle is corked or uncorked . . . the US has been given to understand that the treaty does not constitute an endorsement of the New Zealand port ban (on nuclear armed vessels). Now, having said that, I will keep in mind your alert that when the bottle arrives . . .'

Despite their public mirth, American defence officials were somewhat concerned by the passing of the treaty, particularly as Australia had backed it. There seemed little hope of the US acknowledging the paper by signing the protocols because that would commit America to observing the provisions in regard to American Samoa and agreeing not to test nuclear weapons there. Washington was also determined to ensure that the treaty did not make legitimate New Zealand's stand against nuclear ship visits.

It was that action by New Zealand Prime Minister Lange that has given the United States one of its biggest defence headaches. In January 1985 New Zealand refused to give permission for the conventionally-powered destroyer USS Buchanan from making a port call after an ANZUS exercise with Australian and New Zealand forces because Washington would not give an undertaking that the vessel was not carrying nuclear weapons. The US simply kept to its policy of neither confirming nor denying such weapons were on board.

Lange's move went against the principles of what is known as the ANZUS treaty — an agreement signed by Australia, New Zealand and the United States in San Francisco in September 1951, by representatives of the three nations and which took effect in April the following year. In signing, the nations were reaffirming their faith in the purposes and principles of the United Nations Charter and their desire to strengthen the fabric of peace in the Pacific region. It was a public declaration of unity so no potential enemy could be under the illusion that any of the three governments stood alone.

And as US Assistant Secretary of State Paul Wolfowitz told the House of Representatives Subcommittee on Asian and Pacific Affairs early in 1985, the ANZUS treaty had been of direct benefit to Australia and New Zealand. 'The ANZUS link with the United States has added significant weight to Australia and New Zealand's influence, and ability to preserve stability, within the region — giving those countries enhanced security leverage beyond what they would have in isolation,' Wolfowitz said.

He told the committee that the alliance had its critics, who asserted that participation in ANZUS made those countries nuclear targets and involved them in preparations for a nuclear war. While the Australian Government accepted that Western maintenance of adequate defence, including nuclear weapons, was a regrettable necessity until arms control reduced and eventually eliminated those weapons, the current New Zealand Government had banned nuclear-armed and nuclear-propelled ships in order to get away from, and protest against 'things nuclear'.

According to the New Zealand government that country's location, far removed from potential adversaries, rendered a nuclear defence unnecessary and unwanted.

'The US view is that the safest course in a dangerous world is to make clear our commitment to defend freedom. We believe the best way to prevent a large war is to keep small wars from starting. The commitments of the Western allies to each other over four decades have helped to prevent nuclear war,' said the US Assistant Secretary of State.

The United States was not pro-nuclear, it was pro-alliance. US policy in the event of conflict was to employ the lowest level of defence necessary to turn back an aggressor, to preserve the territorial integrity of the US and its allies and to restore peace on an acceptable basis. The foremost purpose of their alliances was to prevent war from ever occurring. By weakening one of those alliances, New Zealand in a small way, was detracting from that purpose. It was obvious, however, that there was little nuclear threat now in the South Pacific area. It was in the common interest to keep it that way.

The presence of strong naval defence capabilities was the best guarantee against eruption of conflict. The United States had only one navy; not one conventionally-capable navy and one nuclear-capable navy. Not one navy to accommodate one country's policy and another navy for the rest of the world. And it would weaken the deterrent value of US forces to advertise to potential adversaries when they are or are not carrying nuclear weapons.

America's response to New Zealand's action was to reduce its military and security co-operation with New Zealand, which meant that Lange's government was denied intelligence information. As Wolfowitz pointed out: 'Unless our alliance partners bear a commensurate share of military co-operation essential to the alliance, our partnership cannot be sustained practically or politically.'

Despite Wolfowitz's views, a retired American Navy admiral believes the ANZUS treaty is meaningless in today's context. Rear Admiral Gene La Rocque, with 31 years' active navy duty, including commands of nuclear-armed ships, and now director of the US Centre for Defence Information, told Australia's National Press Club in August 1985: 'The treaty is vague. There is no commitment to defend you. We cannot defend you.'

But he defended the right for nuclear tests. America was pushing ahead because it was necessary to maintain a 'first strike' capability. 'If you stop exploding nuclear weapons for test purposes, you won't build new ones. You won't be likely to make a first strike. You will get rid of the ones you have, ultimately, because even nuclear weapons have a shelf life, like a can of beans.'

At Mururoa, meanwhile, France continues her tests, not for 'first strike' capability but, as the country's weapons experts insist, for defence purposes only. As General Jeannou Lacaze, the Defence Ministry's adviser on African issues, said early in 1985: 'Tomorrow's nuclear weapons are being developed at Mururoa. They are indispensable to France's security, whatever neighbouring Latin American and Pacific states may think.

7

Greenpeace and the French

The balloon hung over the horizon like a single white petal of a giant flower. Suspended beneath it like an enormous beehive was the bomb. The three man crew of the ketch Greenpeace 111 — formerly known as the Vega — stared at it through their binoculars, their hearts pounding. Apart from French technicians and military personnel on Mururoa Atoll some 500 kilometres away, they were the only witnesses to the launch of the deadly craft. They were there because they believed that ordinary people had the power to change the course of events dictated by governments.

It was June 1972. The French had been exploding bombs in the atmosphere over the Pacific, defying world opinion, for six years. People and governments had protested from within their own shores. No-one had dared sail into the heart of the nuclear testing ground. It was a far cry from the world McTaggart had grown up with. A former world badminton champion, he had won and lost several fortunes in the construction business. Now, as owner of the Vega, he was taking a gamble with his life.

As he was to admit later, his mind and those of his companions were filled with 'grotesque images . . . of scorching walls of heat, blinding unearthly light, shock waves coming across the water like freight trains and showers of heat-cracked rocks and charred wood. I caught myself looking at my own and the others' skin, wondering how much laceration it could take.'

The voyage to the forbidden zone had been initiated and funded by Greenpeace, at that time not even a year old or even officially founded. For days, the yacht bobbed on the ocean, the crew wearing dark sunglasses in case the sky suddenly became a blinding mass of yellow and orange fire that could cause temporary or permanent blindness. Apart from a 1600 kilometres per hour wind and a tidal wave, there was also the very real danger of being burned by radiation — the official French estimate of the danger zone for shipping was 16,000 square kilometres of water.

In the House of Commons in Ottawa Mr Heath Macquarrie jumped to his feet at the beginning of question time on June 19 and asked the Speaker whether he had any information on the whereabouts of the Greepeace 111 'and its fine, public-spirited crew'.

The Honourable Mitchell Sharp, Secretary of State for External Affairs, told him: 'As I understand it, the Greenpeace is somewhere in the area . . . We understand there is a Canadian aboard, and of course I do hope the ship is not going to get involved in the explosion and that the necessary steps will be taken to see it is removed from the area.'

The French were already taking those steps. McTaggart, sailing with Englishman Nigel Ingram and Australian Grant Davidson, were confronted by the French navy which sent out a fleet of vessels including a 200 metre cruiser, minesweepers and tugboats to divert the Greenpeace 111. A terrifying game of 'chicken' followed while the French tried to force Greenpeace away from the zone. It was during the French harassment, with the huge ships revving their engines perilously close to the yacht and aircraft roaring past just 30 metres overhead that the French exploded the triggering device, the small bomb used to activate the larger bomb, 300 metres over Mururoa. The fallout drifted past the Greenpeace 111 only 80 kilometres to the south.

McTaggart wrote later: 'Lying in our bunks naked, we did not suspect that the ocean south of us was being dusted by radioactivity. And if we had been in the position we had maintained earlier, even now poisoned particles would be settling through our flesh into the fine tissue of our bones . . . A stormfront of death had gone out from Mururoa. A small stormfront — just the triggering device — but still enough to have made us into very old men had we been in its path.'

Trying to get closer to Mururoa, the Greenpeace 111 was crippled when rammed by the 4,000 tonne minesweeper La Paimpolaise. The French towed the yacht to Mururoa where temporary repairs were carried out. Then the Greenpeace 111 was towed out to sea and sent on her way back to Raratonga in the Cook Islands. Now the French could test their bombs in peace . . . or so they thought.

Twelve months later McTaggart and Greenpeace 111 were back in the area. He was accompanied by Nigel Ingram and two New Zealand women, Ann-Marie Horne and Mary Lornie. Other peace boats that had set off earlier, following a wave of publicity about the Greenpeace 111's activities the year before, had dropped back or had been arrested by the French navy. The peace force flotilla had included two yachts, Spirit of Peace and Fri, with five nationalities in their crew — British, American, French, Dutch and New Zealanders — as well as the New Zealand frigate Otago with a cabinet minister on board. The presence of these vessels had already resulted in the test schedule being delayed by two weeks.

Now the real 'troublemaker', Greenpeace 111, was back and sailing right into the heart of bomb territory. The French decided there would be no games this time. On August 15, a high-speed inflatable boat filled with commandoes charged at the ketch and the French set about McTaggart and Ingram with their truncheons. McTaggart was rammed in the right eye by the butt of a truncheon and his sight was permanently affected.

The French naval officers, realising that Ann-Marie had taken photographs of the attack, were triumphant when they found a camera. Again, the Greenpeace 111 was towed to Mururoa, and from there McTaggart was flown to Tahiti where his eye was treated. An armed guard remained near his bed. In Paris, French generals and politicians insisted that McTaggart had not been beaten up. But the small peace team were to dispute that — and present to the world the embarrassing evidence.

The camera that had been found was not the one containing the incriminating film. And at Mururoa, just before the French carried out a thorough search of everyone's possessions, Ann-Marie pushed the 35mm film cannister into her vagina, then walked with a smile past the guards. As the French authorities continued to deny that the boarding party had been armed or that anyone had been beaten up, pictures showing knives on the belts of the men, three showing truncheons and one of Ingram being beaten up were being circulated around the world by the news services. Ann-Marie wrote in her diary later: 'We have done enough. We have drawn attention to the problem.'

Within three months, in November 1973, France announced that tests would be conducted in the atmosphere for one more year, and then the experiments would be carried out underground.

It was a victory for the peace movement. But it had not been won easily. And there were many more battles to be fought in the years to come.

When Greenpeace 111 made its first voyage to Mururoa, the French had been nuclear testing for 13 years against a background of world outrage. And it wasn't just the peace movements who were doing the shouting. It was the Prime Minister of Australia, William McMahon; it was the New Zealand Prime Minister John Marshall; it was Pierre Trudeau in Canada; Sato Eisaku in Japan. It was also the Government of Peru who in 1971 claimed that French tests had precipitated the country's disastrous earthquakes a year earlier. In the Philippines, President Marcos said the tests were the cause of catastrophic floods.

France was prepared to lend an ear to Peru's misgivings. The South American country had threatened to break off diplomatic relations and deprive France of a valuable arms export market. Paris agreed to shorten the seasonal programme from seven to five tests.

However, the French had no intention of listening to Australia's brays. They were nothing but Anglo Saxon hypocrites who had loaned their own territory to the British for atmospheric tests in the 1950s. The Australians had shown no concern then for any Aborigines in the area who would have been affected by radiation.

Interestingly, the British were not among the nations to gang up against the French when the real protests began in the early 1970s.

France insisted that her tests produced less fallout than those conducted by the superpowers in the northern hemisphere before atmospheric nuclear blasts were banned in the region with the signing of the Moscow treaty of 1963.

Mr Gabriel van Laethem, French Ambassador to Australia, gave an assurance to the Liberal Prime Minister Mr William McMahon that France was taking the 'most stringent' safety measures in order to avoid damaging effects the environment. Their precautions had efficiently reduced the hazards of atmospheric tests 'to an extent never before achieved by any other country'. Why, there was more danger of radioactivity from watching television than from nuclear fallout — a 'faithful' viewer received about 10 millirems a year of radioactivity compared to one or two for all the tests performed in the atmosphere in the past 20 years. But Mr McMahon, who had already sent a stiff protest letter to President Pompidou a few days earlier, retorted: 'None of the explanations you have given will in any way, shape or form change the attitude of myself, the Australian Government or the Australian people towards the French atmospheric nuclear tests or towards nuclear tests by any country.'

Australians and New Zealanders were far from impressed with the assurances and with any figures the French produced to show that it was a safer world in the Southern Hemisphere than in the North. Despite the distance, people of both nations claimed that the Pacific was their back yard and pollution was a threat to their lifestyle.

To back up their claim they referred to a new report prepared by a special United Nations scientific committee on the effects of atomic radiation; a report that showed that radio-iodine levels in milk in the Southern Hemisphere had increased significantly since French nuclear testing began. The report had been prepared after three years of evidence-gathering by prominent scientists from 15 countries. Although the average doses absorbed by the thyroid glands of people living in the Southern Hemisphere were lower than those in the Northern Hemisphere following US and Soviet atmospheric tests, the report did come up with a positive finding of radio-iodine in Southern Hemisphere milk after France's tests of 1970 and 1971.

As three out of four Australians and New Zealanders protested that the French should not hold their tests in the Pacific, boycotts were introduced against French products. At Sydney's main post office in mid July 1972, French mail was left in big heaps and French companies were hit by a union black ban which was to last until the current testing was completed. Renault sales fell by 16 per cent in four weeks and the company's telex system was cut off. At the Banque Nationale de Paris in Melbourne and Sydney security was increased after threats to bomb the premises.

Day after day, the protests gained momentum. The Australia Party urged people to impose their own economic sanctions and not to buy anything made in France or use French ships or aircraft. In Brisbane, members of the Union of Australian Women marched on the offices of the French Consul shouting their protests. In Adelaide, students built a bomb shelter from which they issued ban-the-bomb leaflets. In the heart of Melbourne, shoppers and city workers put on gauze masks as a protest and in Papua New Guinea, then an Australian territory, the House of Assembly passed a protest motion. In Auckland, the French consular-agent, Dr R.G. McElroy, a former city Mayor, resigned his post in protest.

Out in the Pacific, 92 descendants of the Bounty mutineers, worried that something might go wrong with the 1972 tests, prepared to flee their homes on Pitcairn island, 800 kilometres south east of Mururoa. The islanders' leader, Tom Christian, a great-great-great-grandson of Fletcher Christian, who headed the Bounty mutiny in 1789, said in a radio message to Australia:

'We are frightened that perhaps this time someone may become over-confident and things could go wrong. We are in the danger zone and the fallout could be a health hazard. We have felt most of the explosions in the past.'

As the outrage from the Southern Hemisphere increased, and the Greenpeace 111 protest yacht began its first cat and mouse game with the French navy, Dr Jim Cairns, a Labor member of Victoria's House of Representatives who was planning to fly from Sydney to Tahiti, was told that he and seven protesters would not be allowed to land.

'In that case,' said Cairns, 'I will fly to Paris and try to see President Pompidou personally. The French are behaving quite unrealistically about all this. They must have a lot to hide in Tahiti.'

Dr Cairns failed to see the President but his efforts gained more publicity for the anti-bomb campaign and in November 1972, the United Nations' main political committee passed a resolution — initiated by New Zealand and co-sponsored by Australia and 11 other Pacific countries — by 106 votes to four appealing for an end to nuclear testing in the Pacific and calling for a halt to nuclear weapons testing in all environments, including underground. The resolution was endorsed later by the General Assembly.

But far from modifying, let alone ending the tests, France announced the intention to go ahead with a fresh series the following year. 'General de Gaulle would be proud,' said one Australian political commentator. 'He made arrogance a way of life, brushing aside Britain when it first attempted to join the Common Market, regarding all opposition to him as lowly and seeing his France as above all countries and destined for greatness. That destiny continues to elude France, yet, in pursuit of it, the republic ignores the safety, tramples on the rights and disregards the protests of many nations. France, it seems, equates greatness with an H-Bomb. This is Gaullist blindness . . .'

In Australia and New Zealand two general elections were due, with forecasts that there would be changes of government in favour of the Labour Party. When that happened in New Zealand at the end of November, Prime Minister elect Norman Kirk pledged that New Zealand would send a warship to the test area, a promise he kept in 1973 with the despatch of the Otago. The following month, Gough Whitlam's Labor Party was swept to power in Australia and the new Prime Minister promised that Australia would take action through the International Court of Justice to stop the tests if France did not volunteer to do so. No-one believed that such voluntary action would be forthcoming. Mr. Alexandre Sanguinetti, a leading Guallist and chairman of the Parliamentary National Defence Committee had declared a short time before: 'The French Government should tell protesters such as Australia that France wants the bomb and is going to have it.'

As Australians despatched 300,000 protest postcards to President Pompidou, Gough Whitlam sent his Attorney-General, Senator Lionel Murphy, to Paris for talks with the French Government as a final move before seeking an injunction against France in the International Court. While in the French capital Senator Murphy recorded a television interview in which he said the tests had contaminated the bodies of 'every man, woman and child in Australia'. Then he began a round of talks with government officials, but his concern fell on deaf ears.

The French utterly rejected the findings of the Australian Academy of Science — secretly commissioned by Mr Whitlam two months earlier in February 1973 — showing that nuclear blasts represented a health hazard to present and future generations of Australians. So the way was now clear for Australia to press ahead with its intentions to take the case against the French to the International Court. In London, Gough Whitlam met Conservative Prime Minister Edward Heath and his Foreign Minister Sir Alec Douglas-Home, knowing full well that Britain accepted French assurances that fallout from the tests did not constitute any health danger and that Mr Heath was extremely reluctant to become publicly involved in such a contentious dispute with a Common Market ally.

However, Mr Whitlam returned to Australia with some satisfaction, having extracted a promise that Britain would 'bring to the attention' of the French the views of the Pacific nations on that year's planned tests. But it was obvious the appeals would be shrugged off in the same way news that Australia and New Zealand were about to bring separate cases before the World Court had been shrugged off. Paris declared, quite simply, that it did not recognise the court's competence to hear the complaints and did not even plan to appoint a representative for the case. In reply Australia referred France to a forgotten treaty signed by the republic in 1928 in which it agreed to accept International Court of Justice rulings. It made no difference. France was still not represented when the case began in The Hague on May 21.

Backed by a team of legal experts, Senator Murphy led the three day case, asking 15 judges from as many countries to declare that the tests were illegal. The Court, the principal legal arm of the United Nations, knew that its credibility was on trial and legal experts predicted that the case would go against France. They were right. The Court, in an interim ruling on June 22 ordered France to stop the atmospheric nuclear tests. The decision was eight votes in favour of them being stopped, six against. The same votes were cast for New Zealand's application for the tests to be restrained.

France issued an immediate statement through its Foreign Ministry: 'The well-known position of France is not to recognise the competence of the International Court of Justice in this affair, which deals with France's national defence.'

There was more to come from France within a few days. In a 114-page White Paper issued on June 28, Paris said all international criticism lacked scientific or legal basis. The tests were to continue.

But the protests from Down Under had not gone completely unheeded. British trade unionists, through the 9,500,000-member Trades Union Congress, called for a boycott of France which began with dock workers refusing to unload a French ship at Avonmouth near Bristol. And the Union of Postal Workers said its members would boycott all mail between Britain and France. In the fashionable Knightsbridge district of London eyebrows were raised when a group of Australian models in the briefest of bikinis staged a demonstration outside a French boutique before marching to the French Embassy to hand in a protest note saying they would no longer model French fashions, or use French cosmetics.

On July 23 France exploded its first nuclear bomb — about a quarter of the size of the one that destroyed Hiroshima — of the 1973 series. Suspended from its silver balloon, it sent an orange-red fireball through a layer of cloud over Mururoa, spreading until it was some 400 metres across. Some 35 kilometres from the blast centre and to the north west of Mururoa, the New Zealand protest frigate Otago was unaffected. A correspondent for the New Zealand Press Association said there had been doubt for a few moments whether the device had been detonated.

'At no time did the ship use its special anti-fallout precautions, but those of us on the bridge all wore goggles and special clothing to protect us from the flash which can cause instant blindness . . . As soon as the (mushroom) cloud began to rise, the entire crew, which had been below decks as a safety precaution for two and a half hours, came out to take photographs.' Several hours after the explosion, the Otago's geiger counters showed no signs of radioactivity.

A few hours after the bomb went off, the leaders of France were out swimming, but a long way from the Pacific. French Prime Minister Pierre Messmer — known as the 'Father of the Bomb' because he was Defence Minister when the tests were launched 10 years earlier — was towelling himself after a swim at Varna beach in Bulgaria when he received the news. He simply smiled and said there would be no statement until the test series finished in September. President Pompidou, on holiday in Brittany, had also just finished a swim when he received the news, but he too reserved all official comment.

In fact he kept publicly quiet on the issue until January 1974, when he told Australia's new ambassador to France, Mr David Anderson, that his country had 'no intention' of stopping the tests. The President told the ambassador when he called at the Elysee Palace to present his credentials: 'The tests are without danger and they are essential for France's security. France hoped that a friendly country and a comrade-in-arms could understand the motives of such a venture. I must tell you very clearly that France cannot give up its nuclear tests . . . I have to tell you in the clearest manner that France cannot renounce them.'

But there was hope on the horizon, metaphorically at least. The first round of Presidential elections were looming up in May. And the Socialist leader Francois Mitterrand gave a pledge to Australia and other Pacific nations to end the testing if he came to power. Although he said he would not get rid of France's nuclear stockpile until the government knew what other powers intended to do with theirs, he firmly declared: 'I do not think nuclear tests are necessary.'

Those words were to be carried in the wind around the world as the Gaullists sank disheartened into history. And in the first round of the 1974 elections French voters in the Pacific and Indian Oceans showed a vast swing towards the man who looked like bringing peace to their regions. In Polynesia, where in the 1965 election Mitterrand pulled only 658 votes, he was carried by a sweeping majority of more than half the 100,000 votes cast. In New Caledonia and the Anglo-French condominium New Hebrides (now the independent nation, Vanuatu) the vote for Mitterand soared from 1,936 in 1965 to 14,521.

In Reunion in the Indian Ocean where France maintained a large naval base, Mitterrand topped the poll with 55,669 votes, compared with 5,806 in 1965. He topped the polls, too, in Guadeloupe, the French department in the Antilles and in French Guiana. But the mainland vote swung for the Conservative candidate, Valery Giscard d'Estaing. Although not a true Gaullist, he showed himself to be a faithful fellow traveller on what the pacifists described as the vainglorious path to nuclear armaments, drawn, as were his two immediate predecessors, by the image of French independence and invincibility. As expected, the announcement many feared came on June 6. In his first speech to the National Assembly the new Prime Minister, Jacques Chirac, said France would continue developing its independent nuclear deterrent, which officials interpreted as indicating that the tests would continue. Within three days the Elysee Palace said preparations were being made for 'the final series of atmospheric tests'. From 1975 on, they would be moved underground. This did not make the nations of the Southern Hemisphere any happier. The French Ambassador in Australia was called to the Department of Foreign Affairs in Canberra where he was told of Australia's concern about the continuation of the experiments.

It made no difference to French resolve. By early July, one bomb had been exploded in the atmosphere — and Australia was back in the International Court to resume the fight against France and seek a permanent ruling.

The Solicitor General, supported by Senator Murphy, said the Australian Government had 'convincing evidence' of the psychological injury caused to Australians by the tests. France had proceeded knowing that fallout over Australia was a strong possibility. New Zealand presented a similar case. However, it became an academic issue. For France sidestepped any censorship by the court by issuing a promise that all future tests would be underground.

As it was, the 1974 series of atmospheric tests proved to be a major success for French nuclear weaponry with the development of a detonating device for multiple warheads. These, it was anticipated, would be in service by 1980 and would be fitted first to the missiles carried by the French nuclear submarine fleet. Defence experts said the determination to develop a successful detonation was why France had obstinately turned her back on the world and continued her programme. Now the tests could go underground, to the satisfaction of her own scientists and the protesters. That, at least, was what France had hoped, but it was not to be.

For as time was to tell, France's cloak of secrecy around the events at Mururoa caused just as much concern. In 1978, rumours abounded that the French had developed and exploded a neutron bomb, just weeks after President Carter halted the production of neutron bombs in America. The reports evoked a swift response from the Elysee Palace. France, it was firmly stated, had not tested a neutron bomb.

On September 22 1979, a mysterious nuclear explosion took place near South Africa, prompting speculation that 'someone' had exploded a neutron bomb. America's Central Intelligence Agency told Congress that if the event seen in the South African skies was a nuclear explosion, it suspected Israel or South Africa. Nine months later, President Giscard announced that France had carried out 'experiments' for her first neutron bomb, but would not make a decision on producing it before 1982 or 1983. Many details were left out for what were seen as political and state security reasons. But the mystery of the brilliant flash of light near South Africa in 1979 became more intriguing when an American scientist, Samuel Cohen, 'father of the neutron bomb', said he had an explanation. 'It was caused,' he declared, 'by France exploding its neutron bomb over the Kerguelen Islands'. These islands form part of France's southern and Antarctic territories, and lie about 2,500 kilometres south west of Capetown.

Meanwhile ecologists and scientists had begun to express concern about the ability of Mururoa Atoll to stand up to constant underground blasting. Ahead was one ray of hope . . . the same hope that had been raised seven years earlier. The French presidential elections were looming, and once again Francois Mitterrand stood high, with his promises to halt the tests. This time Mitterrand was swept to power and at the end of May the good news was passed out from the Elysee Palace: the new Socialist Defence Minister, Charles Hernu, had ordered an end to underground tests at Mururoa pending a thorough study of the whole question.

Some felt this was just too good to be true — and they were right. Against a roar of protest about the suspension from the conservative opposition led by Jacques Chirac and from service chiefs, Hernu issued another statement saying that 'after the time needed to review the matter and in consultation with President Francois Mitterrand, nuclear tests will take place'. Observers remarked that tremendous pressure had been placed upon the President — and he had crumbled. And so the underground blasts continued, the vibrations being recorded by the New Zealand Department of Scientific and Industrial Research's seis-mological observatory in the Cook Islands. By March 1982, the number of recorded underground nuclear explosions had reached 48, their size ranging from one kilotonne to 140 kilo-tonnes. Peace yachts came and went, sometimes being boarded by French marines when the vessels entered the 19 kilometre limit around the atoll, but the confrontations were less severe than the clash involving David McTaggart.

However, they were still unnerving for the crews. The anti-nuclear yacht Pacific Peacemaker was rammed by a French coast-guard vessel in pitching seas near Mururoa in April 1982. The yacht was impounded and Australian skipper Bill Ethell was fined $200 by a court in Papeete for illegally entering French Polynesian waters. On their return to Sydney, two of the crew, David Roberts and Michael Bongiovenni said that when they were rammed they immediately thought of the crew of the Greenpeace 111, attacked and assaulted by the French in 1973.

'Here we were, disabled in steeply-pitching seas with our sails down and engine stopped and the aluminium mizzen mast, which had been snapped by the collision, swinging wildly,' said Roberts. 'We were extremely nervous and thought of the possibility of physical action against us. The mast was also particularly dan-gerous and someone could have been killed if it had fallen from the rigging.'

In Paris, the Socialist Party were now defending the tests as strongly as previous governments. Jean-Francois Bureau, the party's defence specialist commented: 'The French nuclear strike force is a factor of peace. All socialists believe this. But unfor-tunately there is a long-standing misperception of our defence policies ... Our independent nuclear strategy plays a key role in the balance of forces on the European theatre. Warsaw pact nations know they could crush West Germany with conventional weapons. But the fact that French strategy remains an unknown serves as a deterrent. They don't know when or where we might strike, and that's why Yuri Andropov (the former Soviet leader) wants French warheads to be included in the Geneva Euro-missile count.'

A month later in June 1983, France sent its leading vulcanologist, Haroun Tazieff, President of the Commission for the Study and Prevention of Major Natural Hazards, to Mururoa, and although he reported after a six day study that 'there is no danger that Mururoa will vanish under the ocean', he said the tests had caused earth slips and sedimentation which could have resulted in changes in the geological make-up of the atoll, such as the opening or closing of fissures.

His report did not exclude the possibility that radioactivity might 'partially' escape from the cavity caused by the explosions, and he suggested various ways of improving the quality of radioactive controls. Although significant man-induced radioactivity had been found in the atmosphere, in the sea and in living organisms after the atmospheric tests between 1966 and 1975, it did not give rise to concern on health grounds. But he said that long-term underground storage of radioactive waste posed problems that had not been resolved. 'It must be admitted that we have few data on the risks of radioactive material migrating into the environment. A systematic study of the most mobile waste in underground waters and in the sea over a certain number of years would enable us to ensure the quality of storage,' Tazieff concluded.

The most constant cry of the Pacific nations through the years has been: 'If the tests are so safe, why don't the French test them at home?' Paris's answer has always been that there is nowhere suitable away from populated areas. That defence was challenged in November 1984, by Australia's Labor Minister for Foreign Affairs, Bill Hayden. He revealed the existence of a 'technical intelligence assessment' prepared for the Australian Government which showed that the French could safely test nuclear devices within their own geographical borders. The report — believed to have been prepared by the Office of National Assessments, set up by the former Liberal Prime Minister Malcolm Fraser — said there were lightly populated areas where there were large and hydrologically favourable sites in the Massif Central: the Gueret and Margeride Massifs. He also cited almost all the Eastern, Central and Southern area of Corsica.

'The Government's advice is that the significant problems for nuclear testing in these areas would be political, not technical. In other words, it suits the French to export their political problem to the area where we live.'

In Wellington, after France exploded its 67th bomb, the new Labour Prime Minister David Lange said in December 1984: 'What is concerning us now about the French nuclear tests is that they seem hell-bent on increasing the number, a quite appalling escalation of the firepower ... The size of this last blast (70 kilotonnes) means that they have become, in my view, utterly reckless, quite careless of our interests, and it almost looks as though they are having a real splurge there because maybe they accept they are not going to be able to keep doing them. I certainly hope that that's so, but I don't want them to go and foul the Pacific in a sort of pre-departure binge.'

In a mocking response to Lange's concern about a 70 kilotonne weapon, France in May 1985 came up with its biggest nuclear blast yet — a massive 150 kilotonne explosion, the equivalent of 150,000 tonnes of TNT and the maximum allowed under an international treaty covering underground tests. The Hiroshima bomb had an estimated yield of 12-15 kilotonnes. The bomb dropped on Nagasaki was estimated at 22 kilotonnes.

Again, the official protests poured in. And in that same month, the Greenpeace vessel Rainbow Warrior threaded its way through the Pacific for New Zealand from where it would lead the biggest ever protest against the tests. This time, it had been wholeheartedly agreed, France must be forced to listen ...

8

The Players Come Together

From early days French sailors have always battled with the seas off the east coast of the North Island of New Zealand. This occasion was no exception as the Ouvea was tossed around on a wild sea in a force six wind. Since the three DGSE agents and the doctor left Norfolk Island, half way between New Caledonia and the North Cape, the storm had descended and the only glimmer of a welcoming sight on June 22 was the craggy point of Cape Reinga. It was too wet and stormy to sight the famous pohutukawa tree on the cape, through the roots of which the spirits of the Maori dead descend into the sea.

The Ouvea battled past Spirits Bay, Tom Bowling Bay, around the North Cape, then south towards Parengarenga Harbour. More than 200 years earlier the French explorer de Surville, seeking adventure while searching for another Eldorado in New Zealand, had also been lashed by storms as his scurvied crew cried out and died around him. After a confrontation with Maori tribes, de Surville sailed off into the Pacific, where he drowned. Just two years later the French explorer Marion du Fresne sailed down the east coast to the Bay of Islands where, after a month of cordial relations with the Maoris, he was set upon and killed.

There were no threatening tribes to meet the Ouvea as it turned east into the treacherous entrance to Parengarenga Harbour, but there was a pathetic reminder of the shipwreck that had befallen two of their countryfolk just a couple of years earlier — rising out of the sea from the sandbank where it had become trapped was the broken bow of the French yacht Drac II, abandoned to the elements.

Had the crew wished to make a discreet entry into New Zealand waters their hopes would have been dashed from the start. No yachtsmen would try to reach the tiny settlement of Te Hapua through the natural jaws of the harbour in the middle of a winter storm unless they were desperate, did not know the area or, according to tradition, they were French. The Ouvea's occupants fitted the bill perfectly and when they finally moored close to the almost pure glass sand forming the eastern boundary of the harbour the yacht stood out like a beacon in the night.

Late that Saturday afternoon Mr Hector Crene the Park Ranger at Te Paki, a few kilometres from Te Hapua, received a telephone call from a worried neighbour. Her husband was away and there was a foreign yacht not too far from her home, which overlooked the harbour. She had seen a couple of men come ashore.

Such alarm was not so unusual. With the exposure of the notorious Mr Asia narcotics syndicate New Zealand had earned itself a reputation as a drug centre. Private vessels laden with heroin and buddha sticks had sailed up and down the coasts of the North Island during the 1970s and Terry Clark, one of the syndicate's principals who has since died of a heart attack in a British jail, had commissioned a mansion on a headland in the Bay of Islands. Since those days, residents have operated a voluntary 'coastal watch', reporting any vessels which act suspiciously. The Ouvea was just such a yacht. Not only had it defied the elements by entering Parengarenga in a storm — it had not registered with customs.

Hec Crene telephoned the customs office at Opua, further south in the Bay of Islands. There was no record of the Ouvea so Crene was asked to check her out. As darkness was rapidly descending and the yacht was moored some 100 metres off shore, he decided to wait until the following day.

He waved to them from the concrete wharf and they brought the yacht in. He thought it was something of a miracle that they had managed to enter the harbour without mishap for Parengarenga, like most east-coast estuaries and harbours, is exposed to oncoming easterly seas and entry and exit require extreme skill. The channel into Parengarenga was also prone to movement, as a number of frustrated yachtsmen have testified.

'Like to have a word with the skipper,' said Crene. The man who came ashore was fair-haired in his late 30s. He agreed to go with the ranger to a nearby telephone to speak to customs and it was explained he had to register.

'I am sorry,' said the crewman, who Crene now knows to be Dr Maniguet. 'We have had a choppy passage and we had to shelter.'

Crene thought nothing more of it. The crew seemed friendly enough and when they invited him aboard to have a beer, he accepted. They voluntarily showed him the main galley, forward and aft. Everything was tidy and shipshape and gave Crene no reason to be suspicious. On the deck he noticed a rubber dinghy — an orange and black rubber dinghy. There was no sign of a grey one.

After listening to the best English speaker — he had referred to himself as a doctor — describe the rough voyage around the coast, Crene made his exit. The crew said they would set off for Opua first thing in the morning, and they were as good as their word.

Things were happening on another front. On the same day that the Ouvea struggled into Parengarenga Harbour, the DGSE agents posing as the honeymoon couple Alain and Sophie Turenge arrived at Auckland Airport, having flown first from Paris to London. They took a taxi to a suburban car rental company, picked up a campervan, then made their way to a city hotel.

There was one more player to arrive in New Zealand. Twenty four hours after Major Alain Mafart and Captain Dominique Prieur had checked through the airport with their false identities as newly-wed Swiss citizens a man handed a French passport bearing the name Jean Louis Dormand to immigration officials. This was the second false identity assumed by the overseer of the mission, Lieutenant-Colonel Louis-Pierre Dillais. The first thing he did was hire himself a car, a metallic blue Toyota Corolla, for six days. It was no coincidence that he found himself in

Auckland in time for the Turenge couple's second dinner in the North Island city. From the rooftop restaurant of the Hyatt Hotel it is possible to look straight down onto the wharf, less than one kilometre away, where the Rainbow Warrior was due to dock in a couple of weeks . . .

Meanwhile the Ouvea had made its way down the coast and the crew had given their explanations to customs officials at the deepwater port of Opua. During the 150 kilometre voyage they had passed numerous creeks and inlets where their sabotage equipment could have easily been concealed prior to customs inspection. The same regions had been well used by drug smugglers.

Having cleared themselves with the authorities, Chief Petty Officer Verge, Petty Officer Andries, Petty Officer Bartelo and Dr Maniguet then sailed north along the Veronica Channel for three kilometres. Using information gathered by the Greenpeace infiltrator Christine Cabon, they moored some 100 metres off shore, opposite the Beachcomber Motel at Paihia, a small community with a commerical wharf. The motel is the only one in the area facing onto the beach. That same day, June 25, the Turenge couple, still at their Auckland hotel, received a telephone call from Paihia . . .

The Ouvea sailed on south for some 100 kilometres to Whangarei, the capital of the Northland area and a popular spot with international and local yachtsmen. Had they arrived in the summer, the crew would have had great difficulty in finding a berth in the town basin. But this was close to the heart of winter, Friday June 28, and word had already passed along the coast about the terrible passage the crew had had in the north. True to the traditions of its people, Whangarei welcomed the DGSE spies.

On that first day the four sailors made good their time. First, they put a call through to the Turenges in Auckland. Then they went shopping, buying supplies for the yacht and calling at a sports shop where Verge tried to buy a pair of $130 New Balance running shoes, but found his size was not available. He turned down the manager's offer to put the shoes on order, saying his yacht would be leaving Whangarei the following Tuesday July

2. However, a second pair of shoes was purchased for one of the other crew members.

Conversation was not easy with Verge because of his limited English. But working in the shop was a schoolgirl who was studying French and she was able to communicate with him enough to understand his wishes.

One of the most popular spots with visiting yachtsmen is Mrs Reva Meredith's Pizza Parlour in James Street. It is a small place with just a few tables, an old piano, raffia-covered wine bottles and, in one corner, a pair of sun-bleached whale bones. Mrs Meredith emigrated to New Zealand from California with her husband, a former diver, in 1971 and five years later opened what she describes as 'this little hole in the wall'. An old friend, an Italian, taught her the art of pizza-making and word was around town and the coastline that Reva never failed to turn out a good Deluxe, Special or Polynesian. On that Friday night, with more than 20 people already cramming into the small restaurant, four strangers entered with a couple of local people they had met in a pub. The newcomers, she could tell at a glance, were obviously yachtsmen but she didn't pay much notice because she was flat out.

They found a table beside the window and by a strange twist of fate, the steely-eyed handsome man she now knows as Dr Maniguet sat under a poster giving details of the Rainbow Warrior's intended voyage to Mururoa Atoll.

Because it is Reva's custom to ask yachtsmen to sign her visitors' book, she extended the offer to the wine-drinking group of Frenchmen and their lady friends. With a twinkle in his eye, Dr Maniguet took up the pen and wrote:

'Ouvea, Noumea. 28.6.85. For a sailing initiation, Tasman Sea was a good one (. . .). Parengarenga also with a 185 (word illegible) boat and 100-metre water depth (. . .). The main interesting lesson is that a 40 hp engine on a sail ship is very, very useful, very convenient, very efficient and in fact why to get a mast???' He signed his notation 'Xavier Maniguet'.

Roland Verge, using his false name of Raymond Velche, also signed the book, in French, saying that Xavier was not a yachtsman. Towards the end of the page is a sketch which could be of a television set and beside it a matchstick man wearing a hat and basking in the sun. In French, there is the comment: 'Perhaps that is all there is in New Zealand.' Some police officers who have studied the drawing say the figure appears to be wearing flippers — but they agree their suspicions may be nothing more than the power of suggestion. There was one other signatory on the page. The name Carol, written beside the words 'Voila France'.

She is the wife of a police officer. She had met the crewmen shortly after their arrival in Whangarei. She was to dine with them on several more occasions although police were to say later that her connection with them was a 'simple, innocent contact'.

Shopkeepers and restaurant owners around town all knew of the presence of the visiting Frenchmen who made no attempt to keep a low profile. It was their money and the way they used it which attracted the most attention in those first two days. Big tips, lots of wine, no concern about the price of things.

The Golden Palace Sauna and Massage Parlour in Walton Street opens on Sundays from 4 p.m. until ll p.m. Up the stairs shortly after opening came Verge, Andries and Bartelo. The good doctor was no longer with them. He had travelled on down to Auckland en route to the South Island to go skiing and visit a famous landmark, the Fox Glacier. On his way through Auckland he called at the civil aviation section of the Ministry of Transport in a vain attempt to get permission to fly an aircraft onto the glacier. As if he knew it would be denied, he shrugged and proceeded with his skiing plan.

Meanwhile his fellow countrymen were being received in the main lounge of the Golden Palace which was adorned with a big circular red carpet, a large-screen television and a mirror etched with a diagram of Marilyn Monroe. Proprietor Graham Mac-Donald had set a price of $40 for a sauna and massage inclusive and the Frenchmen indulged in the ladies' hospitality for three or four hours. The interlude may have prompted Verge and Bartelo to visit the Grand Establishment Hotel later to ask for rooms with double beds. They left when told there were none available.

However, they were successful the following evening, July 1, Verge finding himself in room 48, containing a double bed and, appropriately, a Renoir print on the wall. Bartelo settled for a smaller room with a single bed. Andries remained on the yacht. Ouvea's crew had also returned to the sports store on that Monday, told the staff that there had been a change of plan and they were not leaving the following day as first arranged, and Verge placed an order for the running shoes he had not been able to buy the previous Friday.

Also moving around the area, but keeping his usual low profile was the man now calling himself Jean Louis Dormand, who had driven up from Auckland in a grey 1984 Holden station wagon. One of his ports of call in the first few days of the Ouvea being moored at Whangarei was Paihia, which happens to have been a spot chosen by the bogus Turenge couple.

Dormand's exact movements in the area are unclear, but posing as a tourist he would not have attracted undue attention as he drove or strolled around parts of the coast. It is possible that as overseer of the mission he checked out the security of the area where the Ouvea crew had concealed the mines before they reported to the customs.

Dormand returned to Auckland on July 4 and checked in at the Hyatt. Within two days the Rainbow Warrior would sail into the harbour under the cold hard gaze of the sabotage commander who had a grandstand view of the wharf from his seventh floor, $121 a day deluxe room. There was time for Dormand to meet up with the Turenge couple that evening, assure them that there were no security problems and discuss their movements for the next few days. Major Alain Mafart and Captain Dominique Prieur must now begin their 'touring honeymoon'. Their brief for the operation was to pick up the mines and transport them and other equipment that the Ouvea crew had brought from Noumea and hidden. The bogus Turenge couple would take care of it until required by the saboteurs.

Travelling in their hired white Toyota campervan, they made their way north to the Beachcomber Hotel, opposite which the Ouvea had moored 10 days earlier. Turning up without the usual luggage that accompanies honeymooners, they asked the manageress, Miss Robin Tanner, for accommodation facing the sea. They were booked into room 12. The date was July 5.

The Beachcomber Motel is now under new management but an employee who was there in July has told police she saw the couple with a 'device' which may have been one of the mines. As an experienced commando, Major Mafart would have felt at ease handing it and would have had no qualms about carrying such a deadly cargo further south. He and his 'wife' would remain in charge of the mines and perhaps the tell-tale re-breather equipment until everything could be handed back to the sabotage team. It would be necessary to meet the crew of the Ouvea soon to clarify their future arrangements.

In Whangarei the three DGSE agents were maintaining their curiously high profile. They dined in a Vietnamese restaurant where they asked the French-speaking manageress if she would like to come on board and cook for them on the trip back to Noumea. Three days later they returned to the restaurant with Carol and continued to joke with the manageress.

Fine food and copious amounts of wine were worked off by visits to the recently opened Kensington squash and fitness centre. They also continued to make purchases from local stores. Among the shops they visited was a marine chandler's run by Mr Deyal McKenzie. The crewmen surprised McKenzie with their purchase of a particular type of grapnel anchor they said they wanted to use to secure their rubber dinghy while fishing in Whangarei Harbour. Although McKenzie suggested that a more traditional mud and sand anchor would be a better choice, the Frenchmen insisted on buying a grapnel that was of little use for anything other than securing a dinghy to rocks. They also bought about 12 metres of 6 millimetre rope and a tool for splicing.

Nothing should be allowed to go wrong at 'zero hour'. To make sure that the 1982 Yamaha outboard motor, coloured blue with black, white and red stripes around the body, worked efficiently they decided to give it a run. They attached it to a small orange dinghy that was part of the yacht's standard equipment and started it up in Whangarei town basin. A yachtsman watching them was asked by one of the crew what fuel mixture should be used.

'What is it running on now?' asked the onlooker.

The crewman replied in broken English: 'Thirty-to-one.'

'She'll go better on a 50-to-one mix.'

In fact the ratio recommended for the engine purchased by Andries in London was vastly different to what they were using — the manufacturers suggested a 100-to-one ratio.

'Where're you heading?' inquired the onlooker.

'After Whangarei, Auckland,' was the reply.

Two of the crew, Verge and Bartelo had now booked into yet another place, the Motel Six, which offers guests the use of a spa pool. From there on July 2 at 10.55 p.m. Verge put a call through to a prominent New Caledonian business who is a financial backer of the right-wing RPCR Party. The following day at ll.35 a.m. Verge placed another call to the French colony, this time to Mr Roger Chatelain at Noumea Yacht Charters. Whether the thought of a stormy passage back to Noumea, or concern about making a speedy exit from New Zealand was behind the call, Verge asked Chatelain if he could arrange for another skipper to fly to New Zealand to sail the Ouvea back to New Caledonia.

The movements to and from the motel by the crew members and their international phone calls were of no concern to proprietors Joan and Barry George. They thought their two French guests were 'nice clean and tidy guys' who gave no indication why they were in town or why they had decided to leave their yacht to stay in a motel. What people did in a motel was their own private business as far as the Georges were concerned.

Not quite so private. A staff member was to recall later that at about 9.30 a.m. on July 6 — the day after the Turenge couple had booked into The Beachcomber 75 kilometres to the north — she saw a white campervan parked outside the Motel Six. Close to this date, two crew members returned for a third time to the local sports store and bought shoes and clothing, including a woman's size sweatshirt.

And what of Dr Maniguet? Skiing quite obviously did not hold his interest, for he returned to Auckland from Christchurch within five days. Instead of staying at Auckland's Sheraton Hotel as he had earlier planned, he hired a car at the airport and drove directly to Whangarei, checking into Motel Six on the night of July 5. He wrote his address as 'Ouvea Boat'. Dr Maniguet's speedy return to Whangarei may well have had something to do with Verge's concern about sailing the yacht back to Noumea. A row broke out between Maniguet and Verge, resulting in each of them placing calls the following morning to the Hyatt Hotel where Dormand-Dillais was maintaining his harbour vigil. The troubled waters were smoothed over for the time being. A replacement skipper was out of the question. Verge was ordered in no uncertain terms by his overseer to get his act together. This was not the time for disputes.

On July 7 the Rainbow Warrior sailed up to Marsden Wharf to a tumultuous reception. The Prime Minister was there. Maoris danced a welcome. Press photographers had a field day. And from the privacy of his room the spy chief moved among them with the aid of a powerful pair of binoculars.

That same Sunday Dr Xavier Maniguet, back from Whangarei, checked into Auckland's Sheraton Hotel. Staff were to remember him as a man who 'splashed bills around' and 'broke' the hotel's foreign exchange bank by trying to change too much money. From room 346 Dr Maniguet made a phone call to Motel Six and another to his father, Dr Gerard Maniguet, who lives near Dieppe.

DGSE spies and their acquaintances, it seemed, were on the move all over the North Island. That they were coming out of the woodwork was literally true. On July 8, in a forest near Wellsford, 65 kilometres north of Auckland, a group of loggers witnessed an extraordinary scene.

Deep in the heart of the Topuni Forest, near State Highway 1 just north of Wellsford, the loggers watched a campervan move slowly along a track, its occupants apparently searching for something or someone. It drove around briefly, then went back to the main road and headed north. Just 10 minutes later, a Holden station wagon with a man later identified as Verge at the wheel sped into the forest and bounced along the same track the campervan had followed. Verge pulled up beside the loggers, got out of the car with his male companion and asked in halting English if they had seen the campervan. They were told they had just missed it. Stunned, they leaped back into the station wagon and raced off. As they swerved onto the main road, they narrowly avoided colliding with another vehicle. In the back of the station wagon, the forestry workers had noticed an outboard motor and blue canvas bundles.

A reason for such panic may well have been that Verge missed the Turenges' vehicle that was to hold the sabotage team's rubber dinghy and outboard motor until it was required in Auckland Harbour.

The run-around spies may have found each other in Whangarei. When a staff member took breakfast to the Ouvea crew's unit on Tuesday, July 9, she was surprised to find at least five people in the room, including a woman. Was it a final briefing? A meeting to discuss the movement of the sabotage team the following night, when the Rainbow Warrior would be scuttled?

By 9 a.m. Dr Maniguet, who had returned once again to Whangarei, was on board the Ouvea with Verge, Andries and Bartelo. The crew reported to customs that they were heading off for Norfolk Island and at 1 p.m. from somewhere off the New Zealand coast, authorities on the island received a radio call saying the Ouvea would probably be arriving on July 14.

Behind in Whangarei the crew had left some bemused ladies, curious shopkeepers and yachtsmen and something of a vacuum. There were few who lived and worked around the central business district who had been unaware of their presence. It was almost as if they wanted to make their mark . . .

Next evening Auckland police received an emergency 111 phone call from two members of a boating club's vigilante committee at Okahu Bay, some two kilometres from where the Rainbow Warrior was moored. On duty to guard against thieves who had been breaking into launches, the men told police of mysterious events surrounding the movements of a Zodiac rubber dinghy. People were seen carrying articles from the boat to a nearby camper van. It took 18 minutes for police to respond to the call.

By the time they had reached the boating club the van and its occupants had gone. The Rainbow Warrior sabotage team had escaped by the skin of their teeth . . . leaving their deadly explosives ticking away on the hull of the boat that had sailed to Auckland with a message of peace.

9

The Players Disperse

They had left the dinghy behind and secured it with a padlock and chain to railings in Hobsons Bay. Whether it was carelessness, panic because they thought they had been spotted or deliberate so as to set investigating officers on a false line of inquiry was to be the subject of police debate in those first days after the sinking of the Rainbow Warrior.

The man given the task of checking the early theories was a softly spoken Scotsman, Detective Superintendent Allan Galbraith. The 48-year-old policeman had a reputation among his colleagues as a stickler for detail, a man who ferreted away until he found the truth. 'If anyone is going to get to the bottom of this affair, it's Allan,' a detective who had worked with him on numerous inquiries commented. 'He has a lot of staying power. He'll charge into this one head on and he'll come up with the goods.'

Such was the confidence instilled in the man who, seeking adventure, had travelled from Glasgow to New Zealand at the age of 20 and had enlisted in the police force in Dunedin, at the bottom of the South Island, within months of his arrival. In his 27 years with the New Zealand police he found his way into the tough armed offenders squad, where he remained for 10 years. Later, while stationed at headquarters in Wellington, he compiled a police pamphlet on explosive devices.

Explosives interested him and to further his knowledge he spent a number of weeks in London with Scotland Yard's Bomb

Squad. The tactics of IRA terrorist squads and the saboteurs of the Rainbow Warrior were not so very different.

Allan Galbraith did not limit his expertise to explosives. A specialist in narcotics, he became National Drug Enforcement Bureau Chief before travelling to Bangkok as a narcotics liaison officer. There he chaired an international police anti-narcotics committee, working alongside officers from Britain, Japan, the United States, Germany, Australia and France. He made good friends with the French detectives.

His background in explosives served him in good stead from the outset. Experts from the Army and Navy who carried out an initial investigation of the sunken peace ship did not have to spell out their theories to any great length. From the beginning, Allan Galbraith had concluded, but certainly not assumed, that the Warrior had been sunk with a powerful explosive charge, probably a mine. And that it was a professional job. But his first public comments were cautious.

'It is possibly murder and possibly terrorism' he said, adding after a pause: 'Probably, I think. Whoever committed it must have known that death was a possibility, if not a probability, depending on where the crew were at the time.'

Navy divers who fumbled around in the oil-blackened water found a hole big enough to drive a car through in the half inch steel plate adjoining the engine room. There was another damaged area closer to the propeller. From the debris on the muddy harbour bed divers started bringing up pieces of metal and other seemingly unidentifiable objects which might, or might not, have some connection with the bombing. The experts all agreed on one point: very powerful mines, each containing as much as 20 kilograms of explosives, had been used.

But how had they been planted? How had the saboteurs carried and attached them?

Already there were whispers around. For once, idle gossip, unfounded rumour and wild speculation was to prove right. It was the French, it was being said. Who else would have wanted to stop the Rainbow Warrior sailing into the Pacific to protest against the nuclear tests? The notion, accompanied by denials and expressions of sympathy from the French Embassy in Wellington, seemed just too obvious to be true. Some thought the CIA might have been responsible. The image of the United States, it was pointed out, had been constantly damaged by Greenpeace; the group's recent voyage through the Pacific to highlight the tragic effects of American nuclear testing being a good example.

Again, the suggestion that the American intelligence agency had prior knowledge of the attack was not so very wild.

From within DGSE headquarters in Paris 'deep throats' had been at work. It was impossible that a major operation such as that launched against Greenpeace could be contained within an airtight quarter of the 'Piscine'. Too many departments, from those who prepared false identity papers, to the accountants, to colleagues of those chosen for the task, became privy to the plan or at least to the general idea. Disgruntled operatives, unhappy with a leader who they say has brought the wrath of the President upon them on numerous occasions, saw an opportunity of bringing further discredit to Admiral Lacoste and a chance to create problems for the left wing President in the months leading up to a general election. These unhappy faceless Gaullists decided to sabotage the sabotage. Word leaked out to a Western agent in Paris that a French plot had been hatched and would be played out in New Zealand.

This cryptic information was relayed to a weekly meeting of English-speaking Western intelligence agency representatives in Whitehall, London in May. This gathering, usually on a Wednesday, is attended by officials from New Zealand, Australia, Canada and the United States, along with high ranking members of Britain's home and foreign intelligence services, MI5 and MI6. The alliance was formed in 1947 when the five countries signed a treaty known as the UKUSA Agreement, a secret decree under which each nation's security service pledged to share information generally only among themselves.

Police forces rarely see the intelligence gathered by their nation's security networks and New Zealand is no exception. The New Zealand Security Intelligence Service (NZSIS) was formed in

The morning after the bombing. The Rainbow Warrior keels over at almost 45 degrees. (*Auckland Star* photograph)

Greenpeace's flagship playing cat and mouse at Mururoa Atoll with a French navy vessel, 5 October 1985. (Copyright: Gamma)

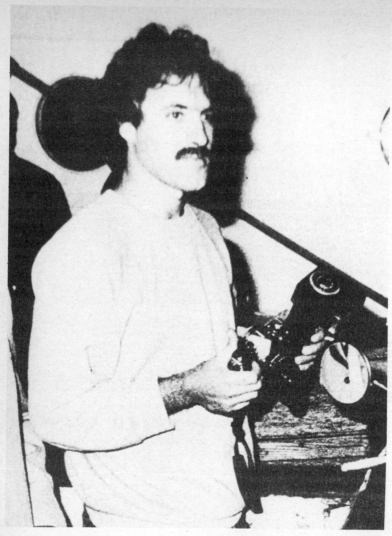

Greenpeace photographer, Fernando Pereira, who drowned as the Rainbow Warrior went down. (*Auckland Star* photograph)

Right: Some of the crew members of the Rainbow Warrior. Bene Hoffman (German, 2nd mate, top left); Steve Sawyer (American, top right), Pete Willcox (American, lower left); and Kelly Rigg (US Greenpeace staff). (*Auckland Star* photograph)

Swimming at Mururoa. In 1970 the then Defence Minister, Michel Debre, dived in just six hours after a small atomic blast to prove that the waters were completely safe. The act was repeated in 1981 by Rear-Admiral Choupin, head of the Pacific Experimentation Centre. (Copyright: Gamma)

Mururoa, a strategically important South Pacific atoll for French nuclear research and testing.

Left: The face of a spymaster? Auckland police think this may be Philippe Dubast who directed the sabotage operation. (*Auckland Star* photograph)

Below: The Ouvea, used by the sabotage team, moored at Norfolk Island after the bombing. (Photograph, Tom Lloyd)

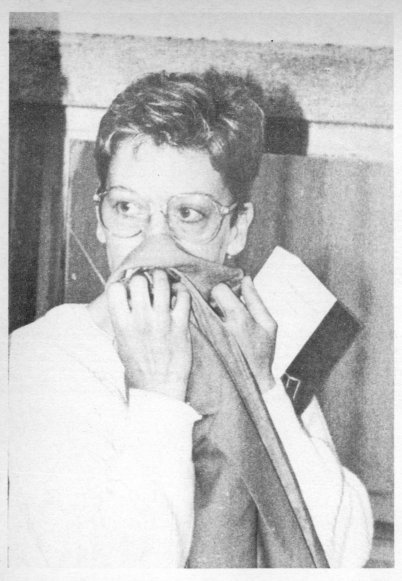

Dominique Prieur, also know at the time of her arrest as Sophie Turenge. (*Auckland Star* photograph)

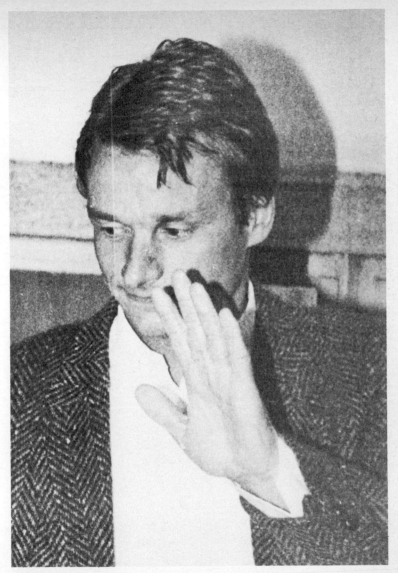

Alain Mafart, who posed as Sophie Turenge's husband, Alain Turenge,
(*Auckland Star* photograph)

The noise from the explosion aboard the Rainbow Warrior becomes unbearable for Defence Minister Charles Hernu, leading him to resign in September 1985. (Copyright: Gamma)

Admiral Lacoste, chief of the DGSE since 1982, was sacked in September 1985 over the Rainbow Warrior Affair. (Copyright: Gamma)

1956 to replace the police Special Branch which had been responsible for state security. Based in Wellington, it has two regional offices in Auckland and Christchurch and with only 170 officers on its staff it is the smallest operation among the five UKUSA members.

The information passed to New Zealand officials in May was far from specific and the French plot referred to may have been understood to have been nothing more than an intelligence mission in the South Pacific. New Caledonia was on the boil and pro-independent groups were being supplied with weapons. It would not have been unusual for French agents to have been active in the region trying to trace the source of the weapons.

Britain's MI5, aware that French agents were on the move, had marked the arrival in London of the bogus 'Turenge' husband, Major Alain Mafart and his pretend wife on their way through to New Zealand. Mafart was no stranger to British intelligence. As deputy head of the underwater warfare school at Aspretto, his record was well known. He had taken part in manoeuvres with Britain's crack Special Boat Service, a commando unit of 300 men trained in land, sea and air operations as well as marksmanship and frogman techniques. During the Falklands War, SBS commandos acted as a reconnaissance squad, mapping out positions of Argentine troops and deciding where British helicopters should land.

New Zealand police sources were to say later that the country's intelligence service did indeed know that French agents were operating in the North Island but this information was not passed to the police. There were at least two good reasons for this. First, the NZSIS did not have enough information to pass on. To raise the alarm about an unknown plot with an unknown target in an unknown place at no specific time was far too vague. Second, the intelligence service may have considered the unspecified French activity to be a state security matter, rather than a police affair, and the intelligence service has to be very careful about what information it makes available, even to its own law officers.

Brigadier Sir Herbert Gilbert, head of the NZSIS from 1957 until 1976, once remarked: 'We depend on our friends abroad for information over a wide variety of fields and they give us this information on the understanding that we will protect it as they do.'

His words were supported by Chief Ombudsman Sir Guy Powles who in 1975–76 conducted a majory inquiry into the service. He revealed that intelligence material from overseas was made available on the clear understanding that it would be afforded in New Zealand substantially the same degree of security as it is afforded in the country of origin. 'This requirement is quite specific, and is specifically attached in the form of tags and stamps to every piece of written material received. In essence, we are required to maintain and enforce personnel and physical security standards comparable to those of our allies, or we face being excluded from this essential intelligence.'

Even after the attack on the Greenpeace flagship, the NZSIS were reluctant to co-operate wholly with the Auckland police. In the long-term intelligence game, the sabotage was regarded as inconsequential, and not worth destroying relations between the DGSE and the NZSIS.

So Superintendent Galbraith and his team of detectives found themselves very much alone in the early days of the inquiry. But they had the clue of the dinghy, a French-made Mark II grey and black Zodiac. The two members of the Okahu Bay Outboard Boating Club who had made the emergency call to the police were questioned intensely. At about 9.30 p.m. they had seen the dinghy approach the shore near Ngapipi Bridge. There was a single occupant on board, a man in a diving suit and wearing a red woollen bonnet. As he stepped ashore carrying bags a woman who appeared to have been waiting on the waterfront hurried away to a campervan parked about 100 metres beyond. She brought it back to the beach and made a half turn. The frogman and another man loaded the bags into the vehicle, then they climbed in and sped away. But not before the suspicious watchers, believing they had witnessed a robbery, had taken the number.

As Prime Minister David Lange in Wellington condemned the sinking of the Rainbow Warrior as a major criminal act with political or terrorist overtones, Navy divers searched Hobson's Bay for clues. A helicopter whirred overhead. There had been reports that the dinghy had been seen in Mechanic's Bay, between Marsden Wharf and Hobson's Bay, and the occupant had dropped the outboard motor into the sea.

The search proved successful. Divers turned up the ditched Yamaha outboard in the sea near boatsheds not far from where the dinghy had been found. There was also one other vital piece of evidence — a small oxygen bottle with French markings, also found in Hobson's Bay.

That bottle was to provide the first clue that the Rainbow Warrior had been sunk by professionals, probably with military experience. The two-litre container was of a size used with closed-circuit scuba gear, also known in military circles as a re-breather outfit. The use of such equipment requires great skill but for those who master it there are great advantages. It is light, compact and, most important for saboteur frogmen, it gives off no bubbles. In addition, the 10-to-15 cubic-foot bottle allows a diver to stay under water for about as long as a frogman using conventional 80 cubic-foot containers.

Superintendent Galbraith in discussions with Naval frogmen learned the workings of the re-breather gear. The equipment is complicated to set up and a mistake can be fatal. Should the mouthpiece slip from the diver's mouth, or it develops a leak, flooding can occur and the operator would be in trouble. Unlike conventional air cylinders, the cannisters use pure oxygen, which is highly inflammable or poisonous under some conditions such as a depth of more than 50 feet.

The equipment creates no surface bubbles because the diver's expelled air is 'cleansed' by a chemical powder, Sodasorb, making it reusable. Strapped around the diver's chest is a plastic box protecting his lifeline equipment. Inside is a breathing bag, which looks something like a large hot water bottle. At first, the diver relies on the breathing bag for his air. As he inhales, the bag goes flat and when he exhales it expands with his oxygen — except there is now slightly less O_2 and slightly more carbon dioxide produced by his lungs. However, this CO_2 is trapped by the special powder before it can circulate around to the breathing bag. Only oxygen gets through, although in a reduced amount. The same good oxygen continues to circulate in one direction, the bag rising and falling as the diver breathes. One bag of air lasts up to two minutes, after which the user has to draw more oxygen from the miniature bottle. By sucking hard on the deflated bag, he opens a valve which releases a fresh supply.

Military divers who wear re-breather apparatus are also usually working under stress. Months of underwater training is required, first using conventional gear, before a diver is even allowed to wear a closed-circuit rig.

Military diving experts also spoke to the police about the methods that could be used to attach mines to a ship and then detonate them. The weapons could be bolted to a protruding part of the vessel, although that could be a noisy operation. They could be applied with rubber suction pads. They could be clamped on with magnets. But attaching mines with suction pads or magnets to an old ship could prove impossible if there were too many barnacles on the hull. Scraping the growth off would also create noise. A reliable trick, it was revealed, was to attach G-clamps to the bilge keels — fin-like strips on each side of the hull — and run a rope between them with the mine held against the vessel by the line.

G-clamps also had another good use. Saboteurs sometimes used them to tie down any buoyancy bags they had used to carry heavy weights under water. To release the bags would obviously send them to the surface and to deflate them would send up bubbles. During an inspection of the Rainbow Warrior later, a clamp was found attached to the keel.

The mines, explosive experts pointed out, could have been detonated in two ways. Radio waves could have been used from a device operated up to 1.5 kilometres away, but the system was not always reliable. The tried and trusted method was a timing device attached to the mine. This could have been electronic or chemical — probably chemical, using a time pencil. Acid released from a phial begins to eat through a strip of copper wire and the length of time taken to activate the detonator depends on the strength of the acid or the thickness of the wire. The attraction of this system is that explosives can be set reasonably accurately to go off any time between 90 minutes and seven days.

As well as the Zodiac dinghy and the oxygen cylinder, police had one more vital clue: the number of the campervan. It was almost too good to be true. The very next day after the bombing of the Greenpeace ship police obtained from the hire firm, Newmans Motor Caravans, the names of those who had rented the vehicle: Alain and Sophie Turenge. A check was made with the immigration department. There was a slight discrepancy in the coding on the passports the 'Swiss' couple had produced.

Staff at every Newmans branch were asked to delay the couple and call the police immediately they showed up to return the campervan. Detectives did not have to wait long. When Becky Hayter turned up for work at the Newmans branch in Bowden Road in the south-east Auckland suburb of Mount Wellington on July 12, less than 36 hours after the bombing, she found the French couple waiting with the van. She wondered at first whether the police had already found them, but after a brief conversation with another staff member, she realised the police had not yet been told they were there. The couple were not unfamiliar. They had visited the depot earlier in the week to change vans because the windscreen on the first one they had hired had been smashed. Ms Hayter and a colleague tried to work out a way to delay them, but in the end it was the French couple themselves who solved that problem. They had, said the man calling himself Turenge, intended to return the vehicle to Wellington city the following Monday but had changed their minds. They would, therefore, like a refund.

While pretending to work out details of the charges, staff phoned the police. Asked how his holiday had gone, the Frenchman replied in good English: 'It went well.'

But the woman appeared nervous and indicated to staff that their trip had not gone well. As Ms Hayter and her colleagues continued to busy themselves with the rental paperwork, a grey Toyota car sped up and three men dashed into the office with handguns drawn.

'Police!' said one. 'Come with us.'

'Why?' the bogus Alain Turenge asked calmly.

'For verification of your travel documents. We have reason to believe they are false.'

Sophie Turenge's face had turned pale. They were taken to Auckland Central Police Station where Special Branch officers began interrogating them. The two campervans the couple had hired were also driven to the police station for fingerprinting and a detailed forensic examination. They refused to divulge their true identities although police, who had arrested them under the provisions of the 1964 Immigration Act, continued to insist they were travelling on false documents. The Swiss Government would soon verify that.

For Major Alain Mafart and Captain Dominique Prieur of the DGSE separate police cells were to climax the end of their fictitious New Zealand honeymoon.

The Ouvea meanwhile had sailed north — and fast. It reached Norfolk Island on July 13, a not altogether impossible feat considering it had sailed twice the distance from Noumea to New Zealand in nine days in worse weather, with a stop-over at Norfolk.

A team of 40 detectives had been assigned to Superintendent Galbraith on the Rainbow Warrior Investigation. That there was a French connection to the bombing now seemed indisputable. The Turenge couple were French speaking. The dinghy was of French design. The oxygen bottle had French markings. And, detectives learned from Greenpeace members who had survived the sinking, a mysterious Frenchman calling himself Francois Verlon had come aboard some four and a half hours before the explosions.

Despite continuing expressions of sympathy from the French Ambassador, detectives began a systematic check of the movements of every French person in New Zealand. A telex message was flashed to police in Tahiti asking them to detain and question Francois Verlon. Detectives also checked out the movements of any French ships that had been in the waters around Auckland at the time of the explosions. There had been one big vessel, the container ship Helene Delmas, which left Auckland for Lyttelton, in the South Island. The crew were questioned by Christchurch detectives, but the officers gained the impression that no-one on board could help them. The same negative response was received from Tahiti. The man calling himself Francois Verlon had repeated to police what he had already told Greenpeace members on board the Rainbow Warrior on that fateful night — that he was a militant pacifist who had visited the ship to express support for the crew. As proof of his sincerity and willingness to help the protest campaign, he had left his name with one of the Greenpeace people.

There was one other French vessel that had been sailing off the east coast, customs officials reported. A yacht, the Ouvea, had left Whangarei Harbour on July 9, the crew saying they were heading for Norfolk Island. But intitial reports gathered by police suggested the yacht had first headed south. Superintendent Galbraith and his men believed it was vital for the yacht to be checked out, and contacted police on the island which has been a self-governing Australian territory since 1978. There are only three men in the island police force, all of them seconded from the Australian Federal Police. Along with a Collector of Customs, there are only three authorised officers in the Immigration Department and the rules applying to visitors are very relaxed. New arrivals are not required to present their travel documents unless they intend to remain for more than a month.

In Dr Maniguet's case, he was well within that time scale. While New Zealand police were in telex and telephone consultation about the the Ouvea, Dr Maniguet was already attending to his onward travel arrangements. And as a team of nine detectives hastily boarded a Royal New Zealand Air Force Andover at Whenuapai air base to fly to Norfolk Island the specialist in diving accidents had also got himself airborne on an East-West Airlines plane — heading for Sydney. The detectives had left New Zealand in such a hurry, in fact, that they had to turn back when it was realised there wasn't enough fuel for the return journey. Dr Maniguet left Norfolk Island barely two hours before the police eventually touched down.

All was not lost. New Zealand detectives had asked the local authorities to detain the remainder of the crew for questioning. As they were being grilled by the New Zealanders and protesting their innocence, Australian Federal Police acting on a request by their colleagues across the Tasman Sea, picked out Dr Maniguet when he arrived in Sydney. He was followed into the city, where he checked into the Southern Cross Hotel in Elizabeth Street and was given a fifth floor room.

That evening his police shadows kept him under surveillance as he made his way along Pitt Street, in the city centre, and entered a cinema. The film took him to another time and another place. Its title: *Passage to India.* An interesting experience was to befall the doctor while he was in the cinema. According to what he was to tell two Australian and two New Zealand police officers who approached him in the foyer during the intermission, no sooner had he taken his seat when he heard a French voice in the seat next to him. Dr Maniguet had introduced himself to the man and they had agreed to continue their conversation in the foyer. That was when the police approached them. Stunned, Dr Maniguet insisted that he and his companion had not known each other before and it was pure co-incidence that two Frenchmen had found themselves sitting side-by-side in the same cinema watching the same performance.

Dr Maniguet's companion, identified later by the French Embassy in Canberra as an expatriate French businessman of high repute, accompanied the doctor to Federal Police Headquarters. The businessman explained he had lived in Australia for 25 years, was a former French trade commissioner in Sydney, and was Australian representative of a group known as the 'expatriate French nationals in the South Pacific'. The French Embassy were to add to his credentials later by pointing out that the man had excellent connections with a number of people of note. One was the Premier of New South Wales, Mr Neville Wran, whom the Frenchman knew through their joint membership of the Franco-Australian Bicentenary Committee.

And what was Dr Maniguet, the man who had clocked up so many kilometres by plane, yacht and car in recent weeks and had given up a brief skiing trip in the New Zealand Alps, doing in a Sydney cinema within hours of his arrival in Australia? Particularly when the yacht he had been sailing had left New Zealand waters around the date that the Greenpeace boat had been sunk.

Dr Maniguet hoped the police would understand his simple explanation. When he checked into his hotel room he switched on the television and saw a news report about the sinking of the Rainbow Warrior. The bulletin stated that New Zealand police were suspicious about the activities of a group of Frenchmen who had left by yacht about the time of the bombing.

Worried, he had left the hotel and gone for a walk. He decided to go to the cinema and, hearing a French voice, had introduced himself. He had explained to his new cinema companion that he might be in trouble with the New Zealand police and was not sure what to do. After questioning, the two men were allowed to leave.

Despite his insistence that he had left the yacht at Norfolk Island because he had pressing professional obligations in France, police asked Dr Maniguet not to continue his flight to Singapore until they gave him permission. He was visited in his room the following day by a New Zealand detective who questioned him closely about his movements and his connections with the Ouvea.

His answer — and he was to repeat it several times in the weeks to come — was that as a single, jet-setting man he wanted to cruise the region between Noumea and New Zealand because it was one place in the world he did not know. He had travelled in the Southern Hemisphere winter because it was summer in France, when everyone took their holidays.

Had he known the three other crew members before embarking on the trip to Noumea?

'No,' said Dr Maniguet, 'I have never met them before'.

When it was put to him that police were suspicious of a link between the yacht crew and a couple touring the North Island in a campervan — witnesses had reported several sightings — Dr Maniguet said he did not know how that could be possible. He pointed out he had been away from the end of June until

July 5 on a trip to Auckland, Christchurch, Queenstown and back so he did not know everything the crew had been up to in Whangarei. He had no reason to ask them any details about what they had been doing. But it was obvious, he added, that they had been seeing some girls while he had been away.

The New Zealand detective then put to him evidence that had recently come to light: Dr Maniguet and a member of the yacht crew, who had been identified as Raymond Velche, had been seen in a car south of Whangarei when they had met up with another man in a camping van. Dr Maniguet explained then, as he was to repeat later, that Velche had asked him to accompany him because he wanted to meet up with two young women who were touring the region. However the girls were not in the van when they found it — just a man who was their 'protector'. If there was ever a rendezvous with the Turenge couple, he was certainly not present.

There was nothing that police could hold Dr Maniguet on. He had ready answers to every question. He was allowed to fly on to Singapore en route for Paris.

Meanwhile on Norfolk Island, New Zealand police had made a startling discovery. A search of the Ouvea had turned up a colour photograph of two frogmen. One was Eric Audrenc (Andries). The other was Raymond Velche (Verge) — wearing a red woollen cap. There was one other intriguing piece of evidence among the pile of papers and maps in the cabin. On the back of part of a map of Auckland, someone had scribbled the address of an art gallery located in the suburb of Ponsonby. The information was relayed back to Auckland. The map was, in fact, one of many Christine Cabon (alias Frederique Bonlieu) had sent back to Paris to assist the plotters.

The owner of the gallery proved she had a good memory. A woman called Frederique Bonlieu, the name of the French voluntary worker detectives had been given by Greenpeace, had indeed called at the gallery a couple of months previously. She had mentioned she was compiling a travel itinerary and had said in conversation she was gathering maps and details about car hire firms. She had also expressed her interest in the Greenpeace movement.

On Norfolk Island, Superintendent Allan Galbraith's men were running into bureaucratic problems in their questioning of the crew. Despite the New Zealanders' suspicions that the crew of the Ouvea were travelling on false passports, local police said there were no grounds on which they could continue to detain the three men on Norfolk Island. It was not enough to be merely suspicious.

The New Zealand team were concerned that the crew were being allowed to go when they considered the grounds to hold them were strong enough. Under Australian law, authorities have the power to detain people who are suspected of having false passports. The Migration Act states that those suspected of having illegal documents can be held, initially, for two days and an order for further detention of seven days can be obtained from a magistrate. However on Norfolk Island the Australian powers do not apply. And because the New Zealanders were unable to say for sure that the crew were using false passports, the local authorities said they could not be held further.

The DGSE spies were delighted. They made known their intention to sail to Noumea and on the evening of July 16 the yacht put out from Norfolk Island.

For Superintendent Allan Galbraith whose team had been expanded to 66 it was a major disappointment. But all he would say publicly was: 'It would be fair to say that we would have liked to have had a longer time to inspect the vessel.'

He would monitor the boat's movements carefully. The crew could still be interviewed in Noumea with the co-operation of the New Caledonian authorities. But already Superintendent Galbraith was wondering just how much help his men would receive. The plot was growing bigger by the day. And he was beginning to have his suspicions about just where the roots lay.

10

The South Seas

It was festival time in Tahiti. Feasts of roast pig, breadfruit and fish were laid out under the shade of hibiscus trees. Colourful kites filled the sky, 50,000 honking vehicles packed the streets and at night native girls danced and sang under coconut frond torches. At the communal feasting ground a couple put on a public display of sexual intercourse. There were shouts of 'Haere mai tamaa!' — 'Come and eat!' — the haunting tones of bamboo flutes filled the air and abundantly filled trays of tropical fruit, fish and meat were offered to Taaroa, the god of the sea. On a low wall, a row of skulls, the ancient heads of battle warriors, were also displayed as a gesture to the god.

The Auckland detective had no time to enjoy it. He sat facing the fair-haired Francois Verlon at the central police station questioning him about his visit to the Rainbow Warrior. The young man recalled eating birthday cake and telling the crew he shared their sentiments. He had gone on board because a crew member had invited him. Still describing himself as a 'militant pacifist', he explained that he had offered his help to the conservationists.

The detective could not establish any direct link between Verlon and the explosion other than that he was French and had been on the Rainbow Warrior a few hours before it was scuttled. There wasn't enough evidence to lay charges. The officer flew back to New Zealand, the laughter of the merry makers in his ears.

With the bomb just 1222 kilometres away, a prophet of doom might have described Papeete as the Sodom of the nuclear age.

For twentieth century hedonists, it is the earthly paradise described 200 years earlier by Cook, Wallis, Bligh and Bougainville. Its beauty is still there — jagged, purple peaks beckon through the low clouds and the sun beams down on crystalline lagoons — but the spirit has been tainted. The landscapes that breathed from Gauguin's canvas have been sliced by a four-lane freeway, signs prohibiting swimming have been erected on Papeete's polluted beach and sometimes a smog settles over the capital.

The French navigator, Louis-Antoine de Bougainville, who called at Tahiti during his voyage around the world between 1766 and 1769, compared the island to the Garden of Eden and helped popularise a belief in the moral value of man in his natural state. This concept had considerable significance among his compatriots of the day. And when Captain James Cook's Endeavour sailed into Matavai Bay in April 1769, the crew saw a people and surroundings that shared an equal beauty. Dressed in brightly coloured toga-like robes, they gazed from dark, liquid eyes and showed perfect gleaming white teeth as they smiled a welcome to the explorers. They shone with an innocence that time, communications and greed would eventually tarnish.

Tahitians today can afford luxuries beyond the reach of those who live on other Pacific islands. The streets are clogged, not just at festival time, with Mercedes and late model Citroens and Renaults. Restaurants serve imported *pâte de fois gras* and wines start at $US20. The women parade in the latest fashions from Paris. The more than 100,000 residents pay no income tax and enjoy the highest per capita consumption of champagne in the world.

These people who only 200 years ago were cut off from the rest of the world, isolated by an endless horizon and the centuries of time, grow fat and have lost their teeth on the proceeds of the nuclear test programme, while many Pacific nations who oppose the French presence and the bomb blasts struggle for economic survival. On this, one of the three remaining French territories in the Pacific, the inhabitants enjoy incomes and living standards found in metropolitan France. By 1980 their gross national product per capita already stood at some $US11,400, compared with $US6390 for nearby American Samoa. The military alone employs 3000 Polynesians throughout the islands — about 15 per cent of the workforce — and is responsible for some 33 per cent of the economy. Tahitians earn a minimum wage of about $US3 an hour, while European public servants earn salaries approaching $US100,000. The wealth acquired by the 15 per cent European population is passed down to the Polynesians, who happily turn deaf ears to the cries of their neighbours who demand that the French must go, taking their bomb with them.

'Why should we turn our backs on a source of income that has kept us for 20 years?' the majority of the inhabitants of the 129 islands of French Polynesia ask. Paris is their Sugar Daddy, forking out some $US320 million in military spending in 1984, close to half the public expenditure in an economy which has little more than tourism, copra, pearls and fisheries to fall back on. The total economic contribution to the area amounted to about $US570 million in 1985.

Take away the French and their military presence and the Tahitian economy will be reduced to the scraping level of its Pacific neighbours. Meanwhile, look at the houses the French government built after the 1983 cyclone; look at the solar-powered telephone booths; look at the cars; look at the televisions, the videos . . . look at the bank accounts!

Partly for these reasons, Tahiti, which became the first island in the Pacific to come under the control of a foreign power, is likely to be the last to cut ties. The anti-nuclear lobby may protest that very little French money actually filters down to the indigenous population, but there are few islanders who would deny they have gained some benefit in recent years. There has been a price to pay, of course: the loss of a culture.

Although colonisation had its drastic effects, some say the real whittling away of Polynesian culture has occurred since the French brought the bomb to the South Pacific. Anthropologists point out that the French used the islanders — then dropped them.

Polynesians were employed during construction of the test base, thousands leaving their islands to earn good money, only to find their incomes cut off when the building work finished. Of course, many hundreds of Polynesians are still employed at Mururoa, but large numbers found themselves out of work after the initial phase and had little inclination to return to their traditional skills and their low incomes.

Fishing and copra production collapsed and without reliable local food production Polynesians tended to rely on imported canned foods. Although virtually everyone now benefits from the French presence, the general acceptance by today's Polynesians of French administration and all its hand-outs is a stark contrast to the islanders of yesterday who fiercely fought the invaders of their land in the first five years. For invade it the French did as a result of what they considered to be a national insult.

The British, busily exploiting Captain Cook's discoveries and entrenching themselves in Australia and New Zealand, had turned their backs for the moment on other Pacific opportunities. America and Russia seemed to be interested only in sending out scientific missions and Spain had given up the colonising race altogether. The gate was wide open for the French. The Napoleonic wars in Europe were over, navigation had improved and government expeditions and private traders from many nations found their way to the South Seas. With them came the missionaries, whose influence on the islanders was to drastically change their whole culture, replacing unashamed free love with Christian guilt. When Otto von Kotzebue, who led a Russian expedition into the Pacific in 1823 landed at Tahiti, he was driven to write down his observations about the effects of evangelicalism.

'A religion like this,' he sadly observed, 'which forbids every innocent pleasure and cramps or annihilates every mental power, is a libel on the divine founder of Christianity. It is true that the religion of the missionaries has, with a great deal of evil, affected some good. It has restrained the vices of theft and incontinence, but it has given birth to ignorance, hypocrisy and a hatred of all other modes of faith, which was once foreign to the open and benevolent character of the Tahitian.'

The evangelical grip tightened. Roman Catholicism was repelled, and when two French priests of the Picusian order tried to settle on the island in 1835 they were tossed out. It happened again the following year. The face had been slapped with the glove. Admiral Depetit-Thouars, cruising with a squadron in the Pacific sailed to Tahiti in his flagship, La Reine Blanche, aimed 60 cannons at Papeete and threatened bombardment unless he was paid an indemnity and shown the respect that was the right of French nationals.

Queen Pomare 1V, monarch of Tahiti and the nearby islands for the previous 16 years, and who travelled around in a coach she had received as a present from Queen Victoria, found no refuge behind the missionaries' Bibles. She was forced to pay up, then ask for French protection. At noon on November 6 1842, 500 French troops began landing from four warships moored in Papeete harbour. Up the beaches and along the wharf marched the artillery followed by the marines and finally the marine infantry.

As a naval band played, they headed for the palace where a Tahitian chief stood waiting under the queen's flag to make a formal protest. He was drowned out by a roll of drums which was followed by a short speech by one of the officers: 'In the name of King Louis Philippe 1, our august master, we plant the French flag over this land and would rather die than abandon it. As for you, the people of the country, we have come to protect you and bring you civilisation and peace.'

Down came Queen Pomare's flag and up went the Tricolore. As the band played the Marseillaise, the French warships let loose a 21-gun salute. A proclamation was issued: Pomare was queen no more. Louis Philippe was the new ruler. Captain Armand Bruat of the French navy was his representative. The hapless queen fled to nearby Moorea and those who showed their allegiance to her by waging a guerrilla war against the French were easily quelled. Years before, the French philosopher Denis Diderot had issued a warning to the Tahitians. One day the Christians would come 'with crucifix in one hand and the dagger in the other to cut your throats or to force you to accept their customs and opinions; one day under their rule you will be almost as unhappy as they are.' He went on to warn of the ravages that would follow the 'wretched caresses' of the European sailors. Now, with the French navy installed, it was too late to heed those prophetic words.

Nevertheless, the Tahitians still harboured the belief that Britain, which had made vague offers of protection in the past, would sail to their aid. London, however, was still too preoccupied with Australia and New Zealand. Unopposed by any outside force, France, realising the commercial and strategic importance of Tahiti, dug in. Their protectorate rule continued until 1880, three years after Queen Pomare's death. By now the Panama Canal was being regarded as a new gateway to the Pacific and the French took steps to convert their protectorate into a colony.

The new century saw the colony embracing all the islands of the Society Group, along with the Austral Islands, the Tuamotu Archipelago and the Marquesas Islands. Nor did it take long for the Europeans to influence the islanders in the way that Diderot had predicted. The French painter Paul Gauguin noticed it when he arrived towards the end of the nineteenth century to perpetuate the nymphs he had heard about. He wanted to capture on canvas their golden skins, their searching animal odour and their tropical savours. Instead he bemoaned that 'day by day the race vanishes, decimated by the European diseases.' He painted unsmiling faces, capturing a people who had only memories of happy days. One picture summed up his feelings. It was the painting of a girl reclining on a bed. The naked teenager gazed endlessly into space, one side of her face cupped in her hand. All life had gone out of her. In the top right hand corner Gauguin had printed in English 'Never More'.

Predictions that the opening of the Panama Canal in 1914 would turn Tahiti into an important shipping centre did not materialise. The French did virtually nothing with the islands that they had undisputed authority over. A new Governor arrived every 18 months, resulting in a failure to stitch together any reform schemes or administrative policy. Among the Europeans, the indifference of Paris to developing fishing and agriculture, sewed the roots of laziness. Government officials on huge salaries lounged under the palm trees soaking in the tropical splendour with native servants, confused and spiritless by the intrusion of early whalers, the missionaries and now their European masters, waiting on them on all sides. Despairing, defeated, the islanders were living the words of an old Tahitian song: 'The palm tree will grow, the coral will spread, but man will cease.'

One hundred years of French occupation were to pass before anyone dared challenge the colonists. A blue-eyed, fair-haired Huahine-born man, marched up to the French Governor, Colonel Georges Orselli, and let him know just what he thought about his economic policies. As a result, the protester, Pouvanaa a Oopa, was thrown into jail before being exiled to a reef islet. The end of the second world war found him back in Tahiti again where be became a champion of his country's war veterans. More than 300 of them had fought for France in Europe and North Africa and now, as reward, they were demanding a greater stake in their own country.

Urged on by Pouvanaa, they named a fighting committee after him and dedicated themselves to giving Tahiti and its achipelagoes more political, economic, administrative and cultural freedom. They proved their determination in June 1947 when, backed by a large crowd of demonstrators, they complained about the landing of three Paris officials who had arrived to take up jobs the Tahitians said they could do. The inevitable happened — they were arrested and held in custody for five months before a court considered whether they were guilty or not of challenging governmental authority. Acquitted, they emerged as heroes, so much so that when elections were held in 1949 for a representative in the French parliament, Pouvanaa swept in, being re-elected twice more through the 1950s. The Comite Pouvanaa had developed into a political party, the Rassemblement Democratique des Populations Tahitiennes (RDPT) — the Tahitian People's Democratic Assembly. Under the RDPT banner, Pouvanaa also got himself elected to the local Territorial Assembly.

In France, General de Gaulle had become President and one of his first moves was to announce referendums for all French territories on the question of independence. Pouvanaa took to the streets, soliciting support for nationalism. Although his associates would have welcomed a form of internal self-government, they were already enjoying some of the spin-offs of colonialism and did not give Pouvanaa their support. Only 36 per cent of the population voted with him. The chance for independence was lost.

In a fit of frustration and rage, Pouvanaa organised demonstrations among his supporters and was soon arrested on charges alleging he threw Molotov cocktails in the streets in an attempt to burn down Papeete. Found guilty, he was sentenced to eight years imprisonment, but the authorities quietly put him on board a ship and took him to France. His son Marcel rose up in his place, only to die in Paris following an operation. His father, released from jail and now ailing, was forbidden from returning to any French territory in the Pacific, including his own. But in 1958, the 50th. anniversary of the end of the first world war in which Pouvanaa had fought for France, he was freed by decree of President de Gaulle. Slightly paralysed by a stroke, he was stunned to see a crowd of several thousand waiting for him when he returned to his homeland. Six months later, President Pompidou came to power and pardoned him along with other French citizens convicted of political crimes. Now free to run for public office, he was elected in 1971 to the French Senate, a victory for those who still pressed for self-government.

One of his fervent supporters was the man who was to rise up as a leading autonomist, Francis Sanford, a Tahitian of American ancestry. He seized every chance to proclaim what he said was his people's desires for independence and when a French Cabinet member visited Tahiti, Sanford and his associates raised the red and white flag of Queen Pomare over the Territorial Assembly building. As another form of protest, he returned all his World War 11 medals to the government, saying he was too ashamed to wear them.

The French made no attempt to placate the autonomists, displaying instead an arrogance that infuriated Sanford and Pouvanaa. By May 1976, with a controversy over nuclear tests tossed in as an added complication, relations were so low between Paris and Papeete that the two men, along with the Speaker of the Territorial Assembly despatched a manifesto to the Elysee saying: 'The French government is keeping its control over Polynesia to avoid having to undertake unpopular nuclear tests at home, and because these 800,000 square kilometres of ocean contain enormous mineral resources coveted by French mining companies. But these desperate efforts will come to nothing. Polynesia will remain French only with the consent of its inhabitants. A prerequisite is that we have good reasons for wanting to remain French, and the best reason France can give us is to acknowledge our right to run our own affairs.'

Four months later, a new constitution was voted through the French parliament, giving French Polynesia the right to internal self government. The Governor was given the lesser role of High Commissioner and Sanford became Vice-President of a new government council. The first session of the council was set for July 1977, but Pouvanaa was not there. He died just six months earlier at the age of 81. Nevertheless, he was remembered. Sanford paid tribute to him as 'the initiator of the autonomist movement' and spoke the words that Pouvanaa himself might well have used. The historic meeting, he said, was 'the gathering of the first fruits of a long and arduous work of cultivation, of a struggle waged without let-up for more than 30 years.'

In September 1984, another statute was introduced giving greater autonomy to the territory's 30-seat elected Assembly. Mr Gaston Flosse, the Parliamentary leader, became President and took over chairmanship of the Governing Council from the Paris-appointed High Commissioner. Paris's gesture meant that it relinquished control of most of the local administration to President Flosse and his Gaullist Tahoeraa Huiraatira party, which holds 15 seats and governs in coalition with three independents. But there is a catch. France has hung on to control of defence, foreign affairs, law, finance and communications.

Although President Flosse, like the majority of Polynesians, Chinese, Europeans and demis — mixed race — is not anxious to cut immediate ties with France, he envisages the day when French Polynesia will become internally self-governing with a 'free association' with France. A similar status is shared by the Cook Islands, a former New Zealand territory which was given self rule in 1965. Those who want the French, and the associated good life, to remain are confident they have at least 20 years ahead of them, and probably much more. What it all really comes down to is just how long France can maintain a military presence in the area. The authorities themselves shrug off any suggestions that pressure from environmentalists and independence movements will force them out. Shout, demonstrate, as loud as they like, the ecologists will not force France to stop the tests.

The future enconomy of Tahiti is on the streets. French sailors amble around the harbourside, mingling with overseas tourists. As long as these two groups are present, the Polynesians know the dollars and the francs will continue to roll in. But the independence movement, like that on New Caledonia, 4,500 kilometres to the west, is gaining strength with an estimated 10 to 15 per cent of the population's support. Some believe the departure of France may be within the decade.

A group of Australian visitors was surprised to hear even their tour leader speak of the imminent departure of France after 145 years of rule. Tiare Sanford, hibiscus in her hair, was explaining why Tahiti needed many thousands of more tourists. 'We have to prepare for the day when the French leave us. Most of us believe we have another 10 years, no more.' Tiare, a hostess with the Tahitian Tourism Board, is the daughter of Francis Sanford and she has watched the growth of the independent movement from close range. Although a number of political agitators are cooling their heels in jail there are enough militants around to nibble away at their colonial rulers. Signs telling the French colonials to 'Go Home With Your Bloody Bomb' pop up here and there and in February and March 1984, 1500 joined in two street demonstrations, the first in 11 years, against 'La Bombe' and militants set fire to buildings causing $US250,000 worth of damage.

The French are well aware of the concern the greying 54-year-old Flosse has about the tests — it was he, after all, who introduced a motion protesting against them in 1981. Since then he has demonstrated his support for the French by signing an anti-independence document with New Caledonian Premier Dick Ukewie, who is also a Senator in the French Parliament. The document agreed to 'an alliance of French Pacific territories to defend their common interests and promote joint action in political, administrative, economic, cultural and social matters.' Flosse's support of the pro-French parties of the white settlers in New Caledonia surprised many, although it was ascribed to the fact that he is a part European and a product of the French mission schools; he taught in such a school before entering politics. Formal opposition to the tests today is usually channelled through the Evangelical Church of French Polynesia, to which most inhabitants belong.

France's constant reaction to any local protest is to point out that, in accordance with the accepted colonial system of government, Polynesians have no control over defence matters. But those who want to see an end to the testing refuse to be beaten back. The initiative that some of them took in 1983 is a good example. Members of the local socialist party, *Ia mana te nunaa*, meaning 'Power to the People', which won three seats in the Territorial Assembly in the May 1982 elections and which can count on about 15 per cent of the popular vote, managed to get an invitation, through wooing an Australian Labor Party official, to a meeting of the Socialist International in Brussels. It was a clever ploy that gave the locals a world platform.

The man who went to the meeting, the Ia mana's secretary-general, Jacqui Drollet, distributed a four-page pamphlet to the 120 delegates representing 30 countries. It told how General de Gaulle 'when France was chased out of Algeria by the victorious patriots of that country, forcibly installed in our Polynesian islands the nuclear testing centre to which his own people had refused house room in France'. It ended with a call for all 'socialist comrades' to persuade or to force President Mitterrand to hold a referendum in French Polynesia on the issue of nuclear testing.

As might be expected, that did not happen, but the anti-French movement had scored a number of points. As if in answer, Paris decided to build a big new navy transport vessel specially to serve the testing programme. More patrol ships, helicopters and air-craft are to be assigned to the programme. During what was regarded by anti-nuclear Pacific nations as a breathtaking display of defiance and insensitivity after the sinking of the Rainbow Warrior, President Mitterrand dashed to Mururoa and declared his country would continue tests in Polynesia for as long as the requirement of its deterrent force made it necessary. Mitterrand also announced that work would begin on the construction of a strategic base at Noumea.

Undaunted by France's clear intention to remain for the fore-seeable future, the pro-independents of Tahiti, with the colour-ful, articulate Mayor of the important municipality of Faaa as one of their leaders, continue to fight on, at the same time sup-porting the battle for independence being waged by the indig-enous Kanak people of New Caledonia. For in the Kanaks, the independents of Tahiti see a mirror image of themselves. In March 1985, the Mayor of Faaa, Oscar Temaru declared that 'if our Kanak brothers are in revolt today it's because colonialist France, without consulting them, took possession of their country. It's because a whole succession of French governments used the country as a human cesspit for 20,000 convicts. It's because the French administration has driven them from their lands to make way for white settlers, who more often than not were freed convicts, or their even more depraved and brutal former jailers. It's because French and multi-national companies have seized their main natural resource, the nickel deposits of New Caledonia.'

Since the arrival of the nuclear testing agency, the Centre d'Expêrimentation du Pacific, Tahiti had been flooded with metropolitan French, and various runaways from other French departments and territories, said Temaru. With the same stub-bornness as in New Caledonia, all governments of the Fifth Re-public have refused to undertake serious decolonisation. Big hotel chains had exploited, and continued to exploit, Tahiti's natural resources for their own advantage.

'The only small difference,' the mayor added, 'is one of numbers: we are not yet quite as dominated and submerged as our Kanak brothers in New Caledonia. But if we don't soon manage to put a stop to this new colonisation, we'll be sunk in a few years. It'll be all perfectly democratic and constitutional, but we'll be sunk just the same.'

Tahiti and New Caledonia are among the last relics of European colonialism in the Pacific. With the exception of the United States, colonial powers in the Pacific — Britain, Australia, New Zealand — have all let the strings go in the past 20 years. Successive governments in Paris have held on in the arrogant assumption that overseas territories are part of France. There is a military argument in favour of them remaining in the Pacific, an argument supported by politicians in all Western nations, but on a local level the militants say they have been exploited long enough.

New Caledonia is heading towards independence faster than Tahiti because the Melanesians who make up 42 per cent of the 146,000 population living on this long strip of nickel-producing French territory just 1500 kilometres from Australia's north Queensland coast, have, among other reasons, been able to compare the wealthy lifestyles of their Polynesian neighbours with their own. Just before territorial elections were held in October, 1985, the death toll in recent clashes between the Kanak independents and police and Caldoches (European New Caledonians) approached 25, marking another black period in the territory's violent history.

While the riots flare up from time to time in New Caledonia, Paris remains worried that they may be contagious and eventually lead to the loss of all their remaining overseas possessions, along with their military bases and nuclear testing facilities. The rumblings of discontent are growing louder in Tahiti and the French are well aware of the need to maintain the good life for those who have tasted of it. The hand-outs are there because the military is there and the military is there because the bomb is there. Paradoxically, it is France's one hope of keeping the peace in its last strategic Pacific outpost.

11

The Net Tightens

As Allan Galbraith and his team tried to pick up the threads of a 20,000 kilometre trail that they were convinced had begun in Paris and led through New Caledonia, New Zealand and north to Norfolk Island, the Ouvea dipped and rolled through the south west Pacific on a course for Noumea.

The crew, who had booked UTA airline seats through the Norfolk Island Bounty Travel Agency to fly from Noumea to Paris on July 26, realised just how precarious their position was. The police were on to them. They were lucky to have been freed. They'd been questioned for hours at the island's South Pacific Hotel and then the police had split them up for further grilling. They had demanded to be freed and the police had reluctantly let them go. But there was little doubt there would be a reception committee in New Caledonia, French protectorate or not. It was time to put an emergency escape plan into effect.

At 6.20 a.m. on Sunday July 21, five days after the yacht left Norfolk Island, a crew member placed a position call through to Noumea Radio. The Ouvea, he reported, was 48 kilometres north-west of the Isle of Pines, a popular holiday island off the New Caledonian mainland.

One other French vessel was on the move in the area at the time — the nuclear-powered submarine Rubis. It is equipped to track and destroy other nuclear warships and submarines. It is equally capable of picking up yachtsmen who scuttle their vessel. The Rubis left Noumea on July 5 carrying a 'Red' crew which had been flown from France to replace the 'Blue' crew who had operated her for 47 days of submerged cruising until the submarine arrived in New Caledonia on May 10.

The Rubis has a top speed of 25 knots and could have reached Tahiti in less than a week. The submarine actually arrived at Papeete 17 days later on July 22. Military personnel in French Polynesia say that among the crew who stepped ashore were the three yachtsmen, although the French Navy denies this. It was certainly an added insult to Greenpeace that the men directly behind the bombing of the group's peace ship should have made good their escape in a nuclear-powered vessel. If, as the Navy claims, the Rubis did not pick up the crew, where did the yacht go? For as New Zealand detectives were soon to establish, the Ouvea with its wealth of forensic evidence had vanished from the surface of the ocean. There remained the improbable notions that the espionage team abandoned their yacht and rowed ashore somewhere on a small rubber dinghy that was always kept on board. Or they sailed the Ouvea into some lonely bay and walked ashore. Or they hitched a lift with a passing vessel. But the captain of any rescue ship would have certainly reported the fact. There was one fantastic notion they did not discount — the crew had drowned after some mishap had befallen the yacht.

Noumea radio continued calling the yacht every 30 minutes but received no reply. Its last reported position would have put it close to Goro Reef, on the southern tip of the mainland, but crews of other vessels who had been involved in rescuing seamen on another yacht, the Phoenix, which had run aground on the reef, had seen no trace of the Ouvea. As police who had dealt with drug smugglers knew all too well, giving false positions requires no skill. Fiddling with a vessel's electronic log, which records its movements, does require some technical knowledge and electrical equipment purchased by the crew in New Zealand would have enable them to by-pass the log when the Ouvea was sailing. According to the log, when the vessel put out from Whangarie it left New Zealand waters on July 9, yet it did not arrive at Norfolk Island until the evening of July 13. This, police established, was a day longer than the Ouvea had taken on its journey south when the weather was particularly bad. New Zealand Prime Minister David Lange refused to reveal whether RNZAF Orion aircraft had been used to photograph and keep a watch on the Ouvea after it had left Norfolk. 'I am not going to disclose that,' he said. 'It is a matter which ought not properly to be disclosed. But there are lots of ways in which you can keep in touch with a particular vessel.'

In fact an Orion was ordered into action to try to track the Ouvea. Without success. But a French navy vessel sighted the aircraft, prompting a report from outraged Noumea authorities to Defence Minister Charles Hernu. The New Zealanders, they protested, had penetrated New Caledonian air space without permission.

At any rate, Mr Roger Chatelain of Noumea Yacht Charters had now become convinced that he would never see the Ouvea again. Three New Zealand police officers, Detective Senior Sergeant Mike Weekes, Detective Sergeant Peter Williams and Constable Nick Hall, were asked to remain in New Caledonia in case the Ouvea crew showed up. For Detective Superintendent Galbraith whom the New Zealand public had flooded with information, had by now obtained arrest warrants for the men calling themselves Raymond Velche, Eric Audrenc and Jean-Michel Berthelo. The charges on the warrants, issued by an Auckland District Court judge, alleged that the crew had committed murder and arson and were involved in conspiracy to commit arson.

It was the second time that such charges had been levelled. Four days earlier Sophie Frederique Clare Turenge, 36, and Alain Jacques Turenge, 34, had appeared in a packed Auckland courtroom on the same accusations. The murder involved the death of Fernando Pereira and the arson charge, as it applies in New Zealand, covered the use of explosive devices. They had also been charged with wilfully damaging the Rainbow Warrior by means of explosives and — relating to their false passports — bringing into New Zealand dishonestly obtained property.

While the Turenge couple were being remanded in custody, New Zealand police were busy tracing the movements of Frederique Bonlieu (Christine Cabon). For Sophie and Alain Turenge, who had access to New Zealand papers which carried the story of her infiltration of Greenpeace, her unmasking as a DGSE agent was bad news. It was certainly a distraction from the tedium of life in Mount Eden Prison where Major Mafart had settled down to reading a biography on Victor Hugo — earning himself the nickname of 'The Philosopher' from his fellow inmates — and Captain Prieur had started knitting a sweater.

Police continued talking to Greenpeace members who had offered Bonlieu accommodation and checked international phone calls made to and from their homes. Often left alone she would use a classic 'blind', making a quick phone call to a 'key' Paris number and asking to be called back immediately. From an office within DGSE headquarters another phone with a different number would be used to return her call.

Evidence linking the Turenge couple with the crew of the Ouvea and with Christine Cabon continued to mount. For as the DGSE were learning fast, New Zealanders did not focus their attention entirely on sheep and making butter. Although not aware of the significance of events and meetings involving the sabotage team, a number of witnesses had now started to come forward with pieces of the jigsaw puzzle.

There was taxi-van driver Peter Gennip, 51, a Dutch migrant who drove the Turenges from Auckland airport to Mt Wellington where they hired their camper van. 'The woman seemed to be the boss,' he was to recall. 'She did all the ordering around.' And there was the rather embarrassing revelation that the two French secret service agents had stayed in a unit owned by none other than Prime Minister Lange at the Hinemoa Motel, at Parakai, south of Kaipara Harbour on the west coast of the North Island. They used the motel twice, checking in the first time on July 1, remaining for two nights, then returning on July 9.

'There was nothing sinister in them staying in my unit,' Mr Lange was to tell an amused Press conference later. 'It was pure coincidence they checked in there.' Whether he learned personally about the sleeping habits of the pretend honeymooners was not revealed, but at least one motel chambermaid told the police

that for a couple who had just been married they behaved un-
usually — they slept in separate beds.

Detectives followed up every reported sighting, moving through
Northland, travelling west to Parakai, south to Hamilton and
east to Thames, at the foot of the Coromandel peninsula, where
Christine Cabon had driven in her hired car two months earlier.
They checked out rented-vehicle numbers and totted up mile-
ages. In a red Ford Telstar car, hired by the Ouvea crew in
Whangarei, a bundle of between 10 and 12 strands of electrical
wire, taped together into a circle, was found. The Telstar had
travelled far, clocking up 1493 kilometres in a week. When hiring
the car the Ouvea crew had told the rental company that they
would soon need a vehicle with a large carrying capacity. The
hire firm made arrangements for the delivery of a station wagon,
but when the blue Holden Commodore arrived the crew did not
take it immediately. Their gear, they said, had not yet turned
up. On July 6 they swapped vehicles and in the next three days
the Commodore travelled 320 kilometres. They did not prove
themselves to be the best of drivers — Bartelo and Andries
bumped into another car while parking one day and although
they caused no damage, backed away from the owner rolling out
their apologies in French.

As well as the bundle of wire, other physical evidence was
being examined. On the week end of July 27 and 28 a walker
on Pollen Island, located in the estuary of the Whau River, about
12 kilometres around the coast to the west of Marsden wharf,
found a two-litre oxygen cylinder, almost identical to that found
to the east of the wharf near the abandoned Zodiac dinghy.

Stories in the local newspapers about the police hunt for evidence prompted more New Zealanders to come forward. One
witness reported that the station wagon seen in the forest with
Verge at the wheel stopped in a lay-by a few kilometres further
north. Also in the lay-by was a white camper van. Packages were
being unloaded from the station wagon to the van.

Erna and Trevor Rogers clearly remembered their encounter
with the Turenges. On Tuesday July 9 they found the couple
waiting outside their shop, the Highway Dairy at Kaitaia in the

far north west of the island, before light. Mrs Rogers thought they looked like they had been up all night. Sophie Turenge bought a large carton of yoghurt and a jar of coffee. As the couple drove off, Mr Rogers noticed their white campervan was towing a Zodiac dinghy.

Examined on its own, each report from a witness of a particular car being seen here, a campervan being seen there, would have had little significance but that the vehicles were often in the same area at the same time and were driven by people fitting the descriptions of the yacht crew or the Turenge couple. True, there were still many holes, but detectives were convinced they had established enough to prove to a court that it was more than coincidence that the group of French were haunting the Northland area in the dead of winter in the days before the Greenpeace vessel was sunk. There was certainly enough evidence to suggest that at the lay-by meeting the packages containing the boat and the outboard motor had been handed over to the Turenges. And the fact that the dinghy, fully inflated, was seen by Mr and Mrs Rogers the next morning indicated that it had been used, or was about to be used, somewhere up in the far north. Had the mines been hidden somewhere in the area at a spot accessible only by water?

The Customs officer who dealt with the crew when they first arrived, Mr Frank MacLean, provided police with his observations after the Rainbow Warrior had been sunk. He had noticed that the men calling themselves Audrenc, Berthelo and Velche had new passports with virtually no stamps in them, whereas Dr Maniguet's was full. Mr MacLean thought it strange that Audrenc, describing himself in his passport as a photographer, had not included any camera gear in his list of personal effects that all new arrivals must provide. Dr Maniguet explained that Audrenc was on holiday and had left his work at home. It wasn't until 16 days later, July 11, when Mr MacLean heard on his radio there may be a French link to the bombing that bells rang in his head. He immediately connected the Ouvea crew with the incident . . . because now everything fitted. They had been too clean cut, too military-like, to have been true yachties on a jaunt down the east coast. And their gear, it had all been neatly packed and stowed as if ready for drill inspection.

But the most damning evidence was the sighting of the Turenge campervan on the waterfront on the night of the bombing when a frogmen pulled ashore in a dinghy and drove away with them.

Based on this wealth of 'sightings', police were able to construct a number of scenarios.

The most popular theory was that the Ouvea, which had now proved its ability to head in other than its intended direction, had made its way south from Whangarei and moored off Leigh, some 80 kilometres north of Auckland. Leaving the Prime Minister's motel unit, the Turenges had made their way across country to pick up the sabotage divers. Whether the mines also spent the night in the unit is unclear. If not, they may have been kept in the van or hidden in the vicinity.

In any case, towards evening the campervan with its team and the explosives headed south to Auckland. Under cover of darkness, the dinghy was launched and headed towards Marsden wharf. After cutting the engine and paddling in towards the Rainbow Warrior, the frogmen had moored the dinghy in a prearranged spot, perhaps behind one of a number of vessels moored in the area, and had then sunk beneath the surface, making use of their re-breather rigs.

The mystery remains of what happened to the second man once the mine planting was over — only one diver was seen returning to the shore in Hobson's Bay. If more than two divers took part in the operation, what did happen to the others?

That two or more men were involved is unquestioned. The discovery of two mini oxygen cylinders supports this. A single frogman working on his own would have taken twice as long to complete the operation and time was of the essence. The longer the saboteurs remained in the vicinity, the greater the risks. And why had the DGSE sent five experienced divers — if Major Mafart-Turenge and Lieutenant-Colonel Louis-Pierre Dillais are included — across the world if only one man was to be used?

How, then, did the others make their escape? One explanation could lie in the mysterious Francois Verlon who was on Marsden Wharf that night. His brief may not have been to get on board, as has been suggested, to make sure none of the crew became suspicious about what was going on underneath the Rainbow Warrior. He may have been there to help a second — or third — frogman get away, perhaps providing a change of clothes concealed nearby.

If the man calling himself Verlon, who has since disappeared, did not help the divers escape there is one other man who could have taken care of that: the commander of the operation, Lieutenant-Colonel Louis-Pierre Dillais, alias Jean Louis Dormand. He booked out of the Hyatt Hotel on the morning of July 10, just as the Turenge couple had checked out of their motel further north on that strike day.

As overseer of the operation, he would not have left Auckland until it was successfully concluded. Much later, detectives were able to piece together some of his movements after the bombing. Evidence suggests that the following day, July 11, he flew to Wellington under yet another false name — no passports or identity checks are made for domestic flights — and then travelled across Cook Strait to the South Island, stepping ashore at Picton.

He had made preparations for the trip to the South Island well in advance. A hire fee of $NZ740 for a campervan was prepaid through a Paris travel agency, Tours 33, three weeks earlier. On July 8 Dillais contacted Horizon Holidays Ltd. in Auckland, who receive much of their French custom from Tours 33, and arranged to pick up the van in the South Island city of Christchurch. After travelling through isolated mountain roads and doing some canoeing, Dillais returned the Toyota hi-top campervan to the Horizon agent in the resort of Queenstown — some 400 kilometres from Christchurch — on July 21. It was the day before he was due to fly out of the country. He had to pay an extra $100 to the Horizon agent for delivery of the vehicle back to Christchurch. He told company representative Miss Raewyn Louden that he had enjoyed New Zealand but could not handle driving on the 'wrong side of the road'. The van was pretty heavy, too, and he preferred to fly straight to Christchurch.

Although he spoke poor English, Miss Louden was to remember that the Frenchman was 'very friendly and chatty'.

As he made good his escape from Christchurch on his false passport, the DGSE agent must have breathed a sigh of relief. The New Zealand newspapers had been filled with the hunt for the Rainbow Warrior bombers and he would have read of the arrest of his two undercover compatriots.

Whether Dormand helped the saboteurs to get away from the wharf that night was to become the subject of police debate. But the discovery of the second oxygen bottle around the coast in the opposite direction to that taken by the diver on the Zodiac suggested that the other frogman — or frogmen — swam further along the waterfront before being picked up. Detectives conceded, though, that the second bottle could have been carried around the coast by the tide.

Why had the divers split up after planting the mines? That was another question raised by Superintendent Galbraith's team. Was it because the man in the red woollen cap, presumed to be Bartelo, had to make a speedy getaway from the area in order to get up to Leigh in the campervan and board the Ouvea so that it could sail hastily from New Zealand? Assuming one other man was working with Bartelo just what had happened to him? Armed with the later knowledge that a fifth underwater expert — Dillais — was in Auckland on the day of the bombing some officers suggested that he was the other diver who had helped plant the mines. As Bartelo made his exit, Dillais swam off to the spot where he had decided to come ashore. Picked up by Verlon, he had vanished into the night. And Verlon caught his plane to Tahiti.

Despite the mass of evidence they had collated, New Zealand detectives were still unable to say with any certainty who had planted the mines. As Solicitor-General Paul Neazor, QC, was to tell a court in November when the 'Turenges' appeared before a judge: '. . . the defendants were responsible for picking up and

removing from the scene one of those responsible for the placement of the explosive devices.

'This recovery was made after the devices had been placed
and the timers had been set, when one of the persons responsible for the placements then made his way in the Zodiac
from the wharves at Hobson Bay to a rendezvous with the
defendants . . .

'The identities of those who actually placed the devices has not
been established.'

Mr Neazor, who was summarising the entire police case, told
the judge that clearly 'the activities were likely to have been
carried out by a number of persons.'

Just why the man in the red woollen cap had left the dinghy
behind is regarded by some investigators as an attempt to create
a false trail. Should the engine be discovered, the dinghy would
be linked to it and the two would eventually be traced back to
London. The purchaser would be found to be a representative
of a Belgian company and by the time it was all checked out the
trail would have gone cold.

But the clearest explanation is that Bartelo simply ran out of
time. Getting rid of the dinghy would have held him up. And
he had to get up to the Ouvea. In their arrogance, the team had
underestimated the ability of New Zealand detectives to piece
the clues together, assuming they would all be well away before
anyone linked the dinghy with the bombing.

Detectives also considered the puzzling high-profile performance of the Ouvea crew in Whangarei. It was suggested they had
deliberately 'hit the town' in a big way so that the presence of
a French crew in the area at the time of the bombing would not
raise too much speculation — that they made themselves so obvious that they could never have been connected with the sabotage.

In that case, there would have been no need for the DGSE to
send a team of trained divers to New Zealand just to entertain
a small town: a bunch of louts could have done the job just as
well. In all likelihood, the DGSE put three divers on the Ouvea
with the intention of using only part of the team, the others
being sent as back up in case of accident or sickness. And, quite

simply, they played up ... entertaining the local ladies and splashing out their money, because they saw the operation as an easy job. Well may they have been qualified frogmen, but as secret agents their subtlety left much to be desired.

Each day brought more bad news for the French secret service. The suspicion in New Zealand that 'Frederique Bonlieu' was a DGSE agent caused great alarm at the 'Piscine'. Desperate to get their operative under ground, the secret service sent an urgent, coded telegram to Israel, where, strangely, the spy was taking part in an archaeological dig near Tel Aviv with University of California students.

The cable said her father in France was very ill and she should return home immediately. But her father had died some years earlier. The telegram meant only one thing: there was trouble, and she should get back to Paris. That same day a second cable arrived in the office of Israeli Police Minister General Haim Parlev. This one was from Auckland police asking that Bonlieu be detained in custody so she could be interviewed by a New Zealand police officer who was on his way. The telegram pointed out Bonlieu had infiltrated Greenpeace in the weeks before the sinking of the Rainbow Warrior.

It was bad news that was relayed back to Auckland. Bonlieu had already left. The telegram from 'her father' had arrived first and she had acted immediately.

Did the Israelis, who had benefitted from the DGSE spy's infiltration of the Palestinian Liberation Organisation and who consider France as one of the country's major trading partners, aid her flight?

Israel said it did not know the woman's father had died years before. Superintendent Galbraith said of the affair: 'We know she was in Israel at the time of our communication to Israeli authorities. We were later advised that she had left the country allegedly to visit her sick father in France.'

So yet another DGSE agent escaped the clutches of the New Zealand police. But the senior detective heading 'Operation Rainbow' was determined to continue the hunt for the Ouvea crew. Warrants for their arrest would remain in force.

Incredibly, a week before her hasty departure from Israel, Christine Cabon penned a letter to Greenpeace in Auckland . . . a letter condemning the sabotage of the Rainbow Warrior.

Dated July 19, the French spy's letter read: 'The news about the sunk (sinking) of the Rainbow Warrior just reached me in the archaeological expedition in Pardes Hanna. What can I say after such a news? I feel so choked.' She added that if the French Government was behind the bombing, its strategy had backfired. The government had inadvertently given more support to the anti-test campaign.

'Why such a monstrosity?' she ended by asking.

Her letter was read with disgust at the Greenpeace office in Nagel House. But members of the organisation agreed with one of the agent's points: only good could come out of such a tragedy. Certainly the sinking of the Rainbow Warrior had not dampened their resolve to send a flotilla to Mururoa. The scuttling of the flagship had focused international attention on the conservation group and members were aware that the time was never better to show just why they were all so concerned about what was happening on and beneath the atoll in French Polynesia.

'We have to make sure that Fernando didn't die in vain,' Dr Patrick Moore, a Canadian executive director of Greenpeace had said shortly after navy divers, under the glare of emergency lighting, had brought the body of Fernando Pereira from the submerged stern of the Rainbow Warrior. 'We've fought tough battles in the past. We're not going to back off now because somebody doesn't like us.'

In all its international campaigns, Greenpeace had its first martyr. The photographer's death had shocked them all. But they had not lost heart.

Early in August, the first of the peace boats, Alliance, sailed off on sparkling waters for the voyage to the French testing grounds.

This time the whole world watched.

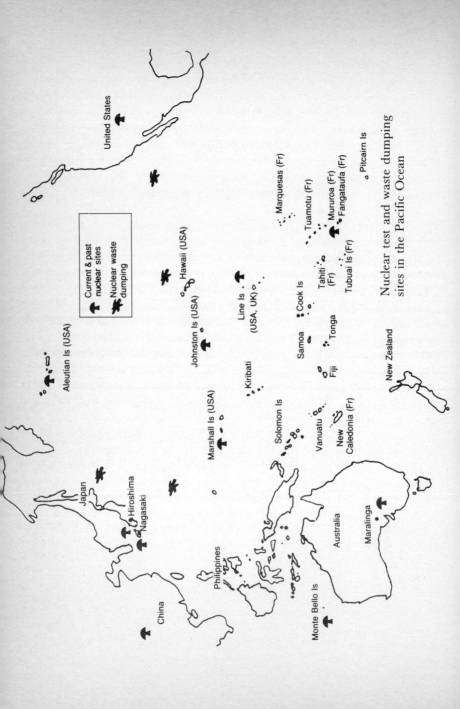

Nuclear test and waste dumping sites in the Pacific Ocean

Current & past nuclear sites

Nuclear waste dumping

United States

Aleutian Is (USA)

Hawaii (USA)

Johnston Is (USA)

Line Is (USA, UK)

Marquesas (Fr)

Tuamotu (Fr)

Mururoa (Fr)

Fangataufa (Fr)

Pitcairn Is

Tahiti (Fr)

Tubuai Is (Fr)

Cook Is

Samoa

Tonga

Fiji

Kiribati

Marshall Is (USA)

Solomon Is

Vanuatu

New Caledonia (Fr)

New Zealand

Japan

Hiroshima

Nagasaki

China

Philippines

Monte Bello Is

Australia

Maralinga

12

'Fallout'

Mururoa Atoll, dawn, March 22 1981. A handful of Polynesian workers walk beside the lagoon, its waters reflecting the grey sky. The hurricane that raged through the night has moved on, but a wind still moves the coconut palms. Lightning licks the horizon and the men can hear distant thunder. It is a dawn the workers may well remember 10, 20 years on.

Floating in the lagoon are gloves, overalls and vinyl bags. More plastic sacks litter the beaches, spilling out clothing. The beach is cluttered, too, with chunks of asphalt and rusty tools. One of the men, sent out on an inspection of the storm damage, reaches for an old glove.

'Ne touchez pas!' shouts one of his companions. But it is too late. In handling the glove, the islander may have signed his own death warrant.

News of the debris littering the beaches and the lagoon spreads rapidly through the housing complex. The implications are terrifying. The material is highly contaminated, threatening the lives of more than 3,000 civilian and military personnel stationed on the tiny Pacific atoll. Many of the staff, as well as people living on surrounding islands, may in time pay dearly for France's total indifference to the storage of its nuclear waste.

When nuclear testing in the atmosphere began, the French military and civil authorities on Mururoa carefully followed international waste disposal guidelines. Irradiated debris was stored in drums, sealed off, cast in cement and sunk at least 300 metres underground.

But the arms race was on. Personnel were needed to attend to current tests, not clear up after the old ones. Packing contaminated material into drums, digging storage holes and filling in documents took up precious time and manpower. It was also costly. So the irradiated left overs were simply crammed into vinyl bags and drums and dumped in a depression on North Beach, well away from the living quarters. A decision would be made in the future, concerned decontamination experts on the island were assured, about proper storage. As tests continued, more tools and clothing were dumped on the beach. And during experiments to improve safety procedures in case of accident, several pounds of plutonium 239 were also deposited there. Soon, the rubbish dump covered 30,000 square metres. As some sort of safety measure a layer of asphalt was spread over the plutonium, which has a life span of 24,400 years, and other material. This was to prevent strong ocean winds blowing any of it away. Again, there was the assurance that it would all be taken care of some time in the future when there was less pressure on nuclear production.

But the nuclear race was never to be won. The Soviets and the Americans continued to build up their arms and France, concerned about its own defences, frantically continued its nuclear tests.

The blasts moved underground, deep in the coral surrounding the atoll, and that is when the lethal chain of events began. Each underground blast sent shock waves through the island's core, causing it to sink 2 centimetres with each explosion. After 100 blasts, the atoll had dropped by 1.5 metres and the roads had to be re-asphalted so often that the surface was more than a metre thick.

The water's edge encroached further inland and, concerned about possible damage in a storm, the Government transferred buildings standing near the waterfront to higher ground. But nothing was done about the plutonium and other material. It was left in its cordoned-off area on North Beach.

On the evening of March 21 1981, the storm clouds rolled in. Decontamination experts looked from their windows and watched the first heavy raindrops hit the glass. Soon the storm was lashing the atoll. Some scientists prayed that the man-made nuclear rubbish dump further up the lagoon would hold out.

The seas grew worse. A powerful swell washed over the beach and pounded the protective asphalt. Man's efforts against the elements were puny. The covering was ripped away and broken pieces of asphalt, clotted with plutonium, were swept into the lagoon or washed along the beaches. At dawn, employees stepped out into the dying wind to inspect the damage. Radio antenna had been torn down, roofs damaged, vegetation pounded. Then the news came in about the devastation at the nuclear waste dump.

A plea was sent from Air Force General Rouyer, Commander of the Mururoa base, to Paris for help to clean up the debris. But his request was ignored. For presidential elections were less than two months away and the last thing former President Giscard d'Estaing's Defence Minister, Yvon Bourges, wanted was a scandal. At all costs, it was decided in Paris, the affair should be hushed up. And the best way to do that was to ignore it. Surely it would stay away for two months.

General Rouyer had no option but to assign men, precious staff, to clearing up the mess. It was then that the seriousness of the situation, as if it wasn't serious enough, became aware to everyone. For as often as the beaches were cleared, more debris floated in. The sea was thick with contaminated material.

The General and his aides, with private encouragement from the Defence Ministry, decided that morale had to remain high among the workers, many of whom were Polynesian. So they encouraged the men to swim in the lagoon and play beach games. 'Just try not to swallow the water' was the only advice given. The radiation danger, they were assured, was minimal, if it existed at all.

But the slapdash way the debris was being collected and stored again concerned a number of civil engineers. Worried by the continued risk of contamination, a group flew to Paris in July.

The man who had emerged as the new Socialist Defence Minister in the May elections was Charles Hernu, but when he contacted the army for confirmation of the engineers' report, he was assured that the situation was far from grave. Hernu bade the delegation good day. If things were as bad as they had made out, he told them, he would be able to see for himself, for he was due to pay an official visit to the atoll on August 4.

Aware of Hernu's plans, military chiefs instituted a rapid, superficial clean up. Three days before the Defence Minister's arrival, the atoll looked a good enough place to take a holiday.

But the engineers were to say later that God or fate must have been on their side. For on the eve of Hernu's arrival, another violent storm swept the atoll. Chaos was restored. And when Hernu stepped from his plane, he must have thought he had landed on another planet. Strange figures in masks and thick, white anti-radiation clothing wandered around. Behind barbed wire enclosures signs dotted the ravaged landscape warning: 'Radiation — Keep Out'.

Hernu promised to take action immediately. The place would be cleaned up in three months. It was a hollow promise. On the Micronesian atoll of Enewetak, the Americans had spent $US100 million over two years in a desperate attempt to dispose of accumulated nuclear waste. They threw it into an old bomb crater as deep as the Grand Canyon on the coral ring and sealed it with a giant concrete lid. Then they placed the dump off limits to islanders for the next 25,000 years. French bombs at Mururoa, ecologists constantly point out, are in no way different from the American bombs that are known for a fact to have polluted Bikini, Enewetak and a number of other adjacent atolls in Micronesia. Such a simplistic view has been an anathema to a succession of colonial governors of French Polynesia appointed by the governments of General de Gaulle, Pompidou, Giscard d'Estaing and Mitterrand.

Despite the example of the Americans' clean-up operation on Enewetak, Hernu believed France could solve its problem in three months, without any concrete. No-one was surprised when Paris did nothing.

Nuclear pollution on the atoll increased with twice as much debris being washed up as was collected. Engineers estimated there was enough radioactive waste on the atoll to fill 200,000 44-gallon drums and restoring the island to its previous state would mean stopping the tests and having extra personnel work full time for more than five years. There was the added concern that workers not in direct contact with nuclear matter were not subject to medical examinations on Mururoa, which made the future detection of symptoms linked to radiation virtually impossible. Tired of waiting for their Government to take action, a CEA (Atomic Energy Commission) branch of the pro- Socialist CFDT (Confederation Francaise Democratique du Travail) Union printed a leaflet, meant only for the eyes of CEA staff. Among demands, it listed systematic X-rays and better medical care for workers. It also appealed to the Government to lift the secrecy ban concerning nuclear contamination on the atoll.

By November the engineers, including decontamination specialists, had made up their minds. They were going to make their grievances public. Defying the Defence Secrets Act, binding them to secrecy regarding Mururoa affairs, but emboldened by a new government, they flew to Paris, aware that the secret service might try to shut them up. 'We're running scared,' one of them admitted, 'but we must do something.' For their own safety, they deposited copies of their information in bank deposit vaults and left statements with their lawyers. They also kept their names secret. Amazingly their cries fell on deaf ears, despite attempts to get the big dailies interested.

Their attitude, they said, reflected that of many of the workers on Mururoa. They all supported France's nuclear policy, saying the nation had to maintain its nuclear independence. The Mururoa tests also provided spin-offs in areas other than defence. But they could not stand by while sheer negligence caused major ecological problems and endangered the lives of the personnel.

The Defence Ministry got to hear about it and at a hastily-convened meeting decided that before the bad word spread too far, the concern had to be played down. And so it was that on December 28 Rear-Admiral Jacques Choupin stepped from the limpid blue water of the tropical lagoon after leading his staff officers on a mid-day swim and beamed a smile of Christmas goodwill at a group of visitors.

'You see, gentlemen,' he said. 'There is nothing to fear. These waters are safe.'

The Rear-Admiral, then head of the Pacific Experimentation Centre, took the swim to prove there had been no leakage of radioactive material into the lagoon or the Pacific Ocean. All he had really proved, though, was that he could swim. The observers, who had been invited to the atoll by the French Defence Ministry had no means of telling whether the waters had been contaminated. There was only the word of either a foolish, brave or confident naval officer. In fact, he hadn't been the first prominent Frenchman to jump into the lagoon to assure mankind. In 1970, the then Defence Minister, Michel Debre dived in just six hours after a small atomic blast to prove that the waters had not been poisoned.

Now, as Rear-Admiral Choupin walked along the sandy white beach with its backdrop of coconut palms he agreed that there had been 'a little problem' nine months earlier. Yes, it was true that radioactive material had been released from an underground wastepile during a fierce ocean storm.

'The asphalt,' the Rear-Admiral said matter-of-factly, 'was partially torn away and thrown into the lagoon, resulting in scattering, which was light and without danger.' He shrugged off suggestions that trade union leaders had spoken of an alarming rise in radioactivy. Everything had been taken care of. 'Through concern for absolute security, we decided to make a systematic check of the entire atoll,' he said. 'We began with the living zone and its beach. Radioactivity was present, I agree, but only in minute quantities. The waters were perfectly clear and can be used for swimming without the least risk. I state, and I take personal responsibility for it, that there is not a single case of contamination here.'

Rear-Admiral Choupin based his conviction on a report by a 130-member radioactivity safety team and a 30-member biological control team which had monitored the atoll's air, water and food products without finding any cause for immediate alarm. The investigation found there was virtually no short-term contamination. But the team warned, as other scientists were to caution later, that long-term underground storage of radioctive waste at Mururoa atoll posed problems.

For Rear-Admiral Choupin, however, along with the Defence Ministry, the immediate assurances were encouraging enough to invite foreign observers to the atoll to see for themselves that all the negative reports had been false. Just to make things extra safe, he pointed out, a radio-biology laboratory kept a check on the 3,200 soldiers and civilians who worked there.

The observers went away satisfied. Rear Admiral Choupin's confidence and swimming display had gone some way towards obliterating concern that had been raised about the safety of the nuclear tests . . . for a while, at least.

But due to the agitation of Greenpeace and other conservation groups, it wasn't long before the old questions bobbed up. Could the French really be trusted to keep their tests safe? After all, the dispersal of waste wasn't the first accident there — at least two others are known, both occuring in July 1979. On the 6th, two men were killed and six seriously injured during a decontamination operation in an underground bunker. Acetone vapour in the bunker exploded, killing one man immediately and injuring others, a second worker dying later. Equally disturbing, the accident released a cloud of plutonium vapour over the atoll which was carried away across the ocean by the wind. True to form, the affair was hushed up because the mishap occurred on the eve of President Giscard d'Estaing's visit to French Polynesia. Bad news would have certainly cast a shadow over the visit. The President went to the atoll on July 21, where he was informed about the accident during an inspection of the technical equipment.

Just four days later, according to workers, another frightening accident occurred. A hydrogen bomb being lowered down a shaft drilled through basalt rock to the explosion chamber some 1000 metres down, became stuck. Technicians tried everything to free it, without success. A quick discussion was held. The bomb obviously couldn't be left where it was because it would hold up future tests. Jammed at 800 metres, it was too close to the surface to explode — or was it? The decision was made to detonate the bomb. The explosion blasted out a piece of the atoll's underlying crater, and three hours later a spectacular tidal wave swept over the atoll, overturning cars, carrying away some bomb shelters and injuring two workers. In New Zealand, seismologists were stunned to see their instruments recording earth waves from the expolosion which were the equivalent to an earthquake measured at 6.3 on the Richter scale. It was the largest explosion to have taken place since underground testing began, and it occurred within a few hundred metres of the surface.

The French nuclear energy commission in Paris was quick to dismiss reports of the accident, describing them as 'fantastic'. Although the commission offered no explanation for the tidal wave, it stressed that a shock wave of the kind produced by a nuclear test cannot cause a wave of this kind. The tidal wave did not coincide with any detonation, and, the commission stressed, Mururoa is normally subject to such tidal waves.

Interestingly, the Government took precautions for the future, installing an on-base seismograph which was connected to a shrill whistle. The idea was that if an explosion severely rocked the earth, the whistle would go off and everyone could expect a tidal wave. At the same time, the blast platforms, reinforced steel, standing on stilts, were erected for use during tests. Able to accommodate 500 people each, they were intended as a refuge from possible tidal waves.

If this wasn't confirmation that something had gone wrong, French scientists in Papeete, Tahiti, finally conceded three months later that the biggest underground blast ever did not go 'according to plan'. The confession came in a report to a special committee set up by the Territorial Assembly to investigate reports of the two accidents. The Assembly had called for a suspension of nuclear tests at Mururoa so the scientists could spend two days there before reporting back to the committee.

Although they confirmed that things had not gone well, the scientific team said they could not find any evidence of leakage of radioactivity from either accident. There might have been a good reason for that — local environmentalists claimed that the team had been specially picked by the French Government and that there was only one radiologist among them. No radiation tests were made, and the team did not examine, because they were not shown them, the medical files of 25 Tahitians who were among 73 people within a 300 metre radius of the accident in the underground bunker.

'We are not convinced by these assurances that there has been no radioactivy leakage,' protested Mr Henri Hiro, President of the local environment society. 'We believe that those people were contaminated and that there was a leak into the sea.'

Medical files of staff on Mururoa and of people living on islands in the vicinity have been carefully guarded by the French. As most doctors and hospital workers are French, it is understandable why 'outsiders' are denied access. Before June 1966, public health statistics for Polynesia were available each month, detailing diseases and epidemics, deaths and their causes.

Then, just before the first atmospheric explosion, publication of health statistics ceased. The local translation of the name Mururoa — 'big secret' — could hardly have been more appropriate. It is only since 1983 that private doctors have again been required to enter the cause of death on a death certificate.

The French authorities have vigorously refused to disclose health statistics to an internationally-sponsored cancer register for the South Pacific, an obvious attempt, say ecologists, to cover up the effects the testing is having on islanders. Some doctors in Tahiti admit privately that there has been an alarming increase in leukaemia and other cancers, among them thyroid tumors. The reason that few will talk about the medical problems is a fear of reprisals. Leaders of Tahiti's indepedence movement, Maohi, who spoke out against the tests and their effects on health, were thrown into jail. Late in September 1982 the self-described Prime Minister of the provisional Government, Mr Tamatea Taero said during a visit to Auckland that his movement was convinced that the only way to stop illnesses among the islanders was for the French to stop their tests. On August 15, three days after his return to Papeete with the president of Maohi, Mr Tetua Mai, both leaders along with their provisional Cabinet and about 30 supporters who were critisising the tests were thrown into jail.

Those opposed to the experiments say the threat of jail has suppressed many who feel strongly about the issue. As well, there is a fear of loss of employment because many Polynesians are employed by the government, or depend on someone who is. But with world attention now focused on the tests, the voices of protest are growing louder. One who talks about the apocalyptical overtones of the experiments is John Doom, secretary general of the Polynesian Protestant Church which has under its wing about 60 per cent of the population.

'There's no evidence, no real hard evidence, you must understand,' says Mr Doom. 'But we can see with our eyes that more people are falling sick around us. There are more leukaemias, there are more cancers. But we cannot prove that these illnesses are directly linked to the tests. God's children are falling sick all around us, and we must find out why.'

His words are echoed by the Mayor of the suburb of Faaa, Mr Oscar Temaru. 'The sick are getting younger,' he says. 'Two of my people have developed cancer and it worries me to have to say that their ages are four and 36. This did not happen before the tests. It makes you think, doesn't it?'

Data on the health of islanders has been collected by Professor Brian Henderson, of the University of Southern California in Los Angeles, who has been in touch with New Caledonia, Fiji, Western Samoa and Papua New Guinea. But assessing the effects of exposure to pollution takes time and scientists rating the incidence of cancer among islanders admit that it is too early to say that the tests are directly affecting the inhabitants of the Pacific.

But one interesting comparison can be made. The types of cancers found in Polynesians are similar to those found among the survivors of the atomic bombs dropped on Hiroshima and Nagasaki. In Tahiti information giving the causes of death has not been published in any official journals since 1963. Those who have tried to obtain details from Tahiti's Chief Medical

Officer have received no response. Neither is it possible to visit a hospital and peek into a cancer ward: most of the island's cancer cases are sent to France, where they are widely dispersed for treatment in public, private and military hospitals. However one independent French investigator has claimed that he knows of 50 Polynesians who were sent to Paris on a military plane, all suffering from brain cancer. All were aged about 35 and when atmospheric tests were being conducted their ages were between 15 and 20 years.

The investigator also claimed that records held by the Secretary of State in Paris showed that 50 patients were sent there in 1976, about 70 in 1980 and 72 in early 1981. Another 57 had been air-lifted to Paris in 1982. According to the Paris records, more than half of these patients had cancer.

The unwillingness of French military doctors who run the hospitals of Polynesia to co-operate with the South Pacific Commission, a multi-national body of islands and major powers, including France, is a constant source of frustration for medical researchers. 'I find them,' said one New Zealand scientist, 'second only to the Russians in terms of difficulty in extracting information.' However, the early figures were enough to interest Professor Henderson. Rates of cancer in Polynesians, he has found, were uncommon in other developing nations. Polynesian women showed a high incidence of breast cancer, unlike women in Africa and Asia. Another anomaly was that increased breast cancer was not accompanied by high rates of colon cancer. Among the general Polynesian population there was an increasing rate of lung and stomach cancer, but the figures for leukaemia were about the same proportion as those in Europeans.

Because of the medical cover-up, independent scientists will continue to have difficulty producing figures proving that people with cancer today developed it when the French were testing their nuclear devices in the atmosphere prior to 1975. It may not be until 1990, or later, that the true effects are known, but the words of one French biologist on the island of Mangareva, downwind from the test site on Mururoa Atoll are ominous.

Speaking of one of those earlier atmospheric explosions, he describes the scene at the lagoon:

'The beach was hot with radiation. All of us in the station wore protective clothing and there was a lot of disagreement about when the natives should be let out of the fall-out shelter, where they had been put before the test. Finally, they were let out and told not to drink water or eat fish, but of course they did, and some became very ill. I remember the birds, the gulls, gannets and sandpipers, flying crazily about before plunging into the ground. Many of them appeared to be blinded.'

The islanders' exposure to contamination was no different to that of the people of Rongelap, a tiny coral atoll in the Marshall Islands. For centuries, life there had been much the same as that of the other islands throughout the Pacific . . . a simple existence with men fishing the lagoon, women caring for their babies, and children running along the beach after scurrying crabs, or scrambling up tall palms to snatch at green coconuts.

Early in the morning of March 1 1954, their world ended. There was a flash of light and a billowing pillar of fire in the western sky. Terrified, the 87 inhabitants ran from their houses and gathered on the beachfront, clutching each other as the giant orange mushroom flared out. They didn't see their blue sky that day. Within two hours a storm moved upon them. They were engulfed in a heavy mist and dust, and debris fell like snow on their heads, on their beach, their thatched roofs and into their drinking water. The 'snow' was the ashes of death.

The fallout was from the world's first deliverable hydrogen bomb, code-named Bravo, one of 96 nuclear devices to be exploded by the Americans in the islands of Micronesia. The first post-war atomic bomb had been tested in 1946 in the region, but then the islanders of Rongelap were evacuated. This time, with a device 750 times more powerful being exploded from the test site at Bikini atoll, 200 kilometeres from Rongelap, no-one had cared about them. The fallout was carried eastward, contaminating the beaches, the coral, the sea and the human and marine life on and around Rongelap. On the Japanese trawler Lucky Dragon 23 fishermen were also contaminated. The United States had told the village chief that a new bomb was to be tested shortly, but neither he nor his people were informed about any preventative measures, Nelson Anjain, the mayor, was to say later.

Within 24 hours, nearly everyone on the atoll complained of itchiness and sore skin. They vomited, suffered from diarrhoea and became extremely tired. Swellings came up on their necks, arms and legs and their eyes burned. Two days later, they were picked up by an American ship and evacuated to a larger atoll, Kwajalein. They were told to wash their bodies with soap and water, but after two months their thick hair began to fall out in clumps and some went completely bald. They were moved on, to the island of Ejet, where they were to remain for three and a half years. In that time, the islanders' pigs and chickens left on Rongelap died from exposure to fallout. All the plants withered and the once-green coconuts dropped lifeless onto the contaminated beach.

Nine years later, the medical problems began to manifest themselves. The first case of thyroid tumour emerged. By 1976, 22 years after the blast, all but one person who were children at the time of the blast, had undergone surgery for the removal of thyroid tumours. One of the victims was the nephew of Nelson Anjain. The boy, Lejoc, was only a year old when the ashes fell. Fourteen years later, his thyroid condition was diagnosed by doctors of the US Atomic Energy Commission and he was flown to Boston and New York for what was termed a successful operation. He returned to his island high school to study but within two years, bruises started appearing on Lejoc's body and in July 1972, he complained of excessive tiredness. His scrotum had swollen too. His father took him to Hawaii and on to Washington. The diagnosis was short and frightening. Lejoc had leukaemia. He died six weeks later.

One sad case alone would not be enough to alarm those who live within the vicinity of the French tests, whether the experiments be above or below ground, but the remainder of the Rongelap story may be a foretaste of what is in store for islanders who have lived in the shadow of La Bombe. When the Rongelap islanders went back to their home from Ejet, the radiation levels in their bodies increased — even in people who had not been on the island in 1954. The main problem was Strontium-90, which poses such a deadly threat for those who breathe the air or drink the water or eat the fish contaminated by the French tests.

This radioactive poison found in fish caught in the waters surrounding Mururoa concentrates in the human thyroid gland and in bone marrow and is a known cause of leukaemia in young children. It is so chemically similar to calcium, that when it is in a cow's body, it replaces some of the calcium in its milk. When children drink this milk, the Strontium-90 goes into their bodies and in some cases becomes part of their bone structure. It remains radioactive for at least 40 years and gives off radiation into the body during the growth period of children.

There is also Iodine-131, a serious hazard to children as it finds its way into milk after fallout, concentrates in the thyroid and irradiates that gland more than any other tissue.

Another fallout chemical is Caesium-137. Once consumed in contaminated food, it rapidly spreads through the body, some 80 per cent finding its way into muscle and eight per cent in the bone. The remainder disperses into other tissue.

Professor H H Bolotin, Professor of Physics at the University of Melbourne explains what happens as radiation continues to bombard the bodies of those unlucky enough to be exposed. 'As the radiation strikes the "glue" of the molecules in surrounding tissue, the molecules may be damaged and harmful effects may result. The genes in our body are the inherited road maps we all possess and which determine the course of our development. They determine the sex of our children, their facial features, growth and future health. But genes are no more than complicated molecules that have a very special function in fixing human traits and development.'

The overriding worry of many biologists and geneticists, he says, is that radiation damage to these gene molecules can lead to genetic damage and change. Such damage, it is argued, is irreversible and may lead to serious long-term consequences that cannot be repaired. Our genes affect and determine our evolution and development and genetic damage may therefore be the most serious hazard faced after exposure to fall-out radiation.

Scientists are still unable to agree on the extent of the harm or damage. Although nearly half a century has passed since the dawn of the nuclear age, radioactive fallout is still a relatively new phenomenon. Not enough time has passed to evaluate the full extent of the damage to mankind. How badly people are affected by small, long term doses, still cannot be confidently assessed. But those directly exposed can expect health problems. Let us go back to Rongelap . . .

Strontium-90 levels increased six times. The levels of Caesium-137 went up by 60 times. Children born to exposed parents have shown some retardation of growth, while others were stillborn. In the first 15 years after Operation Bravo, 16 deaths were recorded in the exposed group, representing 13 deaths for every thousand, compared with 8.3 for the whole Marshall islands. Back in 1975, Nelson Anjain told the Fiji Conference for a Nu-clear-free Pacific: 'For more than 20 years since that experiment, we've been worrying about our health and our lives. Each person who has been exposed asks "Will I be well tomorrow? Will my children be normal?" And when an islander becomes ill, he asks himself "Is this an ordinary illness, or has the ghost of the bomb come to close on me, too?" '

13

Mururoa Atoll

Between July 1976 and May 1984, France conducted about 60 underground tests at Mururoa at depths between 700 metres and 1200 metres of magnitudes up to about 200 kilotonnes. In those eight years the atoll has been blasted by the equivalent of more than 100,000 tonnes of TNT. How, Greenpeace and other ecological groups ask, can a land mass continue to withstand such shocks? The simple answer is that it cannot. French scientists concur with colleagues of other nations that the atoll is showing signs of breaking up and is close to leaking radioactive waste into the ocean — if it isn't already doing so. 'We are already looking at a neighbouring site,' a source within the Defence Ministry reveals.

This is almost certainly Fangataufa Atoll, 25 nautical miles from Mururoa where two underground tests, named after classical heroes, were conducted in 1975. Achilles, a 10-kilotonne bomb, half the size of the Hiroshima weapon, was exploded on June 5 in a shaft 623 metres deep. Its impact was said to be so slight that French seismographs in Tahiti did not detect it. Hector, the second bomb, of similar yield, was fired a few weeks later. The director of the tests, Mr Claude Aycoberry, said at the time that his government was very pleased with the first of the experiments in the underground series. 'They are completely safe. There is no radioactivity outside the cavity of the explosion. There is no radioactivity in the atmosphere or the sea.'

To prove his point, as all French officials are want to do, he led a team of foreign correspondents to the exact place at which the first underground test had taken place on the 10 kilometre-long Fangataufa reef, devasted and denuded by what he described as a 'dirty' atmospheric bomb exploded in 1973 from a barge in the lagoon.

Then, hastily changing into his swimming trunks, he jumped into the lagoon. 'We swam here on the first day after the test,' he declared later. 'In any case, our safety procedures are scrupulous. We test the water every day for two weeks after an explosion and then at frequent periods.'

Certainly underground tests carry little of the drama of the mushroom cloud. But they do produce a brilliant flash, reflecting nuclear shock waves through the surface of the lagoon, and the ground trembles as if seized by a mild earthquake. According to the French description, deep in the ground the enclosed fireball from a 'small' 10 kilotonne bomb melts 10,000 tonnes of rock. The chimney from the blast reaches upwards for 100 metres and the volume of broken stone amounts to 10 million cubic metres.

Just how deep and where the blasts should take place is a burning question. Before 1981, all test devices were lowered down shafts sunk into the coral to a depth of 600 metres to 1000 metres. Then the Defence Ministry ordered that the tests should be moved progressively from the reef to the bottom of a pit, between 1000 metres and 1200 metres below the bed of the lagoon.

Officials on Mururoa anticipate that by 1988, all tests will be conducted under the lagoon, an indication that despite facilities at Fangataufa and the preparatory work said to be taking place there, the present site will have to withstand many more blasts before it is allowed to rest in peace: up to 20 years more, perhaps. General Guy Lewyn, joint director of the test centre, says that by then Mururoa will be 'unsuitable' for further use.

Mururoa Atoll was discovered by the British navigator Philip Carteret in 1767. It was ceded to the French in 1964 by a decision of Polynesia's Territorial Assembly. A condition was that if the tests were dropped, the atoll, along with Fangataufa atoll, 43 kilometres away, would be handed back to Tahiti, along with all the buildings on it, free of charge.

Mururoa is actually a ring of 'stretched' islets which run for 63 kilometres around a lagoon in an approximate horse-shoe shape. From west to east, the atoll measures 22 kilometres while its distance from north to south is 10 kilometres. The partly wooded, part desert islets and the reef are the crown of a 500 metre high coral tower formed on the rim of a submerged volcano, dormant for seven millions years, which rises to an average height of 3 metres above the ocean surface. Tidal waves have become an increasing danger as the atoll sinks with each big boom.

Scientists and geologists say this result is hardly surprising: something has to give when a hydrogen bomb is exploded in a sealed chamber. For the French and Polynesians on Mururoa the testing procedure has become almost a monotonous routine. Drills aboard a floating rig sink holes up to 1200 metres deep in the basalt rock beneath the lagoon. Then a cylinder containing the bomb and super-sensitive measuring instruments is slowly lowered to the bottom. Next concrete is poured into the shaft to seal the bomb in. From then on the instruments have to work fast. When the bomb is exploded, important data is transmitted in the first one thousandth of a second from the instruments, through optic fibres and cables, to registers on a barge, moored on the lagoon. Instruments attached to the bomb are then vaporised. Within one tenth of a second the blast has fused into glass thousands of tonnes of lava which absorb 95 per cent of the resultant radioactivity. After a few seconds the lava becomes solid and collapses as the intense heat and pressure subsides, trapping the remaining radioactivity in the chamber. From the volcano comes the final effect — a seismic shock wave about 100th. of the force of the explosion. Even though the surface of the lagoon bubbles and froths as a result, French technicians insist this has nothing to do with leakages of radioactive material.

However, one crack below sea level is said to be nearly one kilometre long and 30 to 60 centimetres wide. Whether this is as a result of the blasts or a natural landslip has been disputed for some time.

In case any of the military personnel stationed on the atoll for a one-year tour of duty have been listening too carefully to the ecologists, the Centre du Expêrimentation Pacifique headquarters in Tahiti has produced a glossy holiday-style brochure which Club Med would be proud of. It shows swimming pools, white beaches, tennis courts and cinemas. And when the troops arrive they find it is even better than described ... speedboats tow water-skiers across the lagoon, joggers move easily along the beach and sailboards glide across a turquoise sea. It is enough to make the military people ignore the one week off they are entitled to in Tahiti every six weeks.

The French have been praising their test grounds since 1982. In that year, shortly after the detonation of the 48th. nuclear device on the atoll, the French Embassy in Port Moresby issued a fact sheet, saying Mururoa 'could be the place for a holiday village where aquatic sports are daily practised'. It went on to say that Polynesians were surprised to see such a hotchpotch of wrong news, inexactitudes and inventions about the nuclear tests. No trace of radioactivity had been detected on any of the nearest inhabited atolls in the vicinity of Mururoa or in the living systems, such as fish and submarine vegetation. 'Otherwise, how to explain that several thousand people — among them 40 per cent Polynesians — accept to live and work there?'

The producers of such attractive brochures and leaflets have not included official maps that show large areas of the atoll which have been placed out of bounds because of contamination risks or which have been desecrated with bore holes. Neither did the authors of these 'holiday brochures' consult the Swedish anthropologist Dr Bengt Danielsson who has lived with his wife, Marie-Therese, in Tahiti since 1947 specifically to study the anthropology of the area. 'The French, by their insane nuclear tests, have turned a tropical paradise into a place of disaster,' he says. 'People of all Pacific countries will be affected for thousands of years to come.'

He cites the islanders of Mangareva, 450 kilometres from Mururoa, who have existed on fish for thousands of years. Now they have to live on corned beef imported from Australia because the fish are poisoned with radioactivity. In August 1985, the Mayor of Mangareva, Lucas Paeamara, wrote a simple letter to the two Tahitian daily newspapers, *La Depeche* and *Les Nouvelles*, drawing attention to those among his population of 582 who had developed cancer or had deformed children in their families.

His letter said the fish in the lagoon had been contaminated with Ciguatera disease, caused by feeding on organisms which eat damaged coral. When you ate the fish you vomited, trembled, and sometimes you were struck with paralysis. 'My people,' his letter added, 'are a fish-eating people who can no longer eat fish. They are not a happy people.' Mr Paeamara said he was not accusing anyone of polluting the environment but he hoped his letter would prompt scientists to study the problem.

In Bengt Danielsson, Mr Paeamara finds a sympathetic ear. When the Kon Tiki raft was wrecked in French Polynesia he decided to stay and viewed with growing concern Paris's plans to start exploding nuclear bombs into the atmosphere in 1966. Those tests, continuing for nine years, sent a vast amount of high radioactive material into the atmosphere — material that Dr Danielsson says will affect the Pacific for 480,000 years.

'The effects are gradual. Every time it rains, more of this radiactive material comes to earth and gets into the seas and food chains. It will take 20 to 25 years for the cancers caused by those early French tests to show up and longer for any pollution effects from leakage from the coral. Mururoa is the worst place I can imagine to conduct underground tests. The coral has been shattered. It is also very porous material, which leaks easily. The seepage into the sea of radioactivity over the years will be quite massive.'

Until the three-nation team was given limited access to the atoll in 1983, no-one was allowed to inspect it to measure the level of radioactivity. Visitors to the island were forbidden unless they received officially stamped invitations and the use of Geiger counters was banned throughout French Polynesia. The French had perpetrated a systematic pattern of lies and gross deception about the tests and their effects. And just laughing at world opinion.

When the French issued an invitation to Australia, New Zealand and Papua New Guinea to visit the atoll, Dr Danielsson decided to keep a close watch on their study. He believed they would not be shown areas that he thought they should be shown.

The invitation was issued by President Mitterrand's special envoy, Mr Regis Debray, who visited Australia after Prime Minister Bob Hawke decided to suspend all uranium shipments to France for a period as a protest against French nuclear testing. The delegation, made up of two radiation experts from New Zealand, a marine geologist and an environmental scientist from Australia and a biologist from Papua New Guinea spent four days on the atoll in October 1983, and presented a report eight months later which was to provide ammunition for both sides in the nuclear debate.

In favour of the French argument, the team reported that they found there was no present evidence of radioactive leakage from the underground test sites and that there was no statistical support for suggestions that the French Polynesian inhabitants of the area had higher than normal cancer rates. But in a finding that supported the ecologists' case, the team said there had been some damage from the detonations to the coral limestone which comprised the upper level of the atoll. More importantly, the investigators said the movement of water through the upper layers from the underlying volcanic layers could mean some leakage from the highly radioactive underground detonation chambers 'in a period of 500 to 1,000 years'. But there was an added warning:

'It is prudent to remember that this situation ignores potential leakage paths other than those existing. The effects of further testing may serve to reduce the potential contaminant transit time. If the transit time becomes short enough, 50 to 300 years, it is no longer valid to ignore the medium-lived products that have high fission yield.'

The make-up of the inspection team, given the rare privilege of visiting the atoll with the right to ask people questions, came under severe criticism from ecologists, Dr Danielsson among them. For a start, the Parliament on Tahiti, made up of 30 elected representatives of the Polynesian people, had tried to have medical doctors included in the team. They had attempted for years to have a thorough health investigation carried out by a mixed team of French and foreign doctors and felt that the official visit would benefit by such experts being included. Not surprisingly, the French government turned the proposal down. Dr Danielsson was also scathing in his criticism of the inspection team's agenda. The five non-medical scientists, he said, spent most of their time talking, attending lectures, luncheons and dinners and inspecting military installations. Only on the third day did they get down to anything as practical as sample-taking. On the fourth and final day, they visited an abandoned, sealed, underground test site before catching the plane back to Tahiti for more courtesy visits, luncheons, dinners and discussions.

Nevertheless, the team produced a comprehensive report which examined the effects of the early atmospheric tests and the current underground experiments.

According to their findings, radioactive fallout in the South Pacific from atmospheric nuclear testing was made up of two major components — long-lived fission products from largely stratospheric (about 9 kilometres to 24 kilometres above the earth's surface) and short-lived fission products from tropospheric (the atmosphere from the surface to the stratosphere) fallout. In the latitude band in which atmospheric tests were conducted, considerably higher doses than other areas had been recorded, but maximum annual doses in Pacific islands from fallout had remained well below the world average annual natural radiation exposure and very much less than annual rates in areas of the world of high natural radioactivity. In New Zealand and Tahiti, for example, annual doses from fallout were estimated to be about 0.5 per cent of the world average from natural exposure.

All around the Mururoa base accommodation area radiation levels were generally lower than elsewhere in the world, said the scientists, because of the very low natural radioactivity concentration of coral soils. Traces of fallout from atmospheric tests were detectable, but were at levels far below those of health significance. And maximum doses received by personnel involved in handling radioactive material were generally only small fractions of internationally recommended limits for occupational exposure.

Figures handed to the team showed that radiation doses to the French Polynesian population from natural radiation and fallout radioactivity were lower than world average levels and did not lead to the expectation that any radiation-induced disease would be detectable. While the relatively small population of French Polynesia did not allow very precise estimation of cancer rates, cancer statistics for the region did not, according to the visitors, support any suggestion of high rates for types of cancer which might be associated with excessive exposure to radioactive fallout.

Turning to underground testing, the team's findings were less optimistic. The tests, they said, may be changing the make-up of the atoll. This could be seen along the north-east and south-west margins, areas of particularly severe testing, where cracks, subsidence and underwater 'sliding' of the limestone had been found. Some fractures extended up to a 400 metre radius from the detonation points of large tests.

The pattern of past testing beneath the atoll rim had produced a repository of nuclear waste products, the depths probably varying from 500 metres to 1200 metres. Ominously, the team said that the French claim that any leakage from volcanic rock to limestone would be stopped by an impermeable zone of rock was not borne out by the data inspected. This so-called impermeable zone between the volcanics and the limestone varied greatly in thickness and rock type and this cast doubt on its ability to act as a barrier to potential radioactive leakage. The potential existed for leakage of contaminated water from detonation cavities to the biosphere — where life is found — in less than 1000 years.

To have been more precise the team would have had to examine samples from the test bores and have access to extensive geochemical data. These requirements were not met. French information on leakage was not detailed and the team said there was 'no reason to believe' their figure that more than 99 per cent of radioactivity from the underground tests was retained in vitrified material — elements that have been changed into a glass-like substance by fusion due to heat from the blasts.

'Their description of venting as inconsequential is almost certainly true,' the scientists reported, 'but any implicit impression that venting is barely, if not rarely, detectable is almost certainly false. Because of the timing and duration of the Mission's visit, only one approach to the detection of venting was possible; it yielded positive results.'

The claim that the impermeable zone acted as a barrier to long-term leakage could, on the basis of geological evidence available to the team, be discounted. The volcanic rock in its virgin state offered a poor to moderate chemical barrier and a moderate to good water barrier. The testing programme was reducing the effectiveness of both. If the tests were to stop immediately, leakage could be expected, particularly around the southern regions of the atoll, within 1000 years.

Concerning waste management practices at Mururoa, the team admitted it was not possible to verify in any direct way most of the information the French had provided them with but they felt that the 'experience of others at similar facilities' and an inspection of French laboratories gave no reason to doubt its validity. The scientists tried to find out the extent of plutonium contamination in the lagoon but admitted this was made next to impossible by the restrictions on sampling imposed by the French, who did not allow collection of marine life or sediment from the water and restricted the area from which water could be drawn. There was another problem. The team reported: 'As the only avenue available for obtaining a historic record of the transport of plutonium from the lagoon to the ocean was to look at the distribution of plutonium in aged corals, there was a need for coral samples from as close to the lagoon as possible. Collection difficulties were compounded by weather conditions.'

While politicians in Australia and New Zealand found some comfort in the findings that radioactive fallout was relatively low, the report received scathing criticism from ecologists. They claimed the French had clouded over the issues and had been as unco-operative to the scientists as they had been to a French scientific team, headed by eminent scientist Dr Haroun Tazieff, now Secretary of State for the Prevention of Disasters. After his 1982 visit, Dr Tazieff had also concluded that there was virtually no short-term contamination, but warned that long-term underground storage of radioactive waste at Mururoa posed problems and he recommended a systematic study over several years.

Dr Tazieff had asked to monitor a test of the usual 10–70 kilotonne yield but what he got was a test with a yield of less than one kilotonne, the smallest ever detonated and completely meaningless as a comparative study. He was also upset that the French navy did not supply a submarine from which he could inspect the holes torn out by nuclear blasts 700 metres down on the outer wall of the atoll. However, he estimated that the explosions had blown out about a million cubic metres of coral and rock.

Attacking the latest five-member inspection of Mururoa, Dr Danielsson said that once more the French did not detonate a bomb while they were under official observation, and no submarine was made available to them, although one well equipped for this type of research was cruising Pacific waters at the time. This was a small, three-man yellow submarine supplied by the French National Oceanographic Research Institute, and would have been highly suitable for an inspection. It can descend to 3000 metres and stay submerged for up to eight hours at a time. As it was, said Danielsson, nothing could be learned first hand about leaking. As for the pollution threat in the north of the atoll, he claimed it should have been easy for the Australian-New Zealand-Papua New Guinea team to check how serious it was by making the 15 minute trip from their living quarters to the so-called 'safety trial area'. Instead of protesting in the strongest possible way about the limitations imposed on their inspection, he said, they 'meekly' took surface samples of ocean water.

Dr Danielsson's attack brought a strong reaction from Mr Andrew McEwan, Director of the National Radiation Laboratory at the Department of Health in Christchurch, New Zealand, and who was a member of the inspection team. He doesn't believe the French have anything to hide on Mururoa regarding radiation dangers and said he would be prepared to spend a month's holiday with his family on the atoll. Dr Danielsson appeared to harbour the misconception that leakage would occur at the time of tests. In fact, leakage would occur as a slow process over an extended period of time. 'The greater proportion of fission products arising from the underground detonations is fused in rock and only available for water transport at the leaching rate (the porous rate) of the rock,' Mr McEwan explained. 'Radioactive material in solution cannot be transported to the lagoon at a rate faster than that of the rate of movement of water through the volcanic rock strata in which the detonations occur. It is to be noted also that if leakage were to be detected, this is not necessarily to be equated with the development of a local health risk. Apart from the fact that sea water contains considerable natural radioactivity, radioactive material commonly can be detected in concentrations many orders of magnitude below those which might be considered to give rise to a possible long-term risk to health.'

Mr McEwan stressed that although attempts were made to 'raise the bogey of radioactive wastes' dispersed in storms in 1981, the comparatively few people at Mururoa who cleaned it up had all been rigorously monitored and every reasonable effort was being made to clean up previously contaminated land areas.

Mr McEwan's argument was backed by Leslie Kemeny, Senior Lecturer in Nuclear Engineering at the University of New South Wales who pointed out that radiological monitoring stations on the nearest inhabited atolls have never recorded the slightest trace of radioactivity above the normal background. Although underground explosions generate a shock wave, the ground motion some 35 kilometres from Mururoa was less than O.1

millimetre, about the same caused on coral reef by the swell of the ocean.

If there was any problem with underground nuclear tests, it was the shock wave. As a result it had been decided that these tests should be carried out further than 20 kilometres from an inhabited area. As France, with 55 million people in an area of 551,000 square kilometres, could not find an uninhabited region within that radius with a suitable geological structure and where shock waves might not damage historical or important buildings, another test site had to be used.

Mr Kemeny said Mururoa was chosen because it was uninhabited, was located 120 kilometres from the nearest atoll where people lived, provided easy access and had suitable underlying rock. And, of course, it was part of French territory. Although Australia and New Zealand described Mururoa as being in their own 'back yard', it was 6,700 kilometres from Sydney, the distance between Perth and Calcutta — and no-one would describe India as being in Australia's backyard.

Furthermore, Mururoa was the most isolated test site of any of the nuclear-weapon countries, being 1220 kilometres from Tahiti. This compared with the Nevada Range in America, which was 120 kilometres from Las Vegas and less than 500 kilometres from Los Angeles. In China, the Lop Nor test site was 500 kilometres from Urumchi, capital of Sinkaing Province and in Russia, the Semipala Tinsk range was only 560 kilometres from Omsk, which had one million inhabitants.

So the argument continues. But one question the ecologists constantly ask is: Have scientists permitted to visit the atoll been allowed to conduct proper tests? By their own admissions, they have not, but what they have seen, is it enough? They agree with the peace movements that it is not. The only other source of information on the condition of the atoll is the French government whose data cannot be trusted. Four days is not enough time for a scientific team to inspect a land mass subjected to nuclear tests since 1975. To set minds at rest, the French must allow an international team *carte blanche*. Explode one of their big bombs while the scientists are there and provide a submarine for inspection of the atoll. They must be allowed access to hospital records in the islands of French Polynesia and in Paris and be permitted to carry out independent health checks on the islanders.

14

The French Reaction

The black Renault sped through the streets of Paris. It was one a.m. The courier who sat inside was on a mission for the President. He carried a letter addressed to Prime Minister Laurent Fabius. The storm had hit France.

An hour earlier, two police motorcyclists had roared away from the Hotel Matignon to purchase two French magazines hot off the presses. Their contents led to Fabius contacting the Elysee Palace. It was August 8 and half the city was in a holiday mood. But not the President. August had never been a good month for him. In that month in 1982 he found himself under public pressure to do something about a terrorist bombing campaign. The following August he was forced to send the French Army to Chad to repulse Libyan troops. In August 1984 he upset politicians on both sides by recalling them from holiday to discuss referendums.

August 1985 was the blackest yet. The two magazines pointed the first accusing finger at the DGSE in the Rainbow Warrior affair. The agency, it was said, had carried out the bombing because it had learned the Greenpeace ship was equipped with scientific instruments able to record a scheduled neutron bomb test at Mururoa.

President Mitterrand's immediate reaction was to call in his personal assistant and draft an urgent letter to Fabius ordering him to launch a 'vigorous investigation' into the claims. By mid morning it had all been arranged. The weary-eyed Fabius had appointed 65-year-old Bernard Tricot, who was general-secretary of the presidential Elysee Palace during General de Gaulle's final years in power, to conduct a no-holds-barred inquiry. It was not the first time that Tricot had been asked to look into a murky affair with DGSE connections. Twenty years earlier he had investigated, and not got far, the assassination of the Moroccan opposition leader, Ben Barka. Whatever determination he may have had to get to the bottom of the Rainbow Warrior affair, there were many who wondered just how far he would be allowed to probe — or how much he would be allowed to see. On the face of it, he was given carte blanche to talk to whomever he wished, including the highest government officials for in a letter of appointment to Tricot, the Prime Minister urged him to 'establish the truth and determine responsibility without limitation of any sort'. Providing Tricot with the background, Fabius said a link had been put forward between the two people arrested by New Zealand police and the French secret service.

As well as dashing off instructions to his Prime Minister, President Mitterrand despatched an urgent letter to the New Zealand Prime Minister. Referring to a possible link between the arrested French couple and the secret service Mitterrand told David Lange that 'One can only wait . . . to find out how accurate this information is and what persons might be held responsible. Nonetheless, I wish to tell you . . . how much I and the Government of the Republic abhor the criminal attack committed on your territory which no excuse can justify . . .'

The French Prime Minister, added the President, had given orders for 'all possible extra help to be given to your investigations, while we are also naturally pursuing our own. I intend,' he concluded, 'that this matter should be handled with the greatest possible severity and that your country should be able to count on the full collaboration of France.' The President sent his highest regards.

With the door opened onto the affair, the dirt began to fly. Investigative journalists from daily newspapers and weekly magazines dug up truths and untruths and uncovered information that was virtually impossible to confirm. What did emerge was that the DGSE had been trying for five years to discredit Greenpeace and the sinking of the flagship was not the first plot against the organisation. For 18 months, sources close to the secret service revealed, the DGSE had been checking whether any Greenpeace members had been to the Soviet Union, Libya, Cuba, East Germany or North Korea. It was suggested to some journalists that they look into organisations supporting Greenpeace for any possible Communist plants.

As the French press started to probe even further into the matter, President Mitterrand fumed. In this bad month of August he had already faced the wrath of the National Assembly when he recalled them during the sacred French holiday period to debate New Caledonia's independence programme. He declared that those who were guilty, at whatever level, 'will be severely punished'. One by one officials were alerted to be on hand for questioning by investigator Tricot. Even at his country home in the wine-making region of Bordeaux, President Mitterrand busied himself with the Rainbow Warrior affair, summoning his friend, Defence Minister Charles Hernu to fly to him. The two men spoke for two hours. It was not a pleasant affair for either of them.

That hot weekend senior staff of the Direction Générale de la Surveillance Exterieure were called to an emergency session at the Piscine. They were ordered to prepare their files for inspection by Bernard Tricot and make sure their stories tallied. Phones rang hot and the DGSE knew they had their backs to the wall. Former intelligence agents made things worse by declaring that the scuttling of the Rainbow Warrior had all the markings of a DGSE job. Roger Wybot, former chief of the Direction de la Surveillance du Territoire, the French equivalent of the FBI said: 'There cannot be any doubt that the operation against Greenpeace was prepared by the French secret service. From experience I know that this kind of decision cannot be taken without being referred to the highest level of the Defence Ministry'.

The DGSE needed breathing space. And it came up with the classic diversionary tactic — blame somebody else. Gullible journalists with right wing sympathies were fed the story that the real culprits were the British. MI6 were behind it because Margaret Thatcher was angry about French sales of Exocet missiles to Argentina during the Falklands war. Not surprisingly, the main outlet for the misinformation was the State-owned radio France-Inter. Journalist Gilbert Picard said the Warrior might have been bombed by the British to discredit France in the South Pacific. And he claimed to have seen the 'mission order' for 'Sophie and Alain Turenge' which absolved them from any direct involvement in the sabotage.

According to Picard the French couple had been sent to New Zealand on a surveillance mission. Declaring that they were French army officers involved in 'security at nuclear sites', the journalist said their job was to keep a watch on the Greenpeace fleet which was to sail to Mururoa. They were to report to officials responsible for the tests on all means of preventing Greenpeace interference. And they were to attempt to identify the leaders of the protest.

The British reponse to claims that they had been involved was a public 'no comment', but privately Foreign Office officials said the suggestion was absolute nonsense. Nevertheless the seed had been planted and led to further speculation that the CIA had been behind the bombing, supporting France because the two nations were Pacific partners. And if it wasn't the British or the Americans, one newspaper hinted, it had to be the Australians whose secret service had carried out the sabotage and had set an incriminating trail in order to discredit France in the eyes of the South Pacific Forum.

One of Bernard Tricot's first ports of call was DGSE headquarters where he spoke at length to Admiral Lacoste. Not long afterwards he travelled south for a vital meeting — with the three man crew of the Ouvea. For contrary to a number of suggestions as to where they had fled, they had, in fact, made their way straight back to France where they were put up at a secret address. One of the more wild suggestions had been that the three had fled from the South Pacific to Gabon in West Africa where they took up appointments in President Bongo's personal bodyguard. Others said they had fled to the other side of Africa, to the Comoros, where they were working for President Ahmed Abdallah. Nothing so romantic, as Tricot's investigations proved.

As a team of New Zealand detectives arrived in Paris to provide Tricot with assistance and, they hoped, receive help from their French colleagues, journalists tracked down a telephone number for Dr Xavier Maniguet, now back in France after his adventures in the South Seas. New Zealand police had formed their own theories about his role in the affair. While in Whangarei, they had established, Dr Maniguet had telephoned a New Caledonian businessman who had just bought a twin engined Cessna. Whether Maniguet, a qualified pilot had intended to use the Cessna to fly his friends from the Ouvea on a long-distance sight-seeing trip was impossible to establish. Callers to his home were greeted with this message on his telephone answering machine:

'Hello journalists. I have been implicated in an affair which does not concern me. I will explain all later.'

Although Tricot's report was expected to be released well before the end of August, some journalists decided that information they had obtained was strong enough for them to go ahead and suggest that the order to sink the Rainbow Warrior had come from the 'highest level'. Without actually naming the President himself they claimed it was impossible that he did not know something was afoot.

The most extraordinary part of the affair was the initial silence of the opposition parties to join the bandwaggon and attack the government. However, many right wing politicians felt they should not criticise the Socialists because they would be indirectly hitting at the intelligence community they could end up controlling after the legislative elections in March 1986. In fact one centrist opposition leader, Jean Lecanuet of the Union for French Democracy (UDF) said of the Rainbow Warrior affair in a radio interview: 'That is what secret services exist for.'

Another UDF member of the Senate, Jacques Larche, said France had legitimate interests in the Pacific and should defend them. 'The price,' he said, 'is sometimes a high one, but one must know what one wants to achieve. France should not throw in the sponge because of one failure.'

The French public tended to agree with that opinion. Newspaper and magazine polls showed that a national consensus supported the government's readiness to use violence, overt and covert, to protect the nuclear testing programme in the Pacific. If there was any criticism to be laid against the government, it was for ineffective intelligence work. Right wing commentators, referring to the Socialist bid in 1982 to purge the DGSE, said that was a crippling episode and poor management by the Socialists explained why the agents bungled their Rainbow Warrior mission. Certainly, the Socialists had always had strained relations with the DGSE, especially the Action Service.

The opposition, realising that things were looking worse for the Socialist leadership with each new daily revelation and claim, finally decided they could hold their silence no longer. They were damaging their own image by doing so.

Mounting the rostrum under the gilded rafters of the ornate, nineteenth century Senate chamber, Charles Pasqua, Senate whip for the neo-Gaullist Rally for the Republic (RPR) Party shook his fist at government front benchers and declared: 'If it is proved that the French secret services are implicated in this affair, then the responsibility could not be sought elsewhere than at the level of the Premier. For who is to believe that the military can act without orders? France is not a banana republic.' And, in a demand for the resignation of the Prime Minister, he added: 'If, as I fear and believe, the government is incapable of assuming its responsibilites, then the moment has come to tell Laurent Fabius to go away!'

It was the first time since Mitterrand had come to power that the opposition had demanded the resignation of the Prime Minister. In the National Assembly across town the attack against the government was just as strong . . . stronger, in fact. RPR whip Claude Labbe said that responsibility for the Rainbow Warrior affair 'belongs at the summit'. For the Socialists, there was worse to come. The spokesman for the Union for French Democracy (UDF), Jean-Claude Gaudin shouted: 'We will not allow the Government to blame its subordinates. Either the head of state (the President) and the Premier were not informed — in which case they are guilty of negligence — or else they were informed and must assume responsibility for their failure!'

But it was Charles Hernu who many saw as being the man who would lose his position in the government. As head of the Defence Ministry and therefore responsible for the DGSE he would be the first to go. And, it was strongly suggested among government circles, he would take DGSE boss Lacoste with him. Hernu, however, shrugged off reports that he would soon be out of a job. 'I'm not even dreaming of the possibility of resigning,' he said. 'I haven't even written a draft letter of resignation.' And he told friends with whom he dined that he definitely did not give any order to sink the ship.

But that such a scheme could be conceived by the government was confirmed by Mr Bernard Stasi, a former Minister for Overseas Territories who went on television to say that as long ago as 1973 he was told of plans to sink boats protesting against France's nuclear tests in the Pacific.

The plans had in fact been drawn up after David McTaggart in the Greenpeace III had clashed for two successive years with the French navy in French Polynesian waters. Stasi made it clear that when he discovered the plans he strongly opposed them because they were tantamount to committing acts of piracy. 'I learned,' he said, 'that certain authorities intended not only to stop but also to sink a number of boats sailing in prohibited areas of the whole Tahiti region. I let it be known with great energy that I was opposed. I believe France has the right to make nuclear tests . . . but one cannot commit acts of piracy in the name of France.'

Interestingly, one of the strongest attacks against Mitterrand and his Socialists came from the French Communist Party. Mr Roland Leroy, a Politburo member, accused the President of being personally behind 'State terrorism'. Claiming the decision to sink the Rainbow Warrior could not have been made without the President's approval, the Communists called on the people of France to resist the 'flouting of French honour'.

In the midst of the political wrangling Sophie Turenge's real name emerged. Co-operating with New Zealand officers, French police established that she was Captain Dominique Prieur, whose husband had recently been transferred from his job as a fire brigade captain to the employment office of the Ministry of Defence. In fact it may have been a telephone call that the French spy had made from Mount Eden jail to her husband that finally unmasked her. According to a French lawyer who represented her, Captain Prieur was feeling depressed as she languished in jail and a woman prison officer had told her: 'You know, you can telephone from here. You only have to ask permission.'

Dominique Prieur, faced with the prospect of life imprisonment, had jumped at the chance to call her husband. As a result of checks in Paris, New Zealand police established her identity. But it was soon to be officially confirmed within days with the publication of the Tricot report. Alain Turenge's real name was also to be revealed. The police had known for some time that he was not a Swiss businessman; shortly after his arrest he had telephoned a Paris number, 846-8790. It was a DGSE line.

15

Tricot's Whitewash

'I have attempted not to reject any hypothesis, even the most unlikely . . . Of certainties, there are, regretably, few. Briefly, I would say that with the information currently at my disposal I do not think there was any official French responsibility.'

Bernard Tricot's conclusions stunned New Zealand. Speaking for his nation, Prime Minister David Lange sat in Wellington's circular Parliament building nicknamed the Beehive and bellowed: 'This report is so transparent it could not be called a whitewash. It is littered with inconsistencies; it skirts around facts; it has contradictions at key points.'

Thus relations between France and New Zealand cooled further. The respected French investigator had failed to point the finger at anyone. After preparing his 29 page report, based on 17 days of interviews with 'several members of the government' he confessed: 'I might have been duped . . . I did not exclude the possibility that I had been deceived.'

On his official mission to find the truth behind the bombing of the Rainbow Warrior, Bernard Tricot interviewed General Jean Saulnier, former head of President Mitterrand's personal military staff who had since been promoted to Chief of General Staff of the French Armed Forces; Admiral Henri Fages, until June 1985, head of nuclear testing centres; Admiral Pierre Lacoste, head of the DGSE, and a number of its senior officials. He had applied a motto throughout his inquiries — 'do not dismiss any first impression, no matter how unlikely it may seem.'

He began his report with a historical reminder about Greenpeace campaigns, recalling how they had been organised in the 1970s and in 1981 and 1982 including attempted landings at Mururoa. There had been incidents when the French Navy intercepted Greenpeace boats, but there had been no noteworthy developments in 1983 and 1984. The French authorities had made efforts to provide information about facts about the nuclear tests and had extended invitations to French and foreign scientists to visit the South Pacific atoll.

'The announcement that Greenpeace intended to resume its protests certainly irritated a large number of military and civilian personnel concerned, in France or at the site, and who are not the only critics of the organisation's lack of independence and impartiality,' Tricot observed. 'But proposals by the Services were all along the lines of what had been done previously to counter the demonstrations.'

During general discussions emphasis had been placed on the need to establish France's legal right to deny access to its territorial waters in the Pacific and to intensify research on the position and movements of Greenpeace boats. Tricot said that DIRCEN (the head office of nuclear test centres) director Admiral Fages told Defence Minister Charles Hernu in an internal memo last March what he knew of the Greenpeace projects. Fages had requested that French authorities and forces in the Pacific be given legal approval to prevent access to the territorial waters of the test site.

'The Admiral recalls that he raised the question with Admiral Lacoste, head of the DGSE, at the end of 1984 or the beginning of 1985,' Tricot reported, adding that it was with the impression that the DGSE had not taken many initiatives about the planned Greenpeace protests that the commander at the test site had sent his note to the Defence Minister. Admiral Fages had made the recommendation that visitors should be accepted on Mururoa, contact should be made with the governments of other countries and gestures of goodwill made to some of France's neighbours in the Pacific.

'No mention was made of any violence. The tone of the note was calm and moderate.' And a similar tone was evident at a meeting between Admiral Fages and Charles Hernu on March 14. Proposals had been discussed, among them the possibility of sending special naval commandos to the Pacific, equipped to intercept small or medium sized boats and prevent landings. The nature of the requests from Fages showed that the authorities did not intend to stop the ecological mission from leaving New Zealand; rather they showed the wish to thwart the mission at its arrival at the site. Although a note from Fages had revealed concern, because it was not easy to peacefully intercept a large number of boats, it did not betray any nervousness. The authorities at Mururoa were insisting on the need for more intelligence about Greenpeace's intentions and this led to instructions being sent by the Minister of Defence to the head of the DGSE to intensify efforts to gather this information.

'As this meant sending several agents to the South Pacific,' the government investigator reported, 'and . . . hiring a boat, expenses ran over the current budget and called for the allocation of exceptional funds. These were requested and obtained in normal conditions, that is, with the agreement of the Chief of Staff of the President of the Republic. I saw General Saulnier and he recalls that the sole purpose was to increase available intelligence and that he gave his go-ahead.'

The Tricot report stated that when Admiral Fages handed over to his successor at Mururoa in June, he left with him a memorandum, a section of which dealt with Greenpeace. The main points of this section dealt with legal aspects, DGSE information, radio intercepts and jamming, commando intervention as already planned and so on. In addition, the memorandum dealt with the possibility of giving permission for demonstrators to visit the Mururoa base. It was recommended in the document that special attention be paid to the flag displayed by the Greenpeace vessel; in the likelihood that it would be British, care had to be taken not to offend British susceptibilities.

Tricot wrote that as usual, contact between the Defence Minister and the head of the DGSE was essentially by word of mouth.

The civil servant's report stressed that both Hernu and Admiral Lacoste said they had predominantly discussed the need for more intelligence gathering. Hernu said this was the exclusive subject of talks between the two of them. But Admiral Lacoste had added the proposal to infiltrate agents into Greenpeace.

'These agents could also be asked to think of ways and means to counteract the activities of the group. I say "think" and on no account "take action", even if it involved non-violent means.'

Tricot then revealed 'a nuance which troubled me'. He said that if any ambiguity, however slight, got into the transmission of orders at the top of the tree, where would this lead to as the orders were passed down through the bureaucratic ranks to the operative level? Tricot said he was concerned when Hernu showed him that the word 'anticipate' was underlined twice in a Defence Ministry note calling for 'intensified intelligence gathering on the positions and movements of Vega and Rainbow Warrior in order to predict and anticipate the actions of Greenpeace.'

What, Tricot asked, did 'anticipate' mean? It not only meant to foresee . . . it also meant to head off or to forestall. Could not, he wondered, this forestalling action go as far as to physically prevent at least one of the vessels from leaving New Zealand?

Hernu insisted on his interpretation. It was a matter of intelligence gathering, which could nevertheless include infiltration. Lacoste confirmed his interpretation, which went slightly further, but under no circumstances included action, even if these were only 'soft methods'.

Regarding the transmission of instructions within the DGSE, Tricot said the officers he spoke to all defined their mission in a way which conformed to the instruction they had received from their superiors. He concluded that the DGSE had understood its role and that its agents had set out the rules of conduct for their agents' missions in conformity with the directives they had received. 'But I cannot, of course, exclude the hypothesis that these officers colluded to withhold some part of the truth from me.' The investigator added: 'I must not overlook the possibility that the written orders, which I saw, were incomplete or were accompanied by verbal explanations which altered their meaning. But this hypothesis seems unlikely considering the training of the officers, their character . . . and their appreciation of the negative backlash on France of any violent actions against Greenpeace, especially in friendly countries such as New Zealand.'

Tricot pointed out that he had not been able to interview 'Alain and Sophie Turenge' whom he revealed to be Commander Alain Mafart and Captain Dominique Prieur. Neither did he see 'Frederique Bonlieu'. But he had had substantial conversations with the members of the crew of the yacht Ouvea and a 'Monsieur Dubast' sent to New Caledonia in June to set up that side of the operation.

Staff orders dated June 14 to the Turenges, which Tricot was given, were: Provide information on the number, characteristics and programme of the vessels accompanying the Rainbow Warrior to Mururoa; identify the possible new crew of the vessel; identify political and scientific figures and journalists taking part in the campaign; and report on the likely impact the campaign would have in New Zealand.

'It seems unlikely to me,' said the investigator, 'that they (Mafart and Prieur) took part directly or indirectly in planting mines under the hull of the Rainbow Warrior. Directly, because Mme Prieur has never been a Navy frogman and because she has spinal problems which prevent her from over-exerting herself. The choice of Commander Mafart to plant mines would have been unreasonable since this officer was transferred out of the navy frogmen's unit and had not been on the active list of the underwater combat force since 1983.'

The couple's indirect participation was less unlikely, Tricot observed. They would have observed in detail the layout of Auckland Harbour, the habits of those frequenting it and the working methods of the New Zealand police. And after July 7 they could have reported the exact position of the Rainbow Warrior and could have passed on their findings to other agents (in this hypothesis those on board the Ouvea) themselves responsible for planting the mines. This distribution of roles would have been logical. But such a scenario would have been contrary to the orders given. It would suppose that the two showed an astonishing and great lack of discipline, which their superiors believed them incapable of.

These suppositions would imply that other DGSE agents carried out the material part of the operation. The only DGSE agents in New Zealand then were the crew of the yacht Ouvea. It was now time, said Tricot, to turn to them. And for the first time, the true identities of the men who had sailed under the names of Raymond Velche, Eric Audrenc and Jean-Michel Berthelo were exposed to the public. They were, said Tricot: Chief Petty Officer Roland Verge, 15 years of military service, including 11 with the DGSE, a member of the Navy Frogmen Training Centre (CNIC) at Aspretto, near Ajaccio; Petty Officer Gerald Andries (CNIC), 10 years military service, including six with the DGSE; Petty Officer Jean-Michel Bartelo (CNIC), 10 years service, four with the DGSE.

Not surprisingly, Tricot stated that he 'took a lot of interest in what these three agents may have done.'

Their mission, dated May 23, involved navigation training in the Pacific, reporting on the Greenpeace ships and seeing if it would be possible to slip a boat into future Greenpeace campaigns. The idea behind the training was that the crew might be able to run a boat themselves on future expeditions or that Roland Verge might be able to get himself chosen as as skipper of a Greenpeace boat. All this meant trying to get to know that part of New Zealand. That was why they had gone to Whangarei. They were not to go to Auckland itself and, Tricot stated, they were apparently unaware of the presence of the two other agents there. However, reasons to think that the crew had carried out the attack on the Rainbow Warrior were 'not negligible'. The most troubling factor was that there was current indication that the instigator or instigators of the plot could have been someone other than the French government.

There were different possibilities — either an action by politically-impassioned individuals or suspicion that other secret services carried out the attack. And there was no lack of motives for this: to damage Greenpeace, a movement which does not upset only France; to damage 'our country' or to damage both

Greenpeace and France and lay the responsibility for the act 'on our shoulders'.

These were only suppositions, Tricot pointed out. 'If we are led to ask ourselves closely what the three DGSE agents were doing, we must of course be careful not to see this as proof of their guilt. However, other reasons for suspicion of varying seriousness have been evoked: the equipment of the Ouvea with special navigation equipment and means of transmission, the very specialised training of the three men and the many signs which according to the Press were found by the New Zealand police.'

Here he referred to the crew's abandoned rubber dinghy and the oxygen bottles of the type used by the French navy. Tricot said he had to respect his promise towards the New Zealand ambassador in Paris and he could not therefore reveal other elements about the case which would no doubt be revealed when the court hearing against Captain Prieur and Major Mafart opened on November 4. 'I shall only say that the known clues and elements which are still secret certainly deserve to be taken into serious consideration but seem to me to be more disturbing than convincing.'

Tricot then turned to reasons in favour of the crew's innocence. He referred to the short amount of time in which both the Rainbow Warrior and the Ouvea were simultaneously in New Zealand. The Greenpeace vessel arrived on July 7, the Ouvea left on the morning of July 9. And there was coherence between the crew's behaviour and their orders. Asked to collect information on sailing circles, fishing coastal traffic, they were to mix with people and avoid acting like secret agents. If, on the contrary, they had been asked or had themselves decided to sink the Rainbow Warrior, this behaviour would have been extremely imprudent.

From June 28 to July 7, said the investigator, Velche systematically visited the coast. 'These expeditions by land were made by Velche or the others. There were six automobile trips . . . but none as far as Auckland. One day, however, Velche travelled to the city (by other means such as public transport) to try unsuccessfully to buy Satnav equipment which had been stolen. Tricot believed that the crew would have had great difficulty in combining their role as 'tourists' with an attack on the Rainbow Warrior.

These were NCOs of 30 to 35 years of age, he said. All three were excellent sportsmen. They had a very military attitude, but without rigidity. 'I would be very surprised if they were careless. Velche in particular appeared to me very thoughtful and prudent . . . I cannot see these men making a decision contrary to the instructions they had received to the extent of sinking the Rainbow Warrior. Of course, I raised the possibility with each of them and on each occasion they told me that such an act would have been beyond them and they had never thought of it.

After customs formalities lasting from 9 a.m. to 10 a.m. on July 9, the Ouvea left Whangarei. During the evening of July 13 or the morning of July 14 Dr Maniguet heard on the radio that the Rainbow Warrior had been sunk. Tricot stated that Dr Maniguet 'told his companions, who expressed neither joy nor pride. It apparently never occurred to the four that they should press on to New Caledonia and not linger at Norfolk, an Australian island with many ties to New Zealand. When I queried them on this they said that given they had never gone to Auckland and had nothing to reproach themselves apart from their false identity papers, it had never occurred to them to move on rapidly.'

Tricot added: 'Everything I have heard and seen gives me the certainty that on the government level no decision was taken that the Rainbow Warrior should be damaged. This year, as in preceding years, government policy was exactly the contrary. The doubts I had on the manner in which instructions given by the Defence Ministry could have been interpreted were cleared when I assured myself that the margin of possible interpretation was below what I would call the danger zone — that is, one in which the services could have believed they were being asked, or were authorised to use, "soft methods", themselves distinct from acts of violence. There is no reason to believe — and strong reasons to believe the opposite — that the DGSE gave its agents in New

Zealand instructions other than those tending to correctly execute government directives.'

So the crew of the Ouvea were officially cleared of any involvement in the sinking of the Rainbow Warrior. Turning to the couple under arrest in New Zealand, Tricot remarked: 'Although until the court proceedings due in New Zealand it will be impossible to comment confidently on the reality or otherwise of the acts for which Major Mafart and Captain Prieur are accused, I believe, in the present state of my knowledge, in their innocence. The same I believe in the present state of my knowledge about Sergeant Major Verge and Sergeants Andries and Bartelo. A necessarily rapid administrative inquiry can hardly be conclusive. Personally I therefore believe it useful that this report be followed in France by a more detailed examination.'

Not surprisingly, Prime Minister David Lange totally rejected the official report. Demanding an official apology from Paris for the 'invasion of New Zealand territory', Lange declared: 'Of course the French Government is involved. And it is totally unacceptable that a government should authorise, at the highest levels, such clandestine illegal activities in the territory of a friendly country. There is no doubt whatever that it was a heavily funded operation. The removal from the Pacific to Noumea, the abandonment of the ship paid for by the French and the spiriting from new Caledonia to France can only speak of French Government activity. The fact is that we had operators of French Government intelligence agencies in New Zealand for some time and spending at a conspicuous level.'

Lange and his aides — along with the New Zealand police — had studied a translation of the Tricot report with increasing amazement. But there were factors in it which they saw as pointing to official involvement. First, there was the admission that spies from the DGSE had been in New Zealand and that three of them were highly-trained combat divers. There was the abandonment of the yacht and the spiriting back to France of the crew. And while the three DGSE yachtsmen were made available to Tricot for his inquiry, they had not been available for questioning by New Zealand police officers in Paris, even though they were wanted on murder charges. 'This,' declared Lange, 'is an incredible state of affairs to exist between two allegedly friendly countries.'

Pointing to one glaring inconsistency, Lange said that according to one part of Tricot's report the three DGSE divers were charged with watching the Rainbow Warrior and infiltrating the Greenpeace movement. But another section said they stayed at Whangarei Harbour, several hundred kilometres from Auckland where the Greenpeace yacht was berthed.

'Friendship is strained when you have a nation which continually pounds the ocean near us with nuclear testing and which has spies in our country,' the Prime Minister said. 'In the circumstances, I have suggested that the French Government consider recalling the French Ambassador in Wellington for consultation. This might help make it clear in Paris that we take this whole matter more seriously than Mr Tricot. The obsession with pursuing these tests has resulted in an infringement of our sovereignty by the French Government and an unacceptable insult to New Zealand.'

One hour before Tricot's report was made public, the three DGSE crew members reported to Paris police. Despite the international warrants for their arrest issued by a New Zealand court, they were not held. Once it was established they were military personnel they were asked to report back to their superior officers.

Made aware of these events, Lange said: 'I want three people who are wanted on murder charges to be brought to justice. I want that done in New Zealand. I want then after that trial to have French Government culpability assessed in connection with the Rainbow Warrior itself. That is a distinct issue. We know enough now of the spying activity to know that France owes New Zealand an apology right now, with no further proof of anything . . . All that we know now is that France has been dishonourable. They cannot hide from the evidence. If they chose to, it will be the worse for them. The truth might not save them, but untruth will destroy them.'

The Prime Minister seized an opportunity to be interviewed by a Paris television crew and later that day his countenance was beamed into homes across France. He declared: 'France has killed our friendship.'

If the French government hoped that the Tricot investigation would quell the rising storm, they were disappointed. In France his report was greeted with scorn among the Press. And Tricot, barraged with questions, backed away. 'In my report,' he floundered, 'I did not exclude the possibility that I was deceived. I do not exclude that there may have been a kind of general agreement, or agreement at a certain level, not to tell me the truth.'

He agreed there were more expressions of belief than of certainty in his report. But he repeated his conviction that there had been no positive government directive to sabotage the Rainbow Warrior. 'I am sure there was no directive, even veiled in some way. Really no; that is not what happened.' Who then, he was asked, had carried out the attack? 'I cannot say . . . it is possible that it was somebody other than the French.'

As expected, the Opposition tossed the report out of the window. Jean-Claude Gaudin of the UDF party resumed the attack he had begun against the government before Tricot's findings were published. 'Tricot concludes that he cannot reach any conclusions,' laughed Gaudin. 'His report means nothing. The investigation must continue.' Party colleague Alain Madelin was more outspoken. 'The Tricot report takes the French people for imbeciles. It would have us believe that one sends frogmen only to take photographs when it is clear to everyone that France gave itself over to an act of terrorism.'

Two other opposition party leaders, displaying true French pride, refused to condemn the report or launch a fresh attack against the Socialists. 'My country, right or wrong,' was all former President Giscard d'Estaing would say. RPR leader Jacques Chirac, who is also the Mayor of Paris said he would not attack the Government or the intelligence services over the affair. It was a brave stance that they took.

With the French Press screaming headlines such as *Tricot Lave Plus Blanc* — Tricot Washes Whiter — anger spread internationally. The British Government was even lashed by the storm;

MPs of all parties demanding to know why the Foreign Office had remained silent about the Rainbow Warrior affair. Conservative MP Teddy Taylor, claiming the government had insulted New Zealand by maintaining a 'deafening silence', wrote to Foreign Secretary Sir Geoffrey Howe asking why no public statement had been made. Describing the Foreign Office attitude as a 'conspiracy of silence' on what was obviously an international act of piracy, he demanded that Britain protest to France about the bombing and call for an apology.

Because the Rainbow Warrior was a British-registered ship, Labour frontbencher John Prescott demanded that Britain hold an inquiry into the sinking. Underlying the wave of protest was a feeling that Britain's secret service was in some way connected. Certainly Labour's environment spokesman, Dr David Clark, said he remained suspicious that Britain was in some way involved. Liberal leader David Steel was to join the chorus demanding that Prime Minster Thatcher make it clear there was no British involvement. 'I wonder why she is so silent now, particularly in the face of suggestions in Paris that the British secret service is involved,' said Mr Steel. 'I hope it is not our shared membership of the nuclear club with France that stops her criticising this dastardly act.'

The MP raged on: 'This ship is registered in Britain, owned by a British company and had at least one British crew member. It was sunk in New Zealand, a Commonwealth country, to which Britain is intimately connected by ties of blood, history and affection.' Mrs Thatcher should make it crystal clear without delay that there was no British involvement of any sort, he said. 'She would then indicate our anger to the French Government, both at the sinking of the ship and at the cover up of Mr Tricot, who should be awarded the Inspector Clouseau Memorial Prize for preposterous implausibility.'

If there was to be any clue that British intelligence at least knew about a planned action by France, it came through the brief Foreign Office statement that the allegations of MI5 involvement were based on a misunderstanding. The Minister of State at the Foreign Office, Mr Malcolm Rifkind, said he had no plans to make a statement about the affair, although the Foreign Office was ready to give diplomatic support if Greenpeace International asked for it.

That prompted a cynical response from Greenpeace, who contrasted Britain's inactivity with the outspokenness of David Lange in Wellington. Mr Pete Wilkinson, a director of Greenpeace International commented: 'The United Kingdom Government's concern over international terrorism has been evidenced by a resounding silence from Whitehall. It is as though nothing had happened at all, when in fact a British-registered vessel was sunk by an act of terrorism in foreign waters, taking the life of a Greenpeace crew man.'

The 'greens' in France issued a caustic statement saying: 'Monsieur Tricot, the former secretary-general of the Elysee from 1959 to 1969, a period during which the cloak-and-dagger boys and the parallel police had a free hand in France, remains a faithful servant of the state, competent and silent. He has done his work well.'

Not unexpectedly, the Tricot report prompted a new wave of wild speculation. If an official government investigator had found that the DGSE were not responsible it had to be — well, it could be any one of the world's secret services. It was BOSS, the South African Secret Service, declared the daily newspaper *Le Matin*, recently bought by friends of President Mitterrand and edited by his former press spokesman Max Gallo. Basing an article on interviews with 'intelligence services specialists', all anonymous, *Le Matin* said BOSS may have had the help of either the British counter-intelligence service MI6, or the CIA, which 'serve as a firebreak on the terrain of human rights against the position taken by France on apartheid'.

No, it wasn't BOSS or the British or the Americans, declared the Belgian daily, *Le Soir*. The culprits were Greenpeace themselves who had decided to sink their own boat. Greenpeace recently acquired a new vessel, a 190 foot tug donated by the Association of Maryland Pilots, which prompted the Belgian paper to come up with its incredible scenario. Greenpeace, said *Le Soir*, enjoyed friendly and close relations with several independent states in the Pacific and could have been informed by them of the presence of French agents in New Zealand. 'Greenpeace wanted to boost its own stocks and, above all, injure France . . . It's remarkable that Greenpeace could replace the old tub (The Rainbow Warrior) in such an abnormally short time, as if they were waiting to do so, and that they could have, so quickly, such a large sum for the much bigger replacement boat, an amount of money which seems disproportionate to their admitted finances.'

British newspapers were less speculative. Instead they began investigating the movements of DGSE agents in London, establishing the shop where Andries had purchased the rubber dinghy and outboard motor. *The Daily Mail* revealed that British and New Zealand police had established the identity of a French DGSE agent who met the Turenges and two other DGSE agents in London.

French Prime Minister Fabius, clearly aware that the Tricot report was not going to clear his government, tried to calm international anger by declaring that he was determined no element of the Rainbow Warrior affair would remain in the shadows. 'Send me proof of French criminal involvement' he asked the New Zealanders. 'Then prosecutions can take place.' Unfortunately, he said, he had no information to contradict Tricot's report.

Fabius's statement evoked a cynical response from a leading conservative politician, Michel Noir. 'As a habitual reader of St Anthony, I would have said it is unlikely that the Rainbow Warrior was blown up by a simple operation of the Holy Spirit.'

The French Prime Minister had bounced the ball back into the New Zealand court. In asking for proof of French criminal involvement he was challenging Auckland police to show their hand. But Superintendent Galbraith was not prepared to reveal too much of his case. Already he had found to his horror that contents of documents he had sent to assist the Tricot inquiry had been splashed across French newspapers within eight hours. 'Probably we should not have been surprised,' the dour Scottish policeman remarked in Auckland. 'I suppose it was not confidential in that we had not thought to ask that it not be published.'

Despite the policeman's reservations, Prime Minister Lange was quick to point out that Laurent Fabius' words showed that the French acknowledged New Zealand had evidence which would render them absurd if they continued to cling to the Tricot report. 'I think we are getting somewhere,' said Lange with a hint of smugness. 'Tricot has made an international fool of himself.' But he still pressed for justice in the case of the three DGSE yachtsmen. 'I would have thought that the least men of honour would do to vindicate themselves from the appalling allegations that they sabotaged a ship in New Zealand resulting in the death of a person on board would be to come back to New Zealand and go on trial in a court which would offer a presumption of innocence until they are proven guilty.'

If Bernard Tricot had shown himself to be a fool, he also portrayed a gullible soft-heartedness. For he revealed that he had not even tried to interview the mole Christine Cabon because he was concerned for her safety. 'This young woman had already undertaken missions in other parts of the world and some people were not exactly fond of her as a result,' said the investigator. 'She may have carried out infiltration operations in very dangerous movements, capable of taking brutal vengeance. I thought, therefore, that if I tried to make her come in from the cold, she would be exposed to great danger indeed.'

His kid-glove treatment of a spy whose groundwork had helped a team of saboteurs on a mission that had ended in a death only added to widespread conviction that Tricot was an inept choice to investigate the murky depths of the French secret service. According to French Government sources, Cabon was so concerned about the publication of her photograph in newspapers around the world that she had consented to undergo plastic surgery in a secret French clinic to change her features. Certainly her exposure had put her out of action as an infiltrator for many years to come, with or without plastic surgery. Perhaps her time as a spy was up anyway, for as brilliant as she may have been on past missions, she had behaved clumsily in Auckland, asking too many direct questions, placing too many calls to France and displaying an attitude that was at odds with an anti-nuclear campaigner.

Having shown his weakness with Cabon, Tricot, speaking a few days after the release of his report, also displayed a 'Mr Nice Guy' attitude towards the DGSE crew men. 'Did they deceive me by concealing orders that had been given them? I don't think so,' he mused. 'But if they did do the operation, it was almost certainly under orders. I cannot imagine their taking the initiative.'

He suggested, too, that President Mitterrand was unaware of the so-called surveillance operation beforehand, although his military adviser was informed as part of budgeting for the operation. 'The affair,' he said, 'was not sufficiently important to go further than the director of the President's military office (General Jean Saulnier).'

Far from diffusing the political time bomb ticking under the French Government, Bernard Tricot had in fact set it at detonation point. The backlash against the French sent Mitterrand into a rage, storming the corridors of the Elysee Palace and wondering what he could do to divert the accusing fingers. There may have been no sympathies for the government, but the people of France had not forgotten the two imprisoned agents in Auckland. Urged on by one of the couple's legal representatives, families sat down and penned letters to Captain Dominique Prieur and Major Alain Mafart. One old member of the Resistance who had been imprisoned by the Gestapo sent Dominique Prieur a photograph of his grand-daughter. 'Perhaps her smile will cheer you,' he wrote.

Six hundred and sixty kilometres away in Wellington French Embassy staff were not enjoying the same consolation. Threatening and obscene phone calls were being received. Tyres had been punctured. And French children attending local schools were subjected to a jeering song in the playground. Its title: 'Somewhere Over the Rainbow.'

16

The Clean Up

It wasn't going to go away. The Rainbow Warrior affair which Parisians had left behind when they went off for their summer vacations on the Cote d'Azur and all other points south, was still raging when they returned. Tanned secretaries and smiling government officials who had not been involved in the scandal returned to the capital ready to start what they regarded as a fresh new year. For President Mitterrand and Prime Minister Fabius, however, *la rentree* as the return is called, was just an extension of the end of the bad old year. In seven months voters would go to the polls to choose a National Assembly — and show whether France's five year experiment with Socialism should continue.

The cartoonists had been having a field day, showing Charles Hernu swimming ashore in a diving outfit with the Rainbow Warrior sinking behind him . . . and, underneath the caption, 'French Returning Home After a Successful Holiday', a group of holidaymakers stepping off a plane with suitcases and flippers. With his popularity ratings hovering at 30 per cent or below, President Mitterrand saw nothing funny in the cartoons. He was facing the very real prospect of remaining as President until 1988 while co-habiting with a right wing government in the National Assembly.

Whatever truth might eventually emerge from the Rainbow Warrior affair, whatever his personal feelings about the political quagmire the secret service had dragged him in to, the President was aware he had to continue to openly support the nuclear test programme. After all, it was to safeguard the activities at Mururoa that the DGSE had sent people to New Zealand. The French public supported nuclear defence and if there was one sure way of maintaining a relationship with voters it was to show them all that no matter what international opinion said, he would not back down. And so on September 13, buoyed by wide support for his determination to continue the programme, President Mitterrand, accommpanied by his Foreign and Defence Ministers, took off in an Air France Concorde on a 36,000 kilometre public relations exercise to Mururoa. His supporters saw his presence at Mururoa as an eloquent symbol, requiring no words to explain it. Officially, his visit was to preside over the first meeting of a committee of French ambassadors and senior military and civil officials in the Pacific Region. The group, known as the Co-ordination Committee for the South Pacific, had not been heard of before the President's trip was announced unexpectedly.

'Provocative and extraordinary,' was how the New Zealand Prime Minister described the visit. Australia joined the protest, a Foreign Affairs spokesman describing the President's flight as 'highly provocative and contemptuous of countries in the South Pacific'. Seven Australian Democrat senators delivered a letter to the French Ambassador, Mr Bernard Follin saying President Mitterrand had displayed 'incredible impertinence and arrogance' adding: 'At a time when there are more than 50,000 nuclear bombs in the world . . . your government is, in the name of French grandeur and adventurism, increasing that arsenal of death.'

But Mitterrand's ploy to use the nuclear test programme as a popularity booster was working. Even the Conservative opposition newspaper *Le Figaro* sided with him, describing the outcry from Down Under as 'Primitive Reactions'. In a front page editorial it declared: 'The Australians and New Zealanders have a suburbanite's conception of the Pacific, a peasant-like view of their maritime front garden. For them, the Europeans are just people who jib at buying their sheep.'

After the President had officially opened the Co-ordination Committee meeting, his spokesman, Michel Vauzelle said opponents of French nuclear tests would be ignored and anyone who opposed French interests would be seen as adversaries.

'In that case,' responded David Lange, 'France has declared New Zealand an enemy.' The New Zealand Prime Minister had, in fact, offered to meet President Mitterrand when he came into the Pacific, but he had received no response.

Lange, still waiting for an official apology, continued to lambaste France, saying: 'New Zealand did not buy into this fight. France put agents into New Zealand. France put spies into New Zealand. France lets bombs off in the Pacific. France puts its President in the Pacific to crow about it. It's not the New Zealand or Pacific way of doing things, but apparently it's the way to win a French election.'

Determined that Lange's response should not take the shine off his trip to Mururoa, President Mitterrand quickly caught up on his sleep then presented himself in front of the television channels for an official address to the nation. He reaffirmed that tests would continue in the South Pacific, but declared that Paris had no enemies there. Immediately afterwards he answered questions for the first time about the Rainbow Warrior affair, condemning the sinking as 'criminal and absurd'. But he defended a decision to send French agents to spy on Greenpeace in New Zealand. 'Nothing could be more lawful,' he stated. They had been sent to a country 'which serves as a platform and a relay for initiatives hostile to France. And he repeated the findings of the Tricot report, saying the agents' mission had been limited to gathering intelligence. 'There is a large gulf between intelligence and action,' he said.

As Greenpeace vessels headed for Mururoa — the tug Greenpeace passing through the Panama Canal and smaller vessels from New Zealand heading in from the west — Britain at last made a gesture to help the New Zealand authorities.

The government said it was sending an underwater explosives expert to New Zealand to help investigate the sinking of the Rainbow Warrior which had now been raised from the harbour bed, the enormous hole in its side patched, and moved to nearby docks for examination. But that was as far as the British Government were prepared to go. In a letter to Greenpeace, Foreign Secretary Sir Geoffrey Howe confirmed the government did not intend to carry out its own investigation into the sinking. 'The British Government has every confidence in the ability of the New Zealand authorities to conduct a full and fair inquiry,' said Sir Geoffrey.

If Mitterrand thought his visit to the test centre would increase his political stature, all was ruined by yet another damning revelation which now appears to have been the result of confused information supplied to the influential newspaper *Le Monde*. For the usually pro-Mitterrand Paris daily said that if its sources were to be believed, the attack against the Rainbow Warrior was actually carried out by a *third* team working in addition to the 'Turenges' and the crew of the Ouvea. The Turenges, it was said, apparently acted as a decoy and collected the equipment brought by the Ouvea for the perpetrators of the attack who would appear to be two French army frogmen, each of whom fixed an explosive charge against the hull. The sources did not say precisely which base the third team·came from, but it would have to be either the CNIC at Aspretto if they came from the army, or Lorient, if they were from the navy.

The two men specialised in the same sort of thing as Alain Mafart, second in command at Aspretto, and the Ouvea's three crew. The newspaper added that the whole operation would appear to have been co- ordinated by 'Philippe Dubast', who was Commander Louis-Pierre Dillais, boss of the Aspretto base. With the exception of Dominique Prieur, the operation appeared to have been entrusted to military frogmen, which meant that the DGSE, which employed them, certainly did have a hand in it all.

As to who ordered the operation, the paper said the agents could not have improvised an operation on such a scale, if only because of its very high cost and the geographical distances involved. It was logical to assume, then, that they were following instructions from their superior in the chain of command, Colonel Jean-Claude Lesquer, who was appointed head of the DGSE's

Action Division in November 1984. A disciplined officer whose appointment had Defence Minister Hernu's endorsement and was recommended by the then army Chief of Staff, General Jeannou Lacaze, Colonel Lesquer was not the sort of man to order such a mission off his own bat. He was himself following orders from the head of the DGSE, Admiral Pierre Lacoste. In turn, Lacoste was reacting to pressure from the nuclear test centre. But he, said *Le Monde*, was a highly disciplined officer and it was unthinkable that he acted alone. Sources suggested that three other high officials knew what was going on. The operation was either authorised from the top, or was allowed to proceed from there. These people would have to be General Lacaze; General Jean Saulnier, then chief of the presidential staff; and the Defence Minister himself.

It now seems that the newspaper's sources were only partly correct when referring to a third team. If other sources close to the New Zealand investigation are correct, the third team may well be a reference, not to frogmen, but to Commander Dillais and the mysterious Francois Verlon who was invited on board the Rainbow Warrior. Their roles would have certainly involved more than standing around and keeping an eye on what was going on. And there is still the question of why the DGSE would go to the trouble of sending three skilled divers in a yacht to Whangarei when other swimmers were assigned to do the job. Dr Maniguet has, of course, protested his innocence, telling the magazine *Paris Match* that his fellow crew members had cheated him on a grand scale and that he had been very skillfully manipulated. Nevertheless, his presence on the Ouvea as a specialist in 'diving medicine' cannot be overlooked. If a third team, made up of saboteurs who would have used the dangerous rebreather rigs, did exist, did they also have a doctor waiting to care for them in some vehicle parked close by or on board some nearby yacht? And if the frogman in a red woollen cap who brought the Zodiac back was Bartelo, why was a skilled combat swimmer like him wasting his talents by playing courier, delivering equipment back to the camper van?

The 'third team' theory was put forward at about the time New Zealand police realised that Commander Dillais had stayed at Auckland's Hyatt Hotel from July 4 to July 10. However accurate the claim was, its publication had a devastating effect.

Opposition spokesmen screamed for the resignation of both the President and the Prime Minister. While the President remained silent and a spokesman for Fabius said the Prime Minister was determined nothing should be left in the dark, Charles Hernu angrily denied he knew anything in advance about the sabotage. No service and no organisation depending on his ministry received any orders to carry out an attack on the Rainbow Warrior. 'But,' he added, 'if I have been disobeyed or lied to, I will impose pitiless sanctions.' Under further questioning, he conceded he had ordered two agents to spy on the Greenpeace operation in New Zealand but said there was an abyss between gaining information and the murder charges which the arrested agents, the so-called Turenges, were being accused of.

Word was around that Hernu and the DGSE's Admiral Lacoste were in a precarious position; their heads were about to roll. President Mitterrand could stand the rumours no longer. At his weekly Cabinet meeting he angrily turned to his long-time friend the Defence Minister and said: 'I want to know! I want to know!'

The following day the President sent a letter to Prime Minister Fabius pointing out that French newspapers and magazines were uncovering 'new elements that we cannot evaluate because of the absence of information from the appropriate services'. It was an admission that the public were being made privy to information that he, as President, could not obtain from his own government. He found the situation intolerable and told Fabius it could not continue. 'The moment has come,' the President wrote, 'to proceed without delay to changes of personnel and, if necessary, of structures responsible for these shortcomings.'

The following day Admiral Pierre Lacoste was dismissed as head of the DGSE. And President Mitterrand reluctantly accepted the resignation of Charles Hernu.

Lacoste's sacking had been urged by the Prime Minister because he claimed the DGSE head had been unco-operative over the allegations that he had sent a third team to New Zealand. Fabius said after the claims had been made public, the Defence Minister had asked Admiral Lacoste if he had indeed given any orders or received any information about the preparation of an attack on the ship. The same question had been put to the two other senior military officers mentioned in the *Le Monde* article, General Lacaze and General Saulnier. Both officers had given clear negative answers, but Admiral Lacoste had simply said that he had nothing to add beyond what he had told investigator Tricot . . . that he and his service were totally innocent. Hernu, the Prime Minister explained, had then put two precise questions to Admiral Lacoste: Was there another team or other agents of the DGSE in New Zealand? Did initials cited in certain press articles correspond to those of agents in his service?

In his letter to the President urging Lacoste's removal, Fabius said: 'Admiral Lacoste refused to reply to the Defence Minister, citing his conception of his duty. It is obviously impossible to accept such a situation. That is why . . . I request you remove Admiral Lacoste from his functions immediately.'

Hernu, who had denied that a third team had operated in New Zealand, said in his letter of resignation to the Prime Minister that he had known for 24 hours that 'beyond all doubt senior officers within my ministry have hidden the truth from me'.

Despite his public wrath, President Mitterrand was saddened to be rid of the man who had served him so faithfully over the years. Certainly he showed himself to be exceedingly magnanimous by writing to the Defence Minister after his resignation expressing his regret and his gratitude.

But the burning question remained: just how much of the Rainbow Warrior affair did the President know before Hernu's resignation? Was his outburst at the cabinet meeting something of a show?

With such a close friendship between Mitterrand and Hernu, many politicians and observers asked, did the Defence Minister tell the President what he knew about the affair? It seems inconceivable that at the very least Hernu did not say to the President that he had taken steps to have the Greenpeace problem taken care of, even if he was not personally aware how the DGSE would act.

Still the storm raged on. Hernu was replaced by Paul Quiles 43, the Minister of Urban Affairs, Housing and Transportation. The Socialists knew him as Robespaul, a name meant to recall Robespierre, a cruel French revolutionary of the 18th century who authorised the execution of thousands of enemies of the people. The Minister earned his tough reputation when in 1981 he called for a purge of civil servants reluctant to carry out the Socialist programme. On that occasion, paraphrasing Robespierre, Quiles said: 'It's not a question of heads rolling, but of how many.'

He was more conciliatory as Hernu bowed out. After an hour-long meeting with Hernu he declared: 'I want to pay homage to a vibrant man, my friend Charles Hernu. For four years he devoted all his efforts to safeguarding our national independence, and to supporting France and her armies.'

The removals of the Defence Minister and the DGSE head failed to stave off the questions that had arisen from the Tricot report. Did the French secret service bomb the Rainbow Warrior? Who gave the order? Prime Minister Fabius turned to his new Defence Minister for help, ordering him to carry out an immediate investigation and ferret out the truth. It did not take Quiles long. Within 24 hours he reported back to Fabius what his inquiries had uncovered.

Fabius now faced the biggest crisis of his political career. At 39 he was the youngest French Prime Minister this century but he had already proved himself to be worthy of his position. The son of an antique dealer, he became a Socialist Party member in 1974 and climbed to the top with his mentor, Francois Mitterrand. But he had one thing going against him — his wealthy origins. He used to drive a pink Porsche to work and rode show ponies at equestrian events. His wealth and arrogance, even by French standards, separated him from his Socialist colleagues, but after managing Mitterrand's 1981 presidential campaign he found himself being labelled by upper class circles as a class traitor. He had to go one way or the other. His decision was to turn his back on the upper classes and to show that he meant it he introduced, as Budget Director, France's first ever wealth tax.

The contempt that the upper classes now held for him resulted in him being refused service in one posh Paris restaurant and being booed out of another. Fabius distanced himself even further, replacing the Porsche with a small Citroen. As a major influence behind many of President Mitterrand's policy turn-arounds, one of which forced the French Communist Party out of the Government, Fabius became Prime Minister in 1984. 'He is the one who best represents my ideas,' Mitterrand said of him.

On Sunday September 22, Laurent Fabius, who had so bravely turned his back on the upper classes, realised he had to undertake his toughest political assignment. That evening he gave the French media 15 minutes to get to his office. There they found the Prime Minister waiting. Beside him was Paul Quiles. A few hours earlier the External Relations Minister, Mr Dumas, had announced there was no proof of French guilt and ruled out a French apology to New Zealand. The Press expected Fabius to expand on that.

'The new Minister of Defence,' the Prime Minister said, reading from a prepared statement, 'has just informed me of the first conclusions of an inquiry into the Rainbow Warrior affair. I was anxious to inform you of them immediately. These conclusions allow us to get closer to the truth.

'Agents of the DGSE sank this boat. They acted on orders. This truth was hidden from State Counsellor Tricot. I have told the President of the Republic about these serious facts and we have decided that immediate measures must be taken.

'Firstly, a new head of the DGSE will be named at the next Cabinet meeting. His prime task will be to reorganise all of these services. Secondly, the Government favours the creation of a parliamentary commission of inquiry.

'The people who merely carried out the act must of course be exempted from blame as it would be unacceptable to expose members of the military who only obeyed orders and who, in the past, have sometimes carried out very dangerous missions on behalf of our country.

'Ladies and gentlemen, the truth about this affair is cruel, but it must be clearly and thoroughly established, as I pledged.'

Fabius and Quiles then left the room, refusing to answer questions.

Back in Wellington David Lange was far from placated. France had obviously made up its mind that its agents were going to be let off. 'Trials of agents must follow the French confession of guilt for a sordid act of international, state-backed terrorism,' he said. 'This is not a war. This is New Zealand, 1985. The defence of acting under orders is clearly inappropriate. The idea that acting under orders of a foreign power gives anyone licence to execute criminal acts . . . and remain inviolate from prosecution and sanction is, of course, quite absurd.'

The French Prime Minister's confession, of course, opened the wound wider and with two men down he found himself next in the firing line. What was so extraordinary about his admission was that after the change over of Defence Ministers it had taken him only 24 hours to find out what had been hidden from him during the previous 10 weeks. There were claims that the President had been informed by Fabius on July 17 — a week after the bombing — that Hernu and the Elysee military advisor General Saulnier had approved the sabotage.

In order to quell these stories, the polished Prime Minister who had promised 'only one thing — to tell you the truth' agreed to appear on a television programme where he found himself ducking and weaving. He tried to pin all the blame on Hernu and Lacoste saying that his conviction was that 'the two of them had acted and that the idea was taken at their level. It is at their level that the responsibility lies.' Saying it was a 'bad order', the Prime Minister added that the whole truth had been hidden for a long time from the President, Mr Tricot and himself. 'When,' he was asked, 'did you first know about DGSE involvement?' Last Saturday afternoon (September 21), he said. That, according to a radio station, was a lie. He was said to have known everything on July 15 because of the phone call 'Alain Turenge' made to the DGSE in Paris. The conversation was intercepted, it was claimed, and passed on to Fabius's office.

But it did not require a phone call from a spy to alert the government that trouble was afoot. The French Ambassador in New Zealand had sent a series of telegrams to Paris immediately after the arrest of the so-called Turenge couple warning that they were suspected of being French agents and of the disastrous diplomatic consequences that were certain to follow.

Despite claims that the government knew far more than it was saying, despite politicians' description of the affair as France's 'Underwatergate', the public seemed unperturbed. Hiding the truth or telling downright lies in the interests of the State is generally approved on the basis that French leaders know best.

As Greenpeace yachts started gathering just outside French Polynesian waters, watched by a French navy vessel, Paris announced its new DGSE head — General Rene Imbot, 60, chief-of-staff of the French army. His first assignment was to reorganise the secret service and he showed he meant business by ferreting out four French soldiers, including a colonel, who were then charged with disclosing secret defence information to unauthorised people. It was these, said Imbot, who had leaked information to the Press, possibly through a fifth man, Captain Paul Barril, former head of an anti-terrorist squad.

So the clean up had begun. Heads had rolled, confessions had been made. If there were any more leaks, they would not be from the French secret service. But for one remaining problem President Mitterrand could expect the Rainbow Warrior affair to go away at last, giving his party a clearer run down the home straight towards the March elections.

But there was that problem . . . two spies were being held in an Auckland jail. The case could drag on for weeks, bringing the whole affair alive again. Mitterrand, Fabius and their aides now wondered what could be done to avoid another wave of embarrassing publicity.

17

The Final Act

The whisper had been around Wellington for at least a month. The New Zealand Government, anxious not to destroy any chances of gaining the maximum compensation from France following the government's confession, was prepared to come to an 'arrangement'. It involved returning the two DGSE agents to French territory at the earliest opportunity.

Prime Minister Lange, confronted with the rumour, which found its way onto New Zealand television, dismissed it as 'uninformed and irresponsible'.

Nevertheless, as the world's Press descended on Auckland during the first weekend of November the rumour persisted. Major Mafart, who that weekend had celebrated his 35th birthday in jail, and Captain Prieur were due to appear in the Auckland District Court on Monday November 4 for a deposition hearing. The case was originally expected to last for as long as six weeks but as the date approached court officials said it was now likely to be closer to two weeks. Time would be saved because a number of witnesses would not be called — their statements would simply be read to the court instead.

The detention of the arrested spies had not been without drama. Fearing an attempt to 'spring' them amid rumours that a team of mercenaries were on the move in New Zealand, the authorities had moved Mafart to an Auckland maximum security jail, while Prieur had been flown to a women's prison in Christchurch.

But shopkeepers in the South Island reported that they had seen some 'strange French people' wandering around. In the provincial city of Nelson, delicatessen owner Wilhelm Heiner told of three French tourists, two men and a woman, who he said were not like normal visitors.

Shortly afterwards Prieur was moved back to Auckland to an armed services corrective establishment at Ardmore. Police explained this was 'in the interests of her security'. A team of soldiers surrounded the premises with barbed wire. Dominique Prieur was the only occupant.

In the Pacific the Greenpeace protest was hardly gaining momentum — not that the conservationists worried so much this year because they realised they would be gaining maximum publicity through the court case. The Greenpeace ship generator broke down which effectively put it out of action and the brig Breeze decided to return to New Zealand. The yacht Vega was seized by French marines and the crew transferred to a tug. They were banned from returning to French Polynesia. Nevertheless, they had made their point . . .

On Mururoa the French went ahead with their tests of the neutron bomb, detonating two within the space of two days. The new Defence Minister Paul Quiles had flown to the Pacific to be present for the blasts and he behaved in the same way as had a number of officials in the past, taking a swim in the lagoon to demonstrate how safe the waters were.

During the weekend of November 2 and 3, some 80 journalists from around the world, 40 of them from France, joined another 70 from New Zealand at the Hyatt Hotel for a briefing on court procedure. It was, of course, the same hotel at which the sabotage boss Lieutenant-Colonel Louis-Pierre Dillais had stayed four months earlier. A Justice Department official, two members of Auckland District Law Society and a police Chief Inspector spent some time briefing the assembled group. But for a few, something niggled. A lady was present from the New Zealand Tourist and Publicity Department to hand out brochures . . . Auckland Great Time Guide . . . Complete Visitor Guide . . . How to See New Zealand . . . Sightseeing Maps and Accommodation. There were details of harbour cruises, joy flights, tours, golf courses, the opening hours of the Auckland Lion Safari Park and a long list of galleries and exhibitions.

At the old Auckland High Court building police guards stayed on duty throughout the night. And as journalists and the public started to arrive police officers and surveillance cameras watched from the court roof. Everyone entering the court was screened by a metal detector. Some journalists had been allocated seats in the main court, others in a separate court where close-circuit TV screens would relay the proceedings. For the benefit of overseas journalists, it had been explained that the defendants were not required to enter a plea until after the evidence had been heard. The judge hearing the case would decide whether there was a case for them to answer at a higher court.

Mafart and Prieur were brought to the court in a police van that had no windows in the rear section. The back of the court was screened off and no-one saw them entering the building. They were due in the dock at 10 to face murder charges and lesser related charges. Captain Prieur's husband, Joel, sat in one of the jury seats. He had flown from Paris a few days earlier. Not far from him was David McTaggart of Greenpeace. There was an onimous absence of lawyers and the defendants. Finally, at 10.26 a.m. the two agents were led up from an underground cell to the dock. Both were smiling faintly.

The case began sensationally. New Zealand's Solicitor General Paul Neazor, QC, told Judge Ronald Gilbert that the accused had indicated through their counsel recently they were prepared to plead guilty to reduced charges of manslaughter.

An Australian journalist shouted 'The fix is in!' but the judge appeared not to hear.

Said Mr Neazor: 'Whether larger questions arise from the sinking of the Rainbow Warrior, these proceedings are concerned only with the criminal responsibility in New Zealand law of the two accused. It was thought proper to consider the pleas which the accused indicated they wished to make at this stage against the evidence available to support the Crown case.'

The Solicitor General said he had held a meeting with Police Commissioner Ken Thompson, Detective Superintendent Allan

Galbraith, other senior police officers and Auckland Crown Solicitor David Morris to discuss the matter. The issue of prime importance at the meeting was whether the Crown ought to go ahead with the original charges laid against the couple.

'As a result of that consideration, it has been accepted that the evidence available and admissable would not have established the accused were personally responsible for placing the explosive devices.' In addition, the evidence would not have established the French pair intended to kill or injure anyone, or had the knowledge that placing the explosives in such circumstances was likely to cause death. The police also had to consider the actual cause of Fernando Pereira's death in relation to the murder charges. The guilty plea to the manslaughter charge was a 'significant acceptance' of the couple's responsibility for the sabotage. It was also an acceptance that they took part in the act.

After the two spies had signed charge sheets confirming their guilty pleas of manslaughter, Mr Neazor outlined the police case. All charges arose from the scuttling and disabling of the Rainbow Warrior on July 10 when, shortly before midnight, two explosive devices detonated within the space of two to four minutes. The devices had clearly been attached to the hull at some time previously.

The force of the explosions caused a hole eight feet by six feet to the ship below the waterline at the engine room and extensively damaged the stern and propeller assembly. As a result, the ship sank within minutes with the loss of the life of Fernando Pereira, who drowned.

'It is alleged that the two defendants, both of whom are now stated to be serving commissioned officers in the French armed forces, arrived in New Zealand on the 22nd of June and once here took steps in furtherance of a predetermined plan to ensure that the much-publicised intended voyage of the Rainbow Warrior to French territorial waters would not in fact eventuate. For such an action to succeed it was fundamental that the vessel had to be extensively disabled so as to prevent her being repaired and manned in sufficient time to enable the voyage to be undertaken.'

Mr Neazor said that to achieve the mission, the two defendants were associated with 'other members of the French security forces' who travelled to New Zealand in furtherance of the action. These also played significant roles in the scuttling of the ship and the death of Pereira.

'The first step in New Zealand of the undertaking was the arrival here of a young woman known as Frederique Bonlieu. She was clearly sent ahead of the main party to gather intelligence, in particular of what was happening among Greenpeace members, and pass information back so that further steps could be taken. She arrived in Auckland on the 23rd of April last, travelling on a French passport with a false identity. Before her arrival a member of the Greenpeace movement had received a letter from a mutual friend noting the possibility of Bonlieu's visit to this country.

'She was therefore accepted by Greenpeace members and indeed from the time of her arrival partook of their hospitality and friendship up until her departure from New Zealand on the 24th of May. During her stay with the Greenpeace organisation she learned of and reported on the movements of the Rainbow Warrior and that organisation's future plans involving the vessel.'

Mr Neazor said that two days after Bonlieu's departure 'the group' initiated the chartering of a 38 foot sloop, the Ouvea, in Noumea. Charter arrangements were completed by the end of May and on the 13th of June the vessel left Noumea with four people on board. They subsequently arrived in New Zealand under the names of Raymond Velche, Jean-Michel Berthelo, Eric Audrenc and Xavier Jean Maniguet. Their correct identities were subsequently revealed, all except Maniguet being members of the DGSE.

'Inquiries made by New Zealand police officers subsequent to the events on the 10th of July have established that Andries purchased a Zodiac inflatable dinghy and a Yamaha outboard from a marine supplier in London on the 29th of May — five days after Bonlieu left New Zealand. It is the Crown's contention that the Ouvea was the means by which the equipment and explosives necessary to carry out the sinking of the Rainbow Warrior were brought to New Zealand.

'On the 22nd of June, the Ouvea arrived in Parengarenga on the northern tip of New Zealand. On that day the defendants arrived by plane at Auckland. They travelled on Swiss passports in the name of Mr and Mrs Turenge. The passports have been established to be expert forgeries and it is now acknowledged that their identities and all other material particulars were false.

'Subsequent to the 22nd of June the Ouvea moved down the coast to Whangarei from where, according to its log, it left New Zealand waters on the 9th of July. Between the dates of its arrival and departure meetings took place between crew members and the defendants at which it is the Crown's contention the Zodiac dinghy and the Yamaha motor were handed over to the defendants and, no doubt, relevant information on the Rainbow Warrior was exchanged.'

The Solicitor General told the court that crew members also liaised with another Frenchman using the name Jean Louis Dormand, who in turn reported regularly to Paris. During this period Mafart and Prieur also made visits to the waterfront area of Auckland, and more particularly to Marsden Wharf, prior to the arrival there of the Rainbow Warrior. The vessel had a crew, including its captain, of 13. About 10 usually slept on board. It was open to the public during much of its stay.

'On the evening of the 10th a party was held on board to celebrate a birthday and there was a meeting of Greenpeace fleet skippers. Shortly before the explosions, about 30 persons were aboard and at the time of the first explosion 12 persons, including the captain, remained aboard the ship. Some of them had retired to bed in the crew accommodation located on the main deck above the engine room and at the same level immediately aft of it. At about 11.50 p.m. the first explosion occurred causing the damage on the starboard side at the level of the engine room. No warning had been given.

'The reaction of the captain on seeing the massive inrush of water flooding that compartment was to give the order to abandon ship. A number of the crew were in the accommodation area, including the deceased. All of them except for the deceased made good their escape. The evidence available indicates that he, after the first explosion and about the time the order to abandon ship had been given, went to his cabin in the aft accommodation to retrieve his photographic equipment. The evidence suggests that he was there when the second explosion at the stern of the vessel occurred and there was a discernible but limited increase in the inrush of water.'

Mr Neazor said there was no doubt that people trained in underwater warfare had placed the explosives and carried out their detonation. Despite extensive police inquiries, no person had been located who saw any untoward activity in or about the vessel or the wharves that night.

Although the placing of the explosives and detonating them were likely to have been carried out by a number of people, the Crown's investigations did not establish the defendants' role in the affair as other than in support of those who actually placed the explosives.

'As part of their support role, the defendants were responsible for picking up and removing from the scene one of those responsible for the placement of the explosive devices. This recovery was made after the devices had been placed and the timers had been set, when one of the persons responsible for the placements then made his way in the Zodiac from the wharves at Hobson Bay to a rendezvous with the defendants.

'Subsequent to the night's events, a search led to the discovery under Ngapipi Bridge of the Yamaha outboard motor which had been bought by Andries weeks earlier in London. The Zodiac dinghy was left abandoned at the recovery point.'

Mr Neazor said the identities of those who actually placed the devices had not been established. 'During the night of the 11th the defendants claim to have driven to Thames and certainly by the 11th they were in Hamilton, where they telephoned their contact in Paris and altered their plane reservations to ensure the earliest possible departure from the country.

'They were, however, interviewed by the police on the 12th of July and denied all knowledge of the Ouvea, its crew members, and the scheme to sink the Rainbow Warrior.'

The Judge remanded the French couple in custody until November 22 for sentencing.

Obviously angry with the result, David McTaggart emerged from the court building declaring: 'French President Francois Mitterrand said he would call for justice on the highest level. That was certainly not what happened here today. I would call it justice to a certain extent on a very low level.' He said Fernando Pereira's death had been 'premeditated murder' and Mr Mitterrand, Charles Hernu and Pierre Lacoste should have been in the dock.

French consul Lloyd Brown, QC, who was in the court, denied involvement in any 'plea bargaining', saying his instructions from France had always been a watching brief. The French Government had played no part in the court's deliberations. Nor, said Prime Minister Lange, speaking in Wellington, had the New Zealand Government. Both he and the Attorney General emphatically denied any political involvement in the shortened Rainbow Warrior hearing.

However it was clear that the Solicitor General had responded to an offer from lawyers for the French couple and reduced the murder charges in return for guilty pleas. Certainly a fast court case with no witnesses being called had saved Mitterrand from prolonged embarrassment. And the last thing the New Zealand government wanted was a long, tough fight on its hands to obtain compensation from France.

Had the couple pleaded not guilty to murder, the hearing would have run for several weeks, with the prospect that the higher court would still be deliberating in March 1986, when the French elections were being held. A new right wing government might well decide that any talk of deals by the old regime no longer concerned them.

One report from Paris suggested that France had promised to buy colossal amounts of New Zealand lamb to persuade the country to release the two agents. Hit by a Common Market blockade of its produce, New Zealand would welcome a boost to its economy, said the report.

In reality, the immediate concern of Prime Minister Lange's Government was to obtain massive compensation for the French action on New Zealand territory.

The couple's New Zealand lawyer, Mr Gerard Curry, insisted there had been no deal. He had been shown the police file, studied it for a weekend and then advised his clients what he thought they should do. That was followed by some two weeks of formal negotiations, including talks with Solicitor General Neazor. 'There was no political involvement,' Mr Curry said. 'It was made crystal clear from the outset that the Solicitor General would make the decision.'

Police Commissioner Ken Thompson said details of the case against the two convicted agents would probably never be made public. The usual rules had to apply — the court had heard only a summarised version of evidence and there it had to remain. But Greenpeace said it was taking legal advice on the possibilites of obtaining the information. The organisation also wanted to know why the decision was made to reduce the murder charge.

As if to rub salt into the Greenpeace wound, Defence Minister Paul Quiles telephoned the agents shortly before their court appearance congratulating them on their exemplary courage and dignity which he said belonged to the noblest tradition of the French Army.

Admiration spread through the whole of France. A woman living near Dominique Prieur appeared on television to laugh: 'Vive Dominique! We are all proud of her!' One newspaper said 'All of France is rejoicing that the "Turenge" couple will without doubt be free soon after the startling turn of events at their non-trial.'

The official questioning was certainly over. For it was announced in Paris that the French parliamentary investigation that Prime Minister Fabius had promised after his September confession . . . had been scrapped. The National Assembly's Laws Commission, which has to endorse any parliamentary investigation, turned down demands from the Socialists and the Communists for a commission of inquiry. Opposition parties said they would not take part in any commission because it would be dominated by the Socialists. Said one government official: 'As far as the Parliament is concerned, the affair is over. It is ended.'

As France rejoiced for her spies at home and abroad, the crippled Rainbow Warrior remained moored in Auckland Harbour, too far gone to be made seaworthy. Greenpeace auctioned off some of her parts. They had decided what to do with her . . . return her to the sea bed. But it would be an honourable burial, letting her sink into the waters beside the Slipper Island lighthouse on the east coast of the Coromandel Peninsula.

'We could not face the thought of her being cut up for scrap,' said Elaine Shaw of Greenpeace. 'She has travelled so far with us and done so much.'

At the bottom of the sea, the Rainbow Warrior will serve as a monument to the crewman who died.

She will bear no epitaph, except a white dove on her bow . . . a salute to all the old vessel's past campaigns. And those she will never sail on again.

Postscript

On November 22 1985, Captain Dominique Prieur and Major Alain Mafart were each sentenced to 10 years imprisonment for their part in the sinking of the Rainbow Warrior. New Zealand's Chief Justice, Sir Ronald Davidson, told the agents in the Auckland High Court they had taken part in an action of a terrorist nature. The crime called for a heavy penalty in order to underline the seriousness of the offence and to reflect public condemnation of the bombing. Sir Ronald said they would not be given a short holiday and allowed to return home as heroes.

Their defence counsel, Mr Gerard Curry, made a plea for short sentences and asked that the couple be deported. They had acted on orders and played a supportive role in a foolish mission.

'They believed no-one would be injured. They believed they acted in the interests of France and they express remorse at the drowning of Fernando Pereira,' said the lawyer. 'They did not bring the mines to New Zealand, they did not plant them and they were not the strategists who planned the mission.' The plan had proceeded, he said, in the confident belief that when the first explosion occurred all on board would immediately abandon ship.

Crown Solicitor David Morris argued that the pair were an integral part of a well-financed mission which had to be accomplished come what may. 'The plan involved a high risk of injury and possible loss of life of crew members, which was well founded by subsequent events,' he said.

As the French spies left the dock, Captain Prieur smiled at her husband Joel and gave him a half wave. Then she and Mafart were driven back to prison. But for the man who had headed the investigation for more than four months there was still work to do. Superintendent Allan Galbraith left the court making no comment. There were a number of other French people he wanted to talk to. There were warrants for murder to be served. But even this man with a reputation for detail, who had worked doggedly day and night on the Rainbow Warrior inquiry, must have wondered just then what his chances were . . .

In Paris, President Mitterrand spoke for the first time about the bombing and said he did not 'authorise anybody to violate the sovereign rights of New Zealand.' But he said his former Defence Minister Charles Hernu, who was responsible for the DGSE, had put the government in a difficult position. Of Hernu and former DGSE boss Admiral Pierre Lacoste, the President said: 'I retain respect and friendship for them both. But they exceeded their authority.'

Three days later the spies' passport offences were dealt with by the New Zealand Court. The two were returned to jail with the knowledge they would be deported after serving time. Just how long they would remain behind bars would depend on the strengths and weaknesses of the governments involved.